MEDIEVAL FLEGG

Medieval Flegg

Two Norfolk Hundreds in the Middle Ages: East and West Flegg 1086 - 1500

Dedicated to the people of Martham, past and present.

BARBARA CORNFORD

The Larks Press

Published by the Larks Press
Ordnance Farmhouse, Guist Bottom, Dereham
Norfolk NR20 5PF
01328 829207

in collaboration with the author.

British Cataloguing-in-Publication Data
A catalogue record for this book is available from the British Library

Acknowledgements

I would like to thank Chris Barringer for his constant help and encouragement, and for the support I received from two local societies, the Norfolk Archaeological and Historical Research Group, who contributed to the cost of maps and illustrations, and the Great Yarmouth Archaeological Society for their promise of help with the sale and distribution of this book. Thanks are also due to Professor Bruce Campbell who introduced me to the Ormesby Account Rolls in the Public Record Office. I received much needed expertise and encouragement from Susan Yaxley, who edited the book for me, and help from Caroline Bown who organised my notes and periodicals, and helped to get the text ready for publication. I thank my computer-literate sons who rescued me when in trouble and my husband, Arthur, for his patience with me when I despaired of ever mastering the computer or completing the book.

Printed by the Lanceni Press, Garrood Drive, Fakenham

ISBN 0 948400 98 6

Contents

Preface - *11*

Chapter 1. The Geography and Settlement of Flegg - *14*
Geography of Flegg - The Settlement of Flegg

Chapter 2. Flegg in the time of the Domesday Book - *29*
The Population, Economy and Landscape – Population – Households and Plough-teams – Woodland – Meadows – Mills – Saltpans and Sheep Farming – Animal Husbandry – Turbaries and Fisheries – The Landscape.

Chapter 3. Domesday Flegg: Manors and their Lords; Freemen and their Farms - *42*
The Manors – Thurne Manor – Hemsby Manor – Earl Ralph's Manors – The Freemen and Sokemen and their Farms – After the Norman Conquest

Chapter 4. The Monastic Manors of Flegg in the Twelfth and Thirteenth Centuries - *54*
The Estates of the Cathedral Priory in Flegg – Smaller Priory Estates in Flegg - Estates of St Benet's Abbey- Abbey Property leased to Laymen

Chapter 5. Two Lay Manors in the Thirteenth Century: Runham and Mautby - *63*
Runham – Mautby

Chapter 6. Charitable Institutions - *72*
West Somerton Leper Hospital – God's House at Herringby

Chapter 7. A Survey of Martham in the Thirteenth Century - *76*
The Map of Medieval Martham – Martham at the beginning of the Thirteenth Century – Martham in 1292

Chapter 8. The Manor Farm: the Bailiff's Task - *101*

Chapter 9. Tenants of the Martham Manor and the Manor Court in the late Thirteenth Century - *110*
Peasant families in Martham at the end of the Thirteenth Century – Matthew Knight's Farm – The Role of the Manor Court – Appendix 9.1 Corn Prices and Alms

Chapter 10. The Moregrove Manor at Martham, the Clere Lands and the Nature of Lordship in Flegg - *124*
The Manor of Moregrove in Martham – The Clere Lands in Flegg in the Fourteenth Century – Size and Value of Flegg Manors and the Nature of Lordship

Chapter 11. The Fourteenth Century: The Great Famine and the Black Death - *136*
The Great Famine and its Results – Black Death in Flegg – Manor of Rollesby Boyes 1328-1348 – Manor of Martham 1349-1363

Chapter 12. The Peasants' Revolt in Flegg - *147*
After the Black Death in Martham – St Benet's Manor of Ashby and Thurne – The Course of the Peasants' Revolt in Flegg

Chapter 13. The Fifteenth Century: Three Flegg Manors - *160*
The Priory Manor at Martham – St Benet's Manor of Flegg in the Fifteenth Century – A Lay Manor: Ormesby

Chapter 14. Village Life in the Fifteenth Century - *174*
Peasant Agriculture in the Fifteenth Century – The Wealthier Tenants and the Manor Court – Martham Church and Martham Heretics – Fifteenth Century Wills 1424-1505

Chapter 15. Four Centuries of Flegg History - *191*

Glossary *196*

Bibliography *199*

Index *204*

Maps

Drawn by Philip Judge

Map 1.1 Position of Flegg in East Norfolk - *13*
Map 1.2 Flegg in the late Twentieth Century - *15*
Map 1.3 The Hundreds of East Norfolk - *25*

Map 2.1 Households and Plough-teams - *34*
Map 2.2 Sheep and Saltpans in Flegg - *37*
Map 2.3 Domesday Landscape of Flegg - *40*

Map 4.1 The Estates of St Benet's Abbey, early Thirteenth Century - *60*

Map 7.1 Map of Medieval Martham - *75*

Map 15.1 Flegg at the end of the Fifteenth Century - *193*

Explanation of the Maps

The outline of maps of Flegg in this book is based on modern maps. The coastline of Flegg may have extended at least a mile beyond its present position in the eleventh century and the routes of the Rivers Thurne and Bure may have been different. It is possible that the river Ant flowed into the Thurne and so into the North Sea at Fludgates in Winterton. This waterway marked the boundary of the hundreds of Happing and Flegg. The river Bure flowed directly into the North sea at Grubbs Haven, as shown on the Domesday Maps. The coastline was eroding throughout the Middle Ages, and sand was gradually blocking the exit of the River Thurne on the Winterton Horsey border and the River Bure at Grubbs Haven. A sandy spit extended towards Lowestoft hampering the entrance and exit to and from the haven at Yarmouth. I have not tried to represent these developments on the maps, except to show outfall of the River Bure at Grubbs Haven on the Domesday maps. I have used the modern extent of drained marsh and broads to indicate the approximate extent of medieval marsh and meadow.

Tables

Table 1.1. Population of the Isle of Flegg - *28*

Table 2.1. Number of households in Flegg 1086 and 1801 - *30*
Table 2.2. Estimated population in Flegg in 1086 and 1801 - *30*
Table 2.3. Status of tenants in Flegg in 1086 - *32*
Table 2.4. Livestock (excluding plough-oxen) - *38*

Table 3.1. The manors of Flegg listed in order of value - *42*
Table 3.2. Numbers of tenants in groups - *48*
Table 3.3. Size of holdings of single tenants - *48*
Table 3.4. Number of ploughs on the manors, and on free holdings - *51*

Table 5.1. Cropping at Mautby and Martham - *68*

Table 8.1. Harvest 1294 compared with other years - *103*

Table 9.1. Prices of barley in Flegg 1261 to 1425 – *122*
Table 9.2 Alms at Martham, Hemsby and Scratby *123*

Table 10.1. Services on socage holdings at Martham and Burgh - *131*
Table 10.2. Size of manorial demesnes in Flegg - *132*
Table 10.3. Value of arable land in Flegg in 13th and 14th centuries - *133*

Table 14.1. Holdings in Martham 1497 - *175*

Figures

Figure 7.1 Layout of tofts on Common edge - *83*
Figure 7.2 Size and number of holdings in Martham 1192 - *95*
Figures 7.3 Size and number of holdings in Martham 1292 - *95*

Photographs

Aerial view of Flegg from Thurne Mouth to Somerton - *17*
Martham Green - *18*
Winterton Beach - *20*
Stokesby Ferry - *23*
The Muck Fleet near Stokesby - *26*
Mautby Church - *46*
Decoy Farm, Mautby - *50*
Scaring birds with a sling - *71*
Martham Ferry – *77*
Martham Church tower – *79*
View from Martham tower – East to Somerton –*80*
View from Martham tower – South over Welltofts –*80*
View from Martham tower – West towards Cess - *81*
View from Martham tower – North over Moregrove - *81*
The first page of the 1292 Survey of Martham Manor- *84*
Demesne pasture at Dunsyn – *86*
Medwesyk demesne pasture and turbary – *86*
Derelict cottage on the edge of the Common at Cess – *99*
Acorns for the pig - *100*
Martham Hall – *102*
Bailiff's Account Roll 1333-4 – *108*
Moger's Meadow - *117*
Moregrove Farmyard – *126*
Mud block cottage on the edge of Fleggburgh Common – *130*
Braunton Field, Devon – *135*
Blacksmith and assistant at work – *155*
A twentieth century Rollesby blacksmith – *156*
Peasants illustrated in stained glass in Ely Cathedral – *159*
Caister Castle - *169*
Ormesby Church – *171*
Ploughing - *172*
The Acle Causeway, towards Acle Bridge – *184*
Lovers meeting - *189*
Potter Heigham Bridge - *194*
West Somerton Church – *194*
Winterton Church and the Wind Farm - *195*

Foreword

For many years Barbara Cornford's life has focussed on Flegg. She is a Cambridge graduate who gained her expertise with medieval documents through Extra-mural classes in Norwich. With her husband, Arthur, she ran the Youth Hostel at Martham for sixteen years and so was well placed to explore the Fleggs. She contributed to the Yarmouth Archaeological Society's activities and was for years the editor of the Norfolk Research Committee's Bulletin. She wrote papers and gave lectures on the Fleggs to both societies and also taught local history for the Workers' Educational Association.

Gradually the information she collected from her painstaking work, especially on the magnificent collection of the records of Norwich Cathedral Priory in the Norfolk Record Office, began to take shape. Since her retirement from Martham this work has continued; she has immersed herself in the records of Runham, Martham and Ormesby and has followed their evolution from Domesday until 1500.

Each phase of the story brings the people of Flegg and their mode of living to life. From Domesday, when villages and their lands butted up to one another in a densely-populated landscape, she takes us to the pre-Black Death period when no tidy 'Midland' fields system existed but rather a more individualistic pattern of land-use within the manors. For this the 1292 survey of Martham provides a mass of detail. The Black Death had many long-term effects, but the terse remark that in Runham 'all the tenants are dead' is stark enough, as is the picture of cattle straying through unkept hedges.

Martham and Hemsby supplied the Cathedral Priory with wheat for bread and malt for beer. The small estate at Ormesby sent peat for the Cathedral kitchens. The supply of these necessities by boat emphasises Flegg's links by water with Norwich and, of course, Yarmouth.

Barbara Cornford has provided an important picture of a period rich in records, but still too little studied. Together with Roger Virgoe's recent study of the Priory estates, this book provides us with marvellous source material for a distinctive part of Norfolk.

J.C.Barringer

Preface

When I first came from Somerset to live in Flegg in 1967 I thought how dull the landscape was, no hills, no hedges and even the houses seemed mean and skimped after West Country cob and thatch. I began to think differently when I saw the view from Somerton across marsh and broad to Hickling and Horsey, to the red-striped tower of Happisburgh lighthouse in the far distance, and to the sand dunes and North Sea nearer at hand.

There are few places in England where marsh, dune and sea merge together as they do on this coast. I also became fascinated by the little farms and cottages, which lie along the edge of the commons, opening on one side to the cultivated fields and on the other to the common and marshes, as at Fleggburgh Common. Above all it was the friendship of the people of Martham and their willingness to talk about the 'old days' that I valued most. Although their memories dealt with the immediate past, some of the tales I heard helped me to understand a much earlier way of life. So it is to the people of Martham, past and present, that I dedicate this book.

What I had not realised when I came to the village was that Martham had a remarkable collection of manorial documents held in the Norfolk Record Office. For twenty years I studied them and the records of other Flegg villages. Some relevant documents are in the British Museum and the Public Record Office in London. Most are in Latin, a few in Norman French and one essential source, The Domesday Book, is published in translation. It is on these documents that this work is based. The historian is very much constrained by the material available. For some villages, such as Winterton and Caister I found practically no medieval sources. Martham with its wealth of documents was bound to feature largely in this book.

Anyone interested in East Norfolk in the medieval period, and Flegg in particular, must take account of the work of Professor Bruce Campbell of Belfast University, who has made an in-depth study of the rural economy of East Norfolk, and of Flegg in particular. My work is based on his analysis of the agricultural regimes and the patterns of landholding in Flegg throughout the

Middle Ages. I would also like to thank him for his help in the early stages of my studies and especially for introducing me to the Ormesby Account rolls of the fifteenth century in the Public Record Office .

I hope the book will appeal both to the general reader with an interest in Norfolk local history and to the medieval historian, and with this in mind, I would like to give some idea of the scope of the book. An introductory chapter on the geography and settlement of Flegg is followed by two chapters on the Domesday Book of 1086. The Domesday Book has an entry for every village in Flegg and so provides a basis for the medieval history of the area. It gives a picture of a well-populated and widely cultivated land in the late eleventh century, where most of the population were free farmers gaining a viable living from small mixed farms. The Norman landlords encouraged the development of manors that relied on tenant services to work the home farm. The status and standard of living of the tenants deteriorated as the wealth and productivity of the manors increased in the twelfth and thirteenth centuries.

During the Middle Ages, from 1100 to 1500, the most important social unit for the country dweller, whether lord or tenant, was the manor. It was important for the lord to know how his manor was performing economically, and for that he relied on the annual accounts, which his farm bailiff produced. He also needed to keep a check on the activities of his tenants. The records of the manor court told how much land each tenant held, whether he or she obeyed the regulations of the manor and was a peaceable member of the community. The account rolls and the manor court rolls are the best sources for information about economic and social patterns of village life in the Middle Ages, and it is on these mundane records that this book is based. The fullest surviving manorial records for Flegg manors are those for the Priory manor at Martham. Information from the account rolls and the manor court rolls, combined with a survey of the manor taken in 1292, make possible the detailed description of the economy and social organisation of the manor found in Chapters 7, 8 and 9.

The Black Death of 1349 was a human tragedy that, rather like the First World War, fundamentally influenced later economic and social patterns. No longer could the lords of the manors rely on a pool of cheap labour to work their land. A surplus of arable land gave many tenants an opportunity to increase the size of their holdings and livestock farming played a greater part in the peasant economy. Once more Flegg was inhabited by men with mixed farms who were largely free from the restrictions of manorial obligations. Many historians regard the fifteenth century as the 'Golden Age of Peasant Farming'

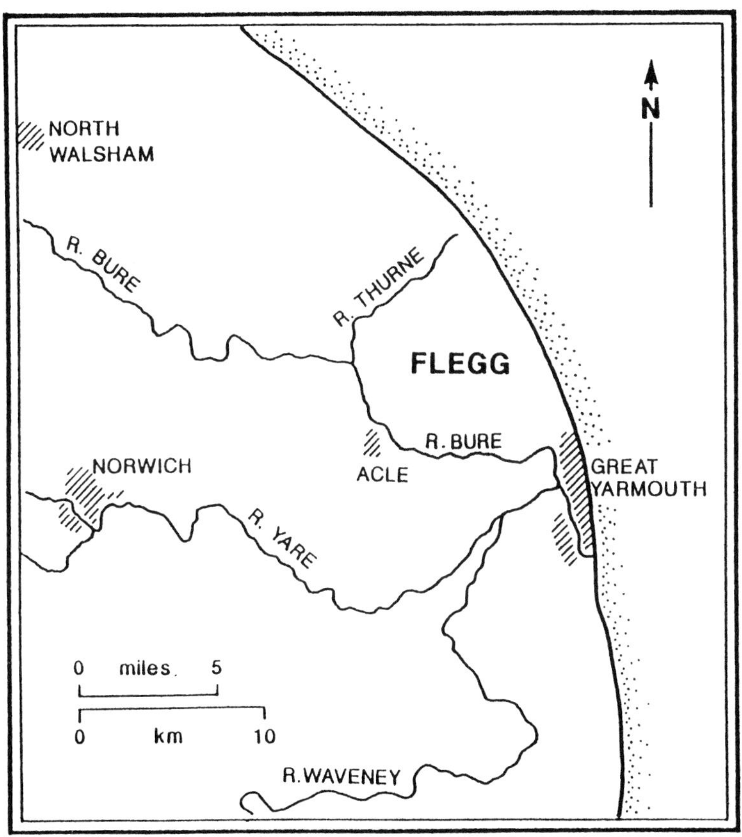

Map 1.1 Position of Flegg in East Norfolk

Chapter 1. The Geography and Settlement of Flegg.

Geography of Flegg

Flegg is the area lying to the north of Great Yarmouth in the part of Norfolk that today is called Broadland or the Broads. These names have no meaning in a medieval context because in the Middle Ages the broads were not lakes, but soggy peat diggings. The name Flegg comes from the Old Danish word *flaeg* used for all kinds of marsh plants, but particularly for reeds.[1] 'The place where reeds grow' is a very suitable description of Flegg with its extensive marshes and water-logged peat soil. The rivers Bure and Thurne form the boundaries of Flegg on three sides, and to the East lies the North Sea. Not surprisingly the area is sometimes called 'The Isle of Flegg'.

Access to Flegg is dictated by the need to cross river or marsh. Two of the four roads on to Flegg still follow the old medieval routes. From Norwich the A1064 crosses the Bure at Acle bridge, built in 1930 to replace the medieval Wey bridge. (The 1930s bridge, which has become quite unsuitable for late twentieth century traffic, is being replaced as I write in 1997). The road runs on the old causeway across the marshes to Billockby, then through Filby and Caister to Yarmouth. Until recently the A149 road from North Walsham crossed the river Thurne by the medieval bridge at Potter Heigham. That bridge still stands, but is less used now because a new bridge was built a few hundred yards to the east in 1969 on the line of the disused railway from Yarmouth to North Walsham. The A149 runs across Flegg, over Rollesby Bridge and so through Ormesby to Caister. The road then follows the old turnpike across the marshland to Yarmouth. A minor road, B1159, quite unsuitable for modern traffic, winds northwards from Caister, by-passing Ormesby and Hemsby, to Somerton, Horsey and beyond. (See Map 1.2) Before that road was made in the mid-nineteenth century, the only way to Horsey was along the back of the sand dunes on a track threatened with flooding at every high

1. Sandred K.I., 1987 'Some Reflexes on Old Anglian and Viking Settlement in Norfolk in *Norfolk Research Committee Bulletin 2nd Series No 38.*

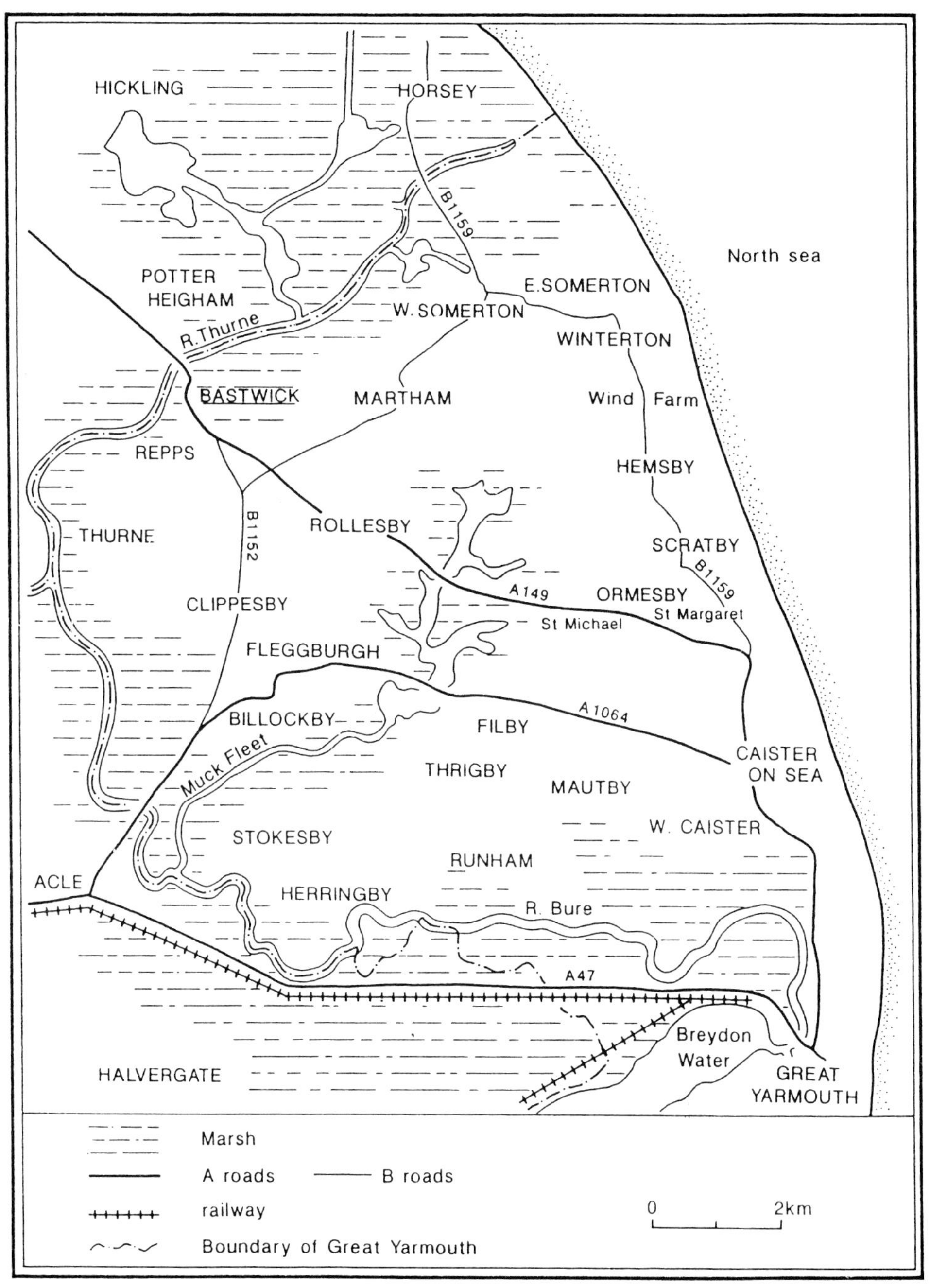

Map 1.2 Flegg in the lateTwentieth Century

tide and sea surge. In the 1970s, before the Caister by-pass was built and the new bridge opened at Potter Heigham, it was possible to find oneself almost a prisoner on the Isle of Flegg on summer Saturdays when holiday traffic jammed the roads to Yarmouth, Acle and North Walsham. Our ancestors were luckier in their choice of routes for they could take the ferry over the Bure at Stokesby. The rivers had not been deepened by dredging and still allowed fording at several places. These crossing places often appear on maps as 'swims' for cattle, as at Runham Swim.

Flegg farmers have always distinguished between the upland and the marsh. (The upland in Flegg is all land over five feet above sea level.) The upland soil is a well-drained, easily-worked fertile loam which has been under constant cultivation for at least a thousand years and probably longer. A seventeenth century author described Flegg as, 'the chiefest Corn Country in the whole shire, and the grounds about Winterton are in the opinion of many the most fruitfull fatte and mouldie of any part of England'. The fertility of the soil has played a major part in determining the history of the area.[2]

Of course there are patches of poorer soil. On the plateau between Ashby and Rollesby lay an area of heath and woodland, described in the Domesday Survey as woodland for nine pigs. It was called *Stefne*, a Danish word meaning 'meeting place', and was almost certainly where the Hundred Court for West Flegg met.[3] (See Map 2.3) The word was pronounced 'Stefen', as the Suffolk village of Hoxne is called 'Hoxen'. In the thirteenth century the hill going up from Martham towards the heath was called *Spachochehil*, which may mean 'the Speech Oak Hill', another reference to the Hundred Court. (See Map 1.3) In the fifteenth century, when the Hundred Court had long since given up its open-air meetings, the heath was known as Stevens Heath, and in the nineteenth century, Rollesby Heath. Although the area has been under cultivation for at least four hundred years, you can still

2. Hood C.M. *The Chorography of Norfolk. An historical and chorographicall description of Norfolk.* Norwich 1938. Written c.1600 and attributed to John Norden.

3. Smith A.H. *English Place-Name Elements.* 1956 English Place-Name Society. CUP. Sandred. K.I. *Norfolk Place-names of East and West Flegg, Happing and Tunstead Hundreds,* English Place Name Society. 1996 p.2.

Aerial view across Flegg from Thurne Mouth, looking toward Somerton Wind Farm

Photo: Courtesy Mike Page of Strumpshaw

feel something of the wildness of the heath as you go over the top of Flegg on the B1152 from Acle to Repps. You will only pass two farms, Heath Farm and Heath Barn Farm, names that still recall the earlier state of the land. Looking east from Heath Barn Farm you can see across Flegg to the ghostly shapes of the ten wind turbines at the Somerton Wind Farm. The electricity they generate is fed into the national grid. (See photograph p. 17)

Small patches of water-logged and ill-drained soil on the upland, not suitable for ploughing, often became village greens where ponds supplied water for man and beast. In Flegg, greens do not usually lie away from the village as in some parts of Norfolk, but are within a quarter of a mile of the church and village centre, as at Martham, Ormesby and Runham. Hemsby once had a green to the west of the church, but that has succumbed to housing in the last two hundred years.

Photo: Eastern Counties Newspapers

Martham Village Green

The cultivated upland of Flegg is fringed by marsh and fen. The state of the marshes depends on the water levels in the valleys of the Bure and Thurne. When the sea levels were relatively low in the Bronze Age (approximately 1,500 BC), peat formed in the fresh-water swamps of the valley bottoms. In the Roman period, higher water levels and the absence of any bar at the mouth of the rivers meant that the valleys became part of the Great Estuary which stretched nearly up to Norwich. The twice-daily tides deposited estuarine clay over the peat. By about 500 AD the sea levels had fallen, the Yarmouth sandbank had appeared and the estuary slowly began to dry out. The resulting clayey peat marshes were sufficiently firm by the early Middle Ages to provide grazing for sheep and cattle. Where the clay was thin or non-existent, fen and carr, that is scrubby woodland, developed on the peat soil. The marshes were an essential part of the local economy in the Middle Ages, providing grazing in summer, hay and litter for winter fodder and bedding, peat for fuel, rushes, reeds and sedge for roofing, wood for tools and implements, and fish and fowl for food.[4]

For most of its way the valley of the Muck Fleet was the boundary between the Hundreds of East and West Flegg, the administrative districts which were formalised in the late Anglo-Saxon period. (See Map 1.3) Peat was extracted in large quantities from the valley and was not only used locally but also taken to Yarmouth and Norwich. The rising water levels of the later Middle Ages gradually flooded the peat diggings thus forming Filby, Rollesby and Ormesby Broads.[5]

The settlement pattern of the Flegg villages has some special characteristics. In every tax list or count of population from the Domesday Survey of 1086 to the 1981 Census, Ormesby, Winterton and Martham are among the five most populous communities, and are usually joined by Caister and Hemsby. (See Table1.1) The villages of Ashby, Billockby, Thurne and Herringby are always near the bottom of the list. Only Somerton does not conform to this pattern, falling, through the centuries, from second or third place in the early Middle Ages to fourth from the last in the 1981 census. The Norfolk Structure Plan, which encourages

4. Lambert, J. et al. 1960, *The Making of the Broads.*

5. For water levels, see: Lambert, J. et al. 1960, *The Making of the Broads, Part 2, Historical Evidence*; Funnnell B.M. 'History and Prognosis of Subsidence and Sea-Level Change in the Lower Yare Valley, Norfolk' in *The Bulletin of the Geological Society of Norfolk* 1979.

the larger villages to grow and discourages growth in the smaller places, is perpetuating a pattern established at least nine hundred years ago.

Yarmouth has always been the market town and urban centre for Flegg. In the Middle Ages corn from Flegg fed the town. For centuries Flegg farmers and small-holders have sold their livestock, vegetables and fruit at the Wednesday and Saturday markets. Now this is changing. New market regulations, the cost of transport and the irksome nature of the twice-weekly trip to market has meant that as the smallholders grow older they relinquish their stalls and younger men are seldom eager to take them over. However, the inhabitants of Flegg still regard Yarmouth as their town and go there for shopping, business and pleasure. The close ties between Flegg and Yarmouth were recognised in the local Government reorganisation of 1974 when all Flegg was included in Yarmouth District. Yet if you walk along the lonely beaches at Winterton it is hard to believe that you are still in the Borough of Great Yarmouth.

Photo: Eastern Counties Newspapers

Winterton Beach

The Settlement of Flegg

In *The Making of the Broads,* published 1960, archaeologist, Charles Green, drew a series of maps showing the pattern of human settlement from the New Stone Age (about 3,000 B.C.) to the Danish invasion in the ninth century A.D. Broadland in general, and Flegg in particular, seemed to have been very sparsely populated until the Danish settlement. Indeed Charles Green emphasises the emptiness of Flegg. In the thirty years since that book was published, aerial photography, metal-detecting and regular field-walking have begun to change our understanding of man's activities in this area. Yet the maps in *An Historical Atlas of Norfolk,* 1993, show that our knowledge of the overall pattern of settlement in Eastern Norfolk has not changed significantly. Even in the Roman period when the regional capital, Venta Icenorum, was built at Caister St Edmund, and impressive forts at Caister-on-Sea and Burgh Castle were established, evidence of settlement in the hinterland is still largely lacking. The constant ploughing of the fertile loam over two thousand years has destroyed much of the evidence, but in recent years Roman coins and pottery have been found by field-walking and metal-detection in the parishes of Martham, Somerton, Ormesby, Filby, Mautby and Caister. The excavation for the Bacton to Yarmouth gas pipe-line has revealed Bronze Age material at Repps, Hemsby and Ormesby.

Place-names suggest that the early Anglo-Saxons settled on the very fertile loam upland between Repps and the North Sea. Repps, Bastwick, Martham, Somerton and Winterton are all names of Anglo-Saxon origin. An interesting recent archaeological find is a piece of a pagan Saxon burial urn and part of an early Saxon cruciform brooch discovered at Martham.[6] These finds are tangible evidence that the Anglo-Saxons settled here as early as the sixth century. This raises the question of the meaning of the village name. The 'ham' of 'Martham' is usually interpreted as 'hamm', meaning 'meadow', but the sixth century evidence suggests that Martham may have been one of the 'ham' villages, which were centres of early Saxon estates. 'Ham' villages often have satellite villages with a 'ton' suffix nearby. Somerton and Winterton may

6. For Anglo-Saxon Pagan Burial Urn see Dawson P. 'A Hill in Broadland' in *Narg News* No 22, 1980.

have been daughter settlements to Martham. The most reasonable explanation of their seasonal names is perhaps that Winterton was the place where fishermen assembled in the autumn and winter to catch herring, while Somerton refers to the abundance of marsh pasture, which provided good summer grazing. The other Somerton on the edge of the Somerset levels is explained as 'the ton of the summer grazing'. Martham means the 'ham of the marten', not the pine marten, but another member of the same family, the polecat. Polecats were native to the marshes, and were treated as vermin in the Middle Ages.

It is tempting to see that other 'ham' village, Runham, as the dominant Anglo-Saxon settlement in East Flegg, but no archaeological evidence has been found to support this. Yet its position sheltered from the north and overlooking the Bure marshes to the south makes it an inviting place to live. At Caister the mid-seventh century cemetery is evidence of a fairly large Anglo-Saxon settlement in East Flegg at that time.[7]

The Danish settlement of East Anglia began after 880 AD, when, according to the *Anglo-Saxon Chronicle*, the Danes occupied the land and shared it out. They must have come to Flegg in considerable numbers for they gave names to thirteen out of twenty-two villages in Flegg. In Scandinavia the suffix *-by* is often used for settlements made in empty or deserted areas. The concentration of *-by* villages in the Muck Fleet valley and round Stefne Heath in south-west Flegg suggests that possibly the Danes found very few inhabitants there. The name Stokesby, which is Saxon in its first element and Danish in its second, is an interesting one. Not only does it suggest the mingling of the two groups, but it may also explain why the Danes found the Muck Fleet valley virtually empty. The Saxon word 'stoc', pronounced with a long 'o', was used to describe an 'outlying pasture near water where cattle are kept for part of the year'. If this is true of Stokesby, then the Danes may well have found only cattle-minders in the valley, with perhaps small and scattered settlements around the Heath to the west. [8]

7. Clarke R.R., *East Anglia,* 1960 p.149.

8. Stokesby, place name, see Smith A.H., *English Place-Name Elements,* 1956.

Stokesby Ferry

This ferry continued into the twentieth century.

Photo: Norfolk Local StudiesLibrary, courtesy J.T.Gotte

Most of the Danish village names in Flegg incorporate a personal name, such as Orm (Ormesby), Malti (Mautby) or Hrodulfr (Rollesby).[9] Dr Sandred believes that these are the names, not of warrior chiefs, but of free farmers, more interested in acquiring land than in pillage and warfare. There appears to be no archaeological or historical support for the local tradition that Saxon and Dane fought a battle at Blood Hills in Somerton, although the name *bloduelle*, 'blood well' dates from about 1300.[10] In the first half of the tenth century East Anglia came under Danish rule, and enjoyed fifty years of relative peace. Danish law was established, including an important legal provision for the transfer of land. Under Anglo-Saxon law, land was transferred only by charter from the King, but in the Danelaw it could be transferred by sale, providing that the transaction took place before witnesses

9. For Danish personal names, see Sandred, K.I. 'Some Reflexes on Old Anglian and Viking Settlement in Norfolk' in *Norfolk Research Committee Bulletin 2nd Series*, 1987, and Margeson, S. 'Viking Settlement in Norfolk' in *Festival of Norfolk Archaeology*, 1996.

10. For 'Bloduelle', See K.I. Sandred. *Norfolk Place-Names of E. and W. Flegg etc.* 1996, p. 78.

at a major town, such as Cambridge, Ipswich, Norwich or Thetford. The law of inheritance was relaxed and a landowner could leave his land freely. This legal pattern seems to have continued for tenant farmers in East Anglia under both Danish, Anglo-Saxon and Norman rule. Later in the Middle Ages the ease with which land was bought and sold in East Anglia was to have important social and economic results.[11]

In 919 Edward the Elder, son of Alfred the Great, conquered East Anglia from the Danes. A further period of relative peace and prosperity followed and Thetford and Norwich flourished. It was at this time that the Saxon pattern of local government in hundreds was probably formalised. The reign of Aethelred in the later tenth century was a confusing period of Viking raids and battles, in which the leading players on both sides frequently changed sides. By the reign of King Canute (1014-1035) Norfolk had been drawn into the flourishing Danish Empire with its widespread commercial activity. In the eleventh century Yarmouth grew from a seasonal settlement of fishermen into a flourishing port and town with seventy burgesses recorded in the Domesday Book.[12] Flegg seems to have experienced something of an economic miracle during that century. By the Norman Conquest it was one of the most populous and widely cultivated areas in Norfolk. It is significant that although two of the smallest in the county, East and West Flegg were full hundreds and not half hundreds like some other small administrative districts. The two Flegg hundreds must have been sufficiently populated and prosperous to undertake the same financial, administrative and military duties as hundreds twice their size. (See Map 1.3)

Danish words have survived in Flegg as they have generally in Norfolk. Holme means an island and is applied to an area of dry ground in the marsh, often a gravel bank. Winterton and Somerton Holmes are sufficiently well drained to be ploughed and contain farms. Medieval field-names include 'gate' for a road, 'wong' for a furlong or collection of strips in the open fields and the 'syk', a marshy strip of land by a stream. These words are still used. Ferrygate and Damgate are roads in Martham, villagers go 'over

11. Judy Sims 'The Vikings in England' in *The Quarterly, Journal of the Norfolk Archaeological and Historical Research Group, No.35 1999.*

12. Presidential talk, 'A Town like Great Yarmouth' given to the Norfolk Research Committee in 1988 by George Rye, reported in *N.R.C. Bulletin Third Series No 1.*

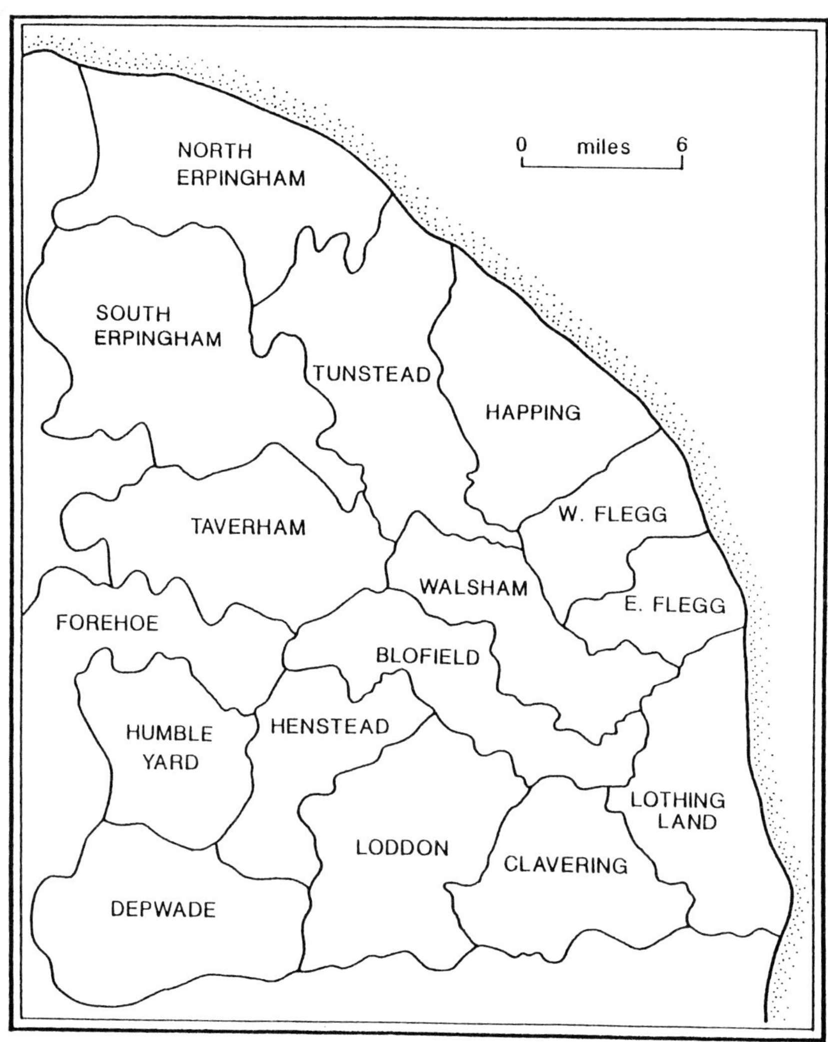

Map 1.3 The Hundreds of East Norfolk

the wongs' from the church to the hamlet of Cess, or through the 'syk' meadow, marshy ground, which was once a navigable stream, marking the boundary between Martham and Bastwick. One Danish place-name has vanished. The hamlet of Sco, mentioned in the Domesday survey, lay where Martham, Bastwick and Rollesby meet around the present Grange Farm (OS TG 437 172), but Sco never became an ecclesiastical or civil parish. The word is Danish, from *skogre*, a wood, and is appropriate for a settlement at the bottom of Speech Oak Hill.

The Muck Fleet near Stokesby

The Hundred boundary between East and West Flegg. The name is probably not medieval, but refers to boats carrying muck from the Yarmouth streets to fertilize the Flegg farms in the eighteenth and nineteenth centuries.

The Domesday Book, although compiled in 1086, gives some information about land ownership and agriculture at the time of the Norman Conquest twenty years earlier. The chief landowners were men of local or national reputation who held estates all over East Anglia and beyond. Gyrth, King Harold's brother, held the large and valuable manor of Ormesby from St Benet's Abbey. He was also the overlord of many freemen in the Flegg villages. Archbishop Stigand held a manor in Somerton. Ralph the Staller, one of King Edward's officials in Norfolk, held a string of estates at Caister, Mautby, Runham and Filby. The wealthy nobleman Alwin of Thetford, the Saxon Sheriff of Norfolk, was the lord and patron of freemen in almost every Flegg village. The Church had many estates, particularly in West Flegg. The Abbey of St Benet's at Holm held eight manors and the Bishop held the valuable manor of Hemsby as well as estates in Martham, Scratby and elsewhere. It is clear from Domesday Book that the manor was firmly established as an economic unit in 1066, and that every freeman was expected to have a lord to answer for him. However, many small groups of freemen in both East and West Flegg had the loosest of feudal ties with their lords before the Norman Conquest.[13]

None of the Saxon overlords lived in Flegg and many probably never set foot there. Their manors were often in the hands of their freemen; for example, Edwin, a freeman of Gyrth held the manor of Stokesby; Wistan, a freeman of Ralph the Staller, held Mautby; at Somerton, Aelfric, Harold's man, held the larger estate and an unnamed freeman held Stigand's manor. His obligations to Stigand were so minimal that he could sell the manor without asking his lord's permission. Before the Conquest these men, and others like them, must have formed an élite group in a society composed overwhelmingly of freemen.

13. *Domesday Book for Norfolk*, ed. Philippa Brown 1984.

Table 1.1 Comparative Population in the Isle of Flegg 1086-1981

Domesday 1086 Households		**Taxpayers 1334**		**Taxpayers 1524**		**First Census 1801 Population**		**Census of 1981 .... Population**	
Caister	113	Martham	124	Ormesby	77	Martham	639	Caister	7,019
Ormesby	95	Somerton	97	Martham	75	Caister	498	Ormesby St Marg. & Scratby	2,967
Somerton	91	Hemsby	92	Hemsby	59	Ormesby St Marg & Scratby	445	Martham	2,219
Martham	87	Winterton	92	Winterton	54	Rollesby	420	Hemsby	1,931
Winterton	59	Ormesby	90	Filby	44	Winterton	378	Rollesby	1,169
Stokesby	58	Filby	56	Caister	39	Hemsby	367	Winterton	1,162
Mautby	56	Caister	54	Somerton	37	Filby	332	Fleggburgh & Clippesby & Billockby	844
Hemsby	53	Fleggburgh	47	Fleggburgh	31	Somerton	257	Repps with Bastwick	349
Filby	49	Clippesby	41	Thurne	26	Ormesby St Michael	219	Mautby & Runham	
Fleggburgh	47	Repps	40	Stokesby	26	Stokesby & Herringby	194	Ormesby St Michael	310
Rollesby	44	Scratby	40	Repps	21	Runham	188	Somerton	263
Runham	42	Stokesby	39	Runham	21	Repps with Bastwick	182	Stokesby	253
Oby	33	Runham	37	Thrigby	17	Thurne	126	Thurne	130
Repps	28	Mautby	32	Clippesby	12	Thrigby	63	Ashby & Oby	69
Ashby	25	Thrigby	22	Scratby	12	Mautby	60		
Clippesby	24	Oby	19	Ashby & Oby	12	Ashby & Oby	47		
Herringby	23	Thurne	19	Herringby	10	Clippesby	46		
Scratby	21	Bastwick	17	Billockby	10	Billockby	42		
Thrigby	21	Billockby	16	Mautby	10				
Thurne	19	Ashby	14	Bastwick	5				
Billockby	19	Herringby	11						
Bastwick	9								
Sco	3								
Ness	1								

Chapter 2. Flegg in the Time of the Domesday Book

The Population, Economy and Landscape

> In the first place the name of the manor; who held it in the time of King Edward, and who holds it now, how many hides there are, how many ploughs in demesne and how many belonging to the men, how many villeins, cottars, serfs, freemen and sokemen; how much wood, meadow and pasture; how many mills and fisheries.[14]

In 1086, twenty years after the Norman Conquest, King William ordered a survey to be made of his realm of England. It became known as the Domesday Book. The entries for Norfolk and Suffolk are particularly detailed. Every Flegg village is mentioned and information is given about the landowners, their tenants and the economy of the area. The extract at the beginning of this chapter shows some of the questions asked by the King's Commissioners. It comes from an account written by a monk of Ely Abbey who had first-hand knowledge of the way evidence for Domesday Book was collected. Information was taken from the priest, reeve and six villeins from each village, from the Hundred Courts and from the Shire Court presided over by the Sheriff, as well as from the new French landlords. In theory at least, every household should have been recorded. The West Flegg Hundred Court, attended by the freemen, would have met in the open air on Stefne Heath. The court would consider the information which the village delegations had brought to the meeting, and then choose a jury to present the evidence to the King's Commissioners at the Shire Court.

A few words of explanation are needed about the terms used in the extract. The hide was a Saxon measurement of land, which notionally contained 120 acres. In Norfolk the Danish word *carucate*, also 120 acres, was used instead of hide. The carucates and acres recorded are not very accurate measurements but they give a rough idea of the size of a manor demesne or a freeman's farm. The demesne was the home farm of a manor and its produce

14. Darby, H.C. *A Domesday Geography of Eastern England*, 1958, p.4.

went to the lord of the manor for his use. Villeins and cottars, or bordars as they are called in Norfolk, were attached to the manors and provided much of the labour force on the demesne. Serfs, possibly slaves, were present in small numbers on a few manors. Freemen and sokemen were both regarded as free tenants. The number of ploughs is always recorded on manors and on the freemen's and sokemen's holdings. The word 'plough' includes its team of eight oxen. The Commissioners were asked to collect information for three different dates: 'then', that is before the Conquest, 'after', that is just after the Conquest in 1066, and 'now', in 1086. Not surprisingly, evidence for all three of the dates was not always recorded. The King, with taxation in mind, was determined to learn about the wealth of his kingdom, so Domesday Book gave in pounds, shillings and pence, the value of every manor and the rent of every freeman's holding.[15]

Table 2.1. Number of Households in Flegg 1086 and 1801.

Hundred	No. of Tenants 1086	No. of Households 1801
East Flegg	468	400
West Flegg	538	541

To estimate the total population it is usual to multiply the number of households by 4½ and then to add the serfs.

Table 2.2 Estimated Population in Flegg in 1086 and 1801

Hundred	Estimated population 1086	Population 1801 Census figure
East Flegg	2,112	1,999
West Flegg	2,417	2,821

15. The most useful books for this chapter are: *Domesday Book for Norfolk*, ed. Philippa Brown 1984, Chichester, which gives a facsimile of the original abbreviated Latin on one page and an English translation on the page opposite, and H.C.Darby, *A Domesday Geography of Eastern England*, 1958, revised 1972, which includes a series of maps showing population density in the hundreds of Norfolk, the extent of recorded woodland and meadow, and the distribution of plough-teams, saltpans, fisheries and mills.

Population

The two Flegg Hundreds, along with others in East and South Norfolk, were the most densely populated in the county. The freemen, villeins and other tenants were heads of households with dependant families. I was surprised to see how very close the number of Domesday households were to returns from the first Census of 1801. (Table 2.1) Many readers will have some idea of what life was like in Norfolk two hundred years ago in the days of Nelson, Parson Woodeford and the Agricultural Improvers. It is important to remember that Norfolk was probably as busy a place in the late eleventh century, as it was seven hundred years later.

Table 2.3 shows the status of the tenants. Over two thirds of the inhabitants of Flegg were freemen and sokemen, that is men and women of free status, but it is not easy to define their position in society. Sokemen are almost always attached to manors and on some manors had specific services to render to their lords. On manors belonging to St Benet's Abbey they were often employed as ploughmen. In theory at least, freemen were free of all feudal control, but most had 'commended' themselves to a powerful lord in order to gain protection. These freemen, in commendation only, as Domesday says, had minimal obligations to their lords. They could sell their land, often without even consulting the lord. They had the right to attend the Hundred Court and take part in its deliberations.

Freemen and sokemen were numerous all over Eastern England, their numbers declining towards the west. Historians have thought that it was a Danish origin or influence which enabled the freemen to maintain their independence from feudal pressures. A more likely cause is now thought to have been the general economic prosperity of eastern England that helped the freemen to withstand the pressures of the feudal lords.[16]

16. Dodwell B (1941) 'The Free Peasantry of East Anglia in Domesday', in *Norfolk Archaeology, 27,* 145-57, links the freemen in Norfolk with Danish settlers. Davies R.H (1954) in *East Anglia and the Danelaw* points out that freemen are most numerous in areas of good arable soil, and it is their relative prosperity that enabled them to resist the landlords' pressures.

Table 2.3 Status of Tenants in Flegg in 1086

Village	Free-men	Soke-men	Villeins	Bordars	Total	Serfs	Est. Pop.
East Flegg							
Caister	108			5	113		509
Filby	22	3	7	12½	44½		198
Herringby	9		12	2	23		104
Mautby	34		7	12½	53½	2	243
Ness*	1				1		5
Ormesby	4	80	4	7	95		428
Runham	20½	11½	10		42		189
Scratby	11	7		3	21		95
Stokesby	24		15	15	54	4	447
Thrigby	18½			2½	21		95
TOTAL	**252**	**101½**	**55**	**59½**	**468**	**6**	**2,312**
West Flegg							
Ashby	5½	13		7	25½		105
Bastwick	9				9		41
Billockby	16			2	18		81
Burgh	36		2	12	50		225
Clippesby	17			7	24		108
Hemsby		4	33	13	50	3	228
Martham	43½	33	7	3	86½	1	390
Oby	20		2	7	29		131
Repps	27½				27½		124
Rollesby	36½		6	5	47½		214
Sco*	1			2	3		14
Somerton	19	26	14	32	91	2	412
Thurne	2½	10		6	18½		83
Winterton	31	3		24	58		259
TOTAL	**264½**	**89**	**64**	**120**	**537**	**6**	**2,455**

The reader may not recognise two villages, or 'vills' as Domesday book calls them, here and in Table 1.1. Sco was a small settlement between Martham and Repps at TG 434172. Ness was the 'ness' of upland to the south of Mautby Decoy in East Flegg. Half a freeman refers not to the man, but to his land. He must have held more land of the same lord somewhere else, perhaps the full holding had been divided.

Villeins and bordars account for only a third of the tenants. Whatever their exact legal status, they were certainly under close control of the manors on which they lived and where they provided most of the labour on the demesnes. They had their own farms, but the size of their holdings is not recorded. A hundred years later the usual villein holding in Martham was about twelve acres, but there were wide variations. Bordars had smaller holdings, perhaps about five acres. Bordars are particularly numerous in West Flegg where small manors sometimes relied entirely on them for labour. Only twelve serfs are recorded in Flegg.[17]

Households and Plough-teams

Domesday Book records the number of ploughs on every manor and farm, for the plough with its team of eight oxen was the essential implement for cultivation. The wooden plough itself was relatively easy to maintain and replace, but the animals that pulled it represented years of regular attention and nurture by their owners. In general the more plough-teams there were on a manor the greater was its value. The well-populated hundreds of East Norfolk had more ploughs to the square mile than any other part of the county. Flegg had both the greatest number of ploughs and the smallest area of woodland, which suggests that much of the land suitable for cultivation was already under the plough. Almost three-quarters of the plough-teams recorded were in the hands of the free tenants.[18] (Map 2.1)

17. Dodwell, B. *Free Peasantry in East Anglia.* 1941. Twelve-acre villein holdings are found in East Norfolk including Martham. The size of holdings tends to increase towards the west of the county, for example to 24 acres around Dereham and Gressenhall. This suggests that on the fertile soils of Eastern Norfolk twelve acres was quite sufficient to support a peasant family. See also Douglas, *Social Structure of Medieval East Anglia,* 1927.

18. J. Macdonald & G. Snooks, in *Domesday Economy,* 1986, show that in general the more ploughs on a manor, the greater its value.

Map 2.1 Households and Plough-teams

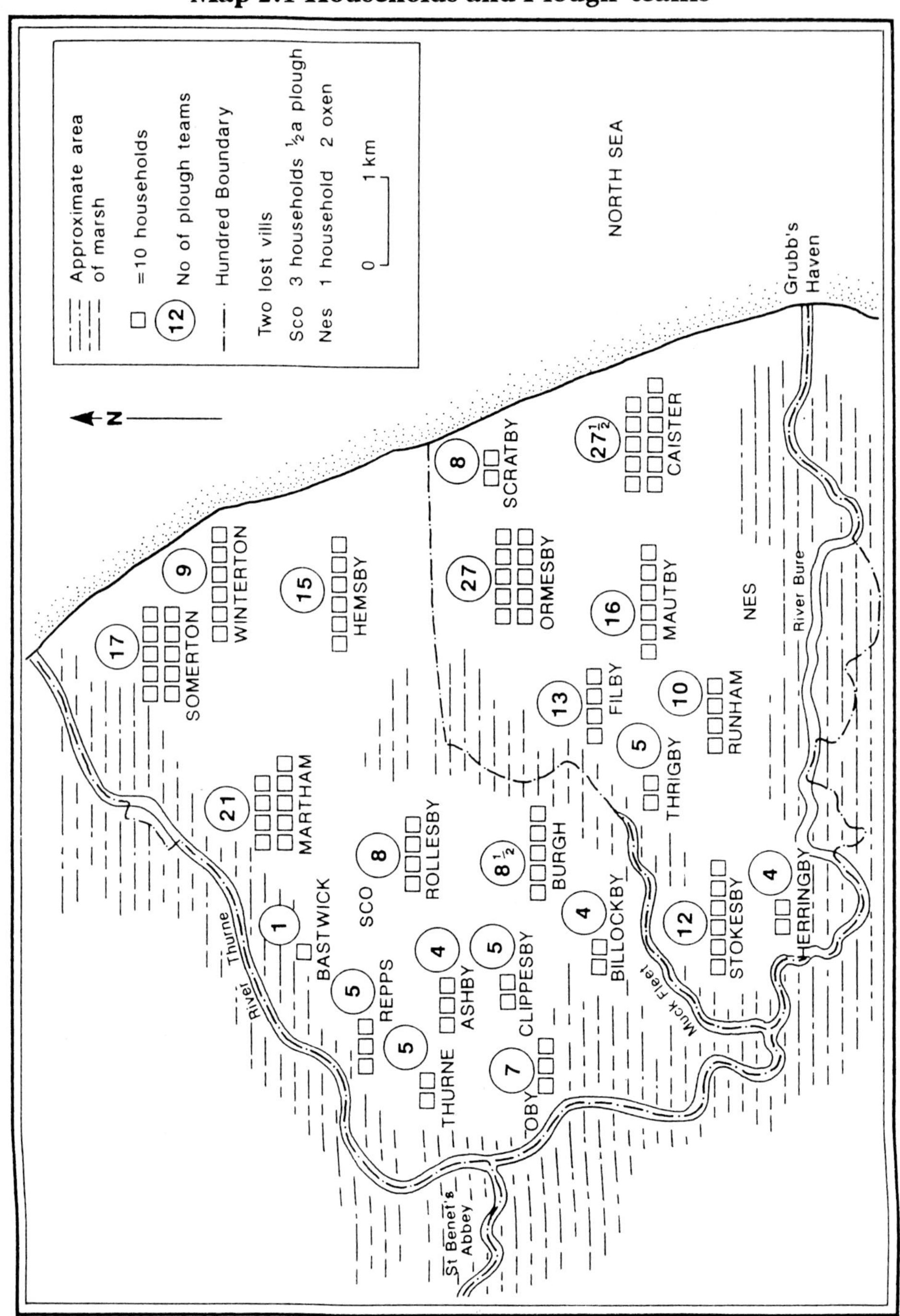

Woodland

Traditionally swineherds took their pigs to the woods to feed on the acorns or beech mast in autumn, and in East Anglia woodland was usually measured by the number of pigs that could feed there. In Flegg woodland is only recorded in Rollesby (wood for three pigs) and in Ashby (wood for six pigs). This must refer to Stefne Heath that lay on the relatively high ground between Rollesby and Ashby. Flegg was unusually short of wood. In the neighbouring hundred of Happing ten villages out of eighteen had woodland and there was a large wood for 180 pigs between Hickling, Ingham and Sutton. In Flegg the absence of any extensive wood must have been a very striking feature of the landscape.

Meadows

Meadowland was important because it provided both summer grazing and winter fodder for the many teams of oxen that Flegg possessed. All manors and most freemen's holdings had private meadows that were distinct from the common marshes used by all inhabitants of the village. Not surprisingly, meadowland was extensive in the Muckfleet valley and along the river Thurne. Martham and Somerton had exceptionally large areas of meadow. Comparatively little meadow is recorded for the coastal villages.

Mills

Caister: King's Manor: half a mill:
Mautby: King's Manor: half a mill.

These are the only two references to mills in Flegg in the Domesday Book. Most of the short, sluggish streams in Flegg were unsuitable for water mills. One of the few streams that might have provided a satisfactory millpond was the Pickerell Holme, which separates Caister from Mautby. It is possible that the two half mills refer to one mill serving both communities, for Earl Ralph held a manor in both villages. In the rest of Flegg, corn was ground on hand querns, as it had been since the Stone Age. The lords of the manors must have welcomed the new-fangled windmills that were introduced to England in the next century.[19]

Saltpans and Sheep Farming

Corn was not the only valuable commodity produced in Flegg. Both salt production and sheep farming brought in extra income. The spring tides up the river Bure flooded pools in the estuary with salt water that gradually evaporated in the summer sun and wind. The resulting brine was taken to earthenware pans on the marsh edge where the brine was heated until the salt crystallised. At the time of Domesday, Flegg was the centre of salt production in East Norfolk and no doubt provided the town of Norwich and the townsfolk and fishermen of Yarmouth with this essential commodity. Caister had forty-five saltpans, more than any other village in Norfolk, and every community near the banks of the Bure had its own saltpans, the number decreasing with the distance from the sea. It is possible that in the eleventh century the salt water may have reached as far as Acle bridge and beyond, and the saltpans of such inland villages as Filby may have been three or four miles away on the lower reaches of the Bure.[20](Map 2.2)

Sheep are found on the marsh pastures along the river Bure, up the Muck Fleet and near the banks of the Thurne, as Map 2.2 shows. Sheep are only recorded on the eight richest manors in fairly large flocks of a hundred or more. The smaller manors do not appear to have kept sheep, certainly not in numbers large enough to be recorded. On the small manor at Herringby no sheep are recorded, although there was said to be pasture for a hundred. In other areas of East Norfolk sheep are kept on both large and small manors and in flocks of very varying size. Unless there is some quirk in recording the facts, sheep farming in Flegg was in the

19. The name Pickerell Holme is somewhat strange for a stream, since the word 'holme' is usually applied to a gravel bank in a marsh. A pickerel is a small pike. There is a bank where the footpath from West Caister to Mautby crosses the stream, which might be the remains of a dam. Further investigation is called for.

20. The only evidence for a salt works in Flegg is the remark of a nineteenth century clergyman. It is shown on the older Ordnance Maps at Herringby. The court rolls of Burgh record 'the salt marsh' down by Acle Bridge, as distinct from the fresh marsh along the Muck Fleet. So salt-making may once have been possible as far up the Bure as Acle.

Map 2.2 Sheep and Saltpans in Flegg

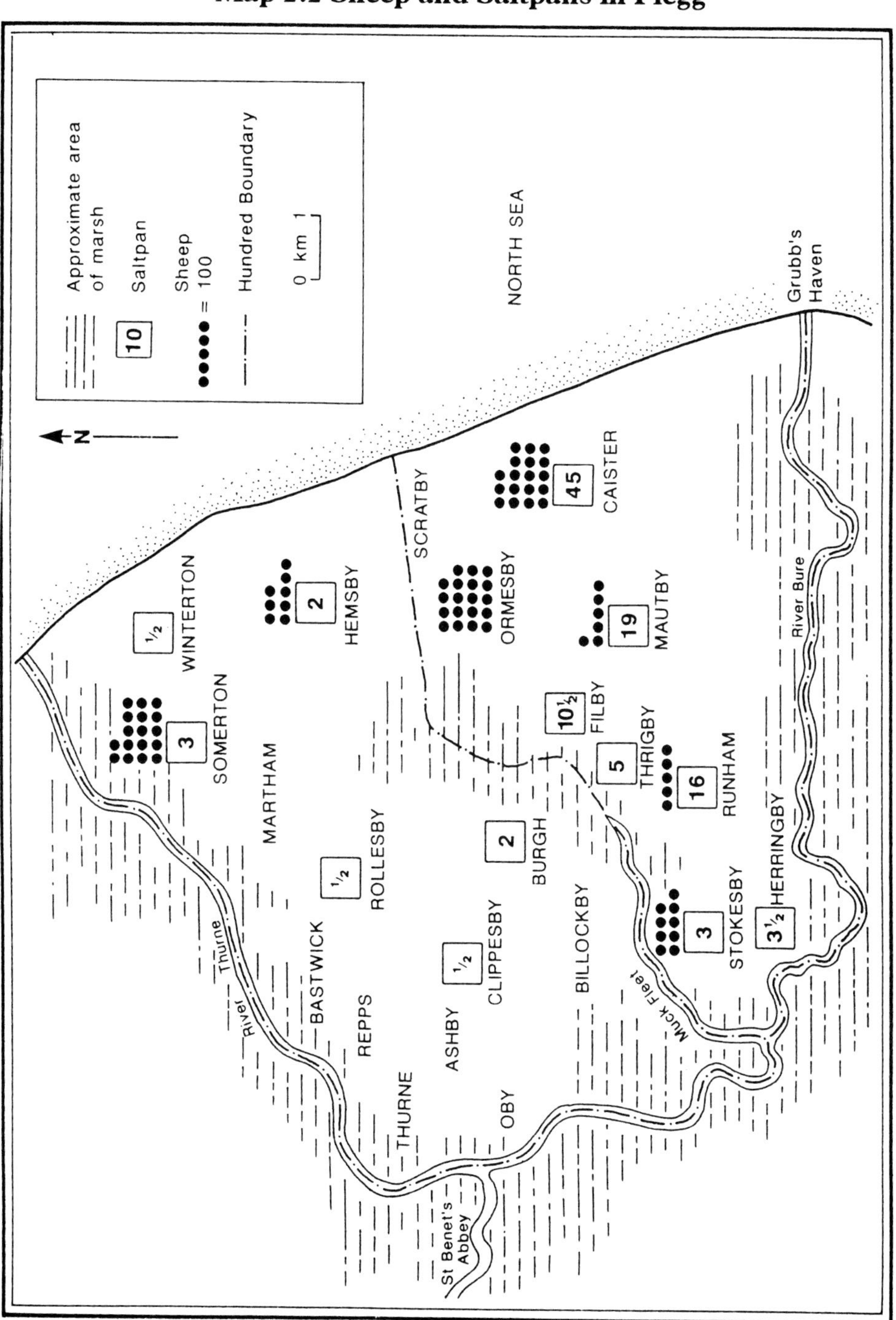

hands of the wealthier landlords. It was a relatively large-scale operation and the wool and skins must have gone to the markets of Yarmouth and Norwich.

Animal Husbandry

As well as the plough oxen, the manor farmyards contained a number of familiar animals. (Table 2.4) The animals (*animalia* in Latin) were most probably bulls or breeding cows. The horses were only used for riding, not for work on the farm at this date. The table shows clearly that only the larger manors had flocks of sheep. Pigs, on the other hand are found on most manors in small numbers, but on Count Alan's manor at Somerton, his steward, Wymarc, had a herd of thirty-four. Count Alan or his steward seems to have specialised in livestock for the flock of sheep at Somerton had doubled in the twenty years since Domesday. Wymarc also kept a herd of twenty-four pigs five miles away at Hickling, in Happing Hundred.

Table 2.4. Livestock (excluding plough-oxen)

Village	Lord	Horses	Animals	Pigs	Sheep	Etc.
Caister	King	3	8	12	360	
Filby	Rabel	2	1	10		
	St Benet's	1				
Herringby	Reinbald				Pasture For 100 sheep	
Mautby	King		7	2	112	
Runham	King	1	1	9	101	
Ormesby	King	3	4	6	381	
Stokesby	Ecouis	2	6	10	180	
Hemsby	Bishop			12	160	
Oby	St Benet's	3	2	6		
Rollesby	St Benet's			7		
Somerton	King	3	8		145	2 bee-hives
	Count Alan	3	2	34	200	
Thurne	St Benet's	2		6		
Winterton	St Benet's			6		

Turbaries and Fisheries

Domesday has many omissions. No mention is made of peat-digging although peat was certainly the main fuel in east Norfolk at that time. In fact Domesday Book only mentions turbaries in one or two places in England. I think it possible that in Flegg all the inhabitants of a village could cut peat freely in the marsh and that the lords of the manors had no private turbaries and so no income was recorded from that source. Nor are any fisheries mentioned in Flegg although the Domesday Commissioners were specifically required to note them and did so along the rivers of west Norfolk. Perhaps in Flegg, fishing, like peat-digging, was free for everyone, and was not a direct source of manorial income.

The Landscape (See Map 2.3)

Would we have recognised Flegg in the eleventh century? Perhaps it has changed less than many parts of England. There was little untamed land, and the cultivated fields of one village must often have run up to the fields of the next. The marsh was not a watery wilderness, but a well-used and valuable resource. We would see hay-making on the meadows, sheep on the marshes (a sight which has again become familiar to us in recent years), and the unfamiliar activities of turf-digging in the Muck Fleet valley and salt-making in the Bure estuary. On the arable fields we would recognise the crops of barley and wheat, although not perhaps the rye. Bullocks and cows would be everywhere, pulling the ploughs, harrows and carts, feeding in the meadows and the marsh pastures or tethered on the grassy verge of the field paths. The fallow fields where pigs rooted and a few horses grazed would be unfamiliar to us, but not unlike the neglected rough grazing of the years of depression between the two World Wars, or the 'set-aside' land of today. There would be more trees than today in copses or groves and along the field paths, but as now, no large woods. (Map 2.3)

We would easily recognise the village names that have changed very little in the last nine hundred years, but would we recognise the villages? Most villages had a church that probably stood on the same site as today. Both the Domesday Book and the records of St Benet's Abbey tell of the existence of churches in the eleventh century. (Map 2.3) We cannot be sure that the villages had the same pattern as they have now, although one or two seem to have

Map 2.3. Domesday Landscape of Flegg

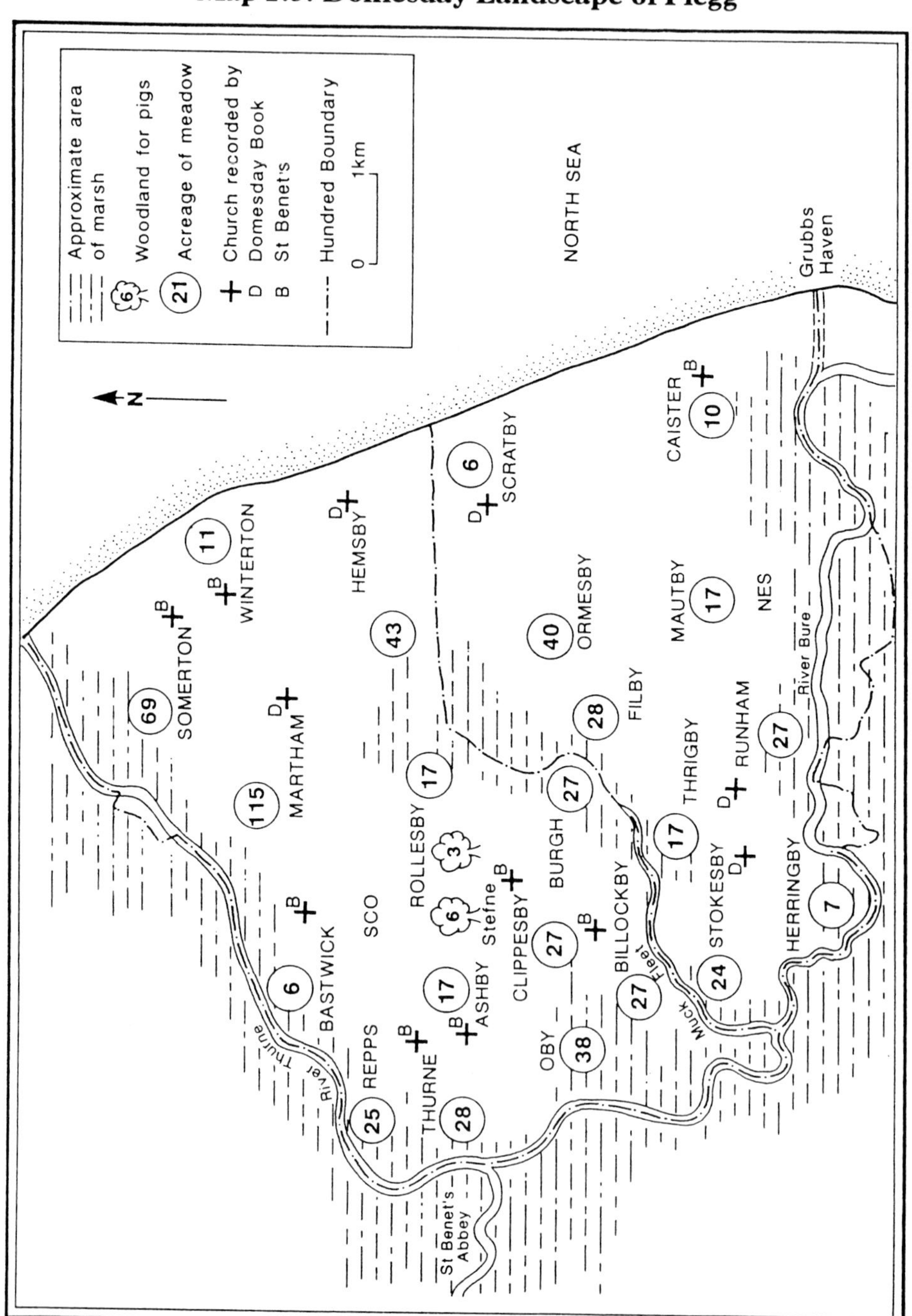

retained their eleventh century shape. Hemsby, which at Domesday had only one manor and one feudal lord, has always had a nucleated, compact settlement. The three small manors at Filby were spaced along the main road to Yarmouth as the farms, cottages and residential estates are today. We know that Count Alan's large manor at Somerton became the parish of West Somerton, while the king's smaller manor became East Somerton. On the whole, villages full of freemen, such as Repps and Clippesby, developed a dispersed pattern. Above all, Flegg was a busy place and we would be very much aware of people out and about, working in the fields and farmyards, meadows and marshes. Oby, Ashby and Somerton record more households in 1086 than they had in 1981, and this is probably also true of Stokesby, Herringby, Mautby and Runham. Throughout the Middle Ages Flegg was not a remote and backward part of England but a well-populated area with excellent agriculture and traversed by an an important trade route from Norwich to Yarmouth and so to the continent.[21]

21. For some indication of the relative sizes of Flegg villages over the period from 1086 and 1981 see Table 1.1 on page 28.

Chapter 3: Domesday Flegg: Manors and their Lords; Freemen and their Farms.

The Manors

Table 3.1 The Manors of Flegg listed in order of Value

The acreage is given in 'carucates' (120 acres). This refers to the demesne, but it is very approximate.

Village	Lord	Acreage	Tenants Unfree	Tenants Free	Ploughs	Salt-pans	Sheep	Values
Hemsby &	Bishop	3c.	49	4	15	2	160	£29
Martham		2c.	11	27	3			
Ormesby	King	3c.30a.	10	80	25½		381	£28
Caister	King [1]	4c.		80	22	39	360	£14
Stokesby	Ecouis	3c.	33	24	12	3	180	£10.1s.
Somerton	Count Alan	3c.	15	16	9	1½	200	£9
Mautby	King [1]	1½c.	11	30	15½	17½	122	£6
Runham	King [1]	1½c.	10	23	8	16	101	£5
Caister	St Benet's	1c.	4	28	5½	6		£3.5s.
Filby	Rabel	2c.47a.	8	17	6			£2.10s.
Oby	St Benet's	1½c.	4	10	4½			£1.16s.
Ashby	St Benet's	2c.	7	13	3½			£1.6s.
Rollesby	St Benet's	1c.	6	11	3½			£1.6s.
Thurne	St Benet's	1c.	6	10	3½			£1.6s.
Winterton	St Benet's	1c.	14	10	4½			£1.6s.
Billockby	Bishop	57a.	8	1½				£1
Burgh	St Benet's	1c.	2	6	1			£1
Burgh	Bigot	106a.	9	17	4½			£1
Herringby	Reinbald	100a.	14	8	4			£1
Somerton	King [3]	1c.	23	19	5½	1½	145	£1
Filby	Warenne	1c.	3		1½	2		16s.
Scratby	St Benet's	109a.	3		1½			10s.
Filby	St Benet's	1c.20a.	5	3	2½	1		3s.?

1 - Manors formerly belonging to Earl Ralph. 2 - Stokesby was in fact let for £15 4s a year. 3 - Somerton had been held by Archbishop Stigand.

The Normans thought of the manor as the normal economic and agricultural unit. Table 3.1 gives the names of the tenants-in-chief who held manors in Flegg, and the details of their estates. Most were either dignitaries of the Church or Normans of national importance, such as Count Alan, who was the King's son-in-law, or William Warenne who held land in thirteen counties. None of the Flegg manors were large estates like Count Alan's manor of Costessey with its deer park and dependent manors all over South Norfolk. Most of the tenants-in-chief probably never even visited Flegg, but sent their stewards to collect the rents; only Reinbald the Goldsmith at Herringby and Rabel the Engineer at Filby may have lived on their manors.

Thurne Manor

Manors differed very much in their size and composition, and I want to compare the small manor at Thurne, with the larger and much more valuable manor at Hemsby. Thurne manor belonged to St Benet's Abbey. Here is the entry from Domesday Book:

> St Benedict has always held Thurne,
> 1 carucate of land.
> Always 6 bordars
> Meadow, 8 acres; 1 plough on demesne; ½ men's plough;
> 2 horses, 6 pigs.
> 10 sokemen, 45 acres; meadow, 6½ acres; 2 ploughs.
> Value then 20s.; now 26s. 8d.
> It has 5 furlongs in length and 4 in width; tax 9d.
> Others hold there.

The manor farm was a small one, reckoned at one carucate. A bailiff, appointed by the Abbot of St Benet's, would have lived in the manor house, managed the farm, and sent corn and other produce by boat two miles up the Bure to the monastery, 'for the supplies of the Monks' as it says in Domesday Book. Towards the river lay the eight acres of meadow that provided the plough-beasts with summer grazing and hay and rough grasses for winter feed.

Most of the labour on the home farm was supplied by six bordars. As well as these unfree tenants, ten sokemen were attached to the manor. Their two plough-teams would mean about sixteen head of cattle to maintain on their six acres of meadow. As on other manors belonging to St Benet's, it is likely that the sokemen were required to do ploughing and harvesting work on the demesne.[22]

The value of the manor reflects the annual rent that could be obtained if the estate was let. The value had risen in the twenty years since the Conquest but not as much as on some of the larger manors. The measurements at the end of the entry refer to the size of the village, and bear some relation to the amount of tax Thurne had to pay. It is difficult to interpret the area of a village from the Domesday measurements, but then as now, Thurne was one of the smallest villages in Flegg. Like most small manors it had no flock of sheep to increase its value. The final statement is 'Others hold there'. The 'others' were in fact one man, Roger Bigot, who was the lord of two freemen who each had a holding of about twenty acres. One of them was an outlaw who had returned to claim his land.

To sum up, in 1086 Thurne was a community of about twenty households with a probable population of nearly a hundred. It was one of the smaller villages in 1086, as it still is today. In 1981 there were forty-five households in the village and a probable population of a hundred and thirty. The village does not seem to be very much larger now than it was nine hundred years ago.

Hemsby Manor

The Bishop's manor of Hemsby was the most valuable estate in Flegg. The entry is given below.[23]

Lands of the Bishop.
In Lordship 3 carucates of land.
Always 33 villeins; 13 bordars.
Then 6 serfs, now 3.

22. R.G.West.1932 'First Register of St Benet's Abbey', *Norfolk Record Society*. Vol.2. This shows it was customary for sokemen to do ploughing and harvest services on Abbey estates.

23. The Bishopric was at North Elmham before 1071, at which date it was moved to Thetford. Bishop William of Thetford, appointed in 1085, was Bishop at the time of Domesday. In 1094 or 5 the See was moved by Bishop Herbert de Losinga to Norwich.

Always 3 ploughs in demesne; 11 men's ploughs.
Meadow, 40 acres; 2 salt-pans
1 church, 20 acres; value 16d
Now 12 pigs; 160 sheep.
4 Sokemen 60 acres; meadow 3 acres, always 1 plough
To this manor belongs 1 outlier, Martham. 2 carucates of land Always 7 villeins; 3 bordars; 1 serf.
Always 2 ploughs in demesne; 1 men's plough
Meadow, 50 acres.
Further 27 sokemen, 30 acres of land; meadow 5 acres.
In Winterton 2 freemen; 10 acres; always ½ plough.
Value then £26; now £29
The whole has 1½ leagues in length and in width 1 league; tax 30d., but more hold there.
In Sco 2 bordars, 6 acres. They belong to Hemsby.[24]

Hemsby manor is quite a contrast to St Benet's little manor at Thurne. The forty-six villeins and bordars with their eleven ploughs make Hemsby look very similar to the text-book manors of the Midlands. Like many large manors it had a smaller manor attached to it at Martham, and tenants in Winterton and Sco. Unlike Thurne it had a flock of sheep. The large number of villeins is so untypical of Flegg that it seems possible that an earlier owner had remodelled the estate and perhaps reduced a group of free tenants to villein status in order to get greater control over them and their ploughs. If human memory did not distort the facts, this manorial pattern had already been established by 1066, at which time Hemsby, valued at £26, was over twice as valuable as any other manor in Flegg. By 1086 the value of Hemsby although still the highest in Flegg, had only risen by £3 to £29, while the value of other comparable manors had often doubled.

Earl Ralph's Manors

The prosperity of Hemsby manor must have impressed other landlords, some of whom appear to have tried to improve their estates after the Hemsby model. Such a landlord was Earl Ralph

24. For information about Sco, see Chapter 1, page 25.

whose father had not taken part in the Battle at Hastings and so continued in the possession of his estates. At Caister Earl Ralph, 'made a manor' from the land which eighty freemen had held in the time of his father. The freemen were no doubt deprived of some of their land to form the demesne, and were required to work on the manor farm. The estate included thirty-nine salt-pans, by far the largest number on any Flegg manor, and a flock of 360 sheep. Its value increased from £8 in 1066 to £14 in 1086.

Earl Ralph was also busy on his other manors. At Mautby he added fourteen freemen with nine ploughs to the manor. The estate more than doubled in value. He may have built the mill on the

Mautby Church

The round tower with its layer of dark stone (ironstone conglomerate) is typical of twelfth century churches.

Photo: J.C.Barringer 2000

stream between Mautby and Caister. (See page 35) Was he also responsible for the round tower of Mautby church with its striking bands of warm, brown, ironbound, conglomerate stone? At Runham the value of his manor increased from £1 10s. to £4 10s. However Earl Ralph did not enjoy his success for long. In 1075 he rebelled unsuccessfully against William and went into exile in Brittany. His lands were confiscated and were in the King's hands in 1086.

The five wealthy manors of Hemsby, Stokesby, Ormesby, Caister and Somerton and Earl Ralph's rather smaller manors at Mautby and Runham had certain features in common. The combined labour force of free and bond tenants attached to these estates was large. Four of the manors had serfs. Except at Hemsby, which seems to have been a special case, the freemen and sokemen outnumbered the unfree tenants, and it was these men with their ploughs who contributed substantially to the value of the estates. All the manors had flocks of sheep and most had salt-pans. They all lay in an arc, close to the coast or along the estuary of the river Bure. Perhaps the proximity of the sea, the river system and Yarmouth had also favoured their development.

However these wealthy estates were not typical of Flegg, and were outnumbered by smaller, less valuable manors, like St Benet's manor at Thurne. The smaller manors had fewer tenants, no serfs, and far fewer ploughs. Their values had generally increased by about a third in the twenty years after the Conquest, while the values of the larger manors had often doubled. All St Benet's manors fall into this group of small manors. During most of the twenty years between the Conquest and the compiling of Domesday Book, the Abbot, a supporter of Harold, was in exile in Denmark. Whoever managed the Abbey's property during the period of the Abbot's exile did not follow Earl Ralph's example of reorganising the estates and maximising profits. It is not surprising that the monastery lost some land and influence during this period, in particular to Roger Bigot. In 1105, twenty years after the survey was written, the Abbot drew up a list of the tenants whom he accused Roger Bigot of taking from the Abbey. In Oby there was Ringolf, who went to Denmark with the Abbot, and Lefchild, Elfred, Sunning and Scotlande who remained at Oby. Godric the priest at Clippesby and Tukke the smith of Ashby and his son, willingly or unwillingly, transferred their loyalty to Roger Bigot. Is the Ashby smith the ancestor of the many 'Tookes' who now live in Flegg? The Abbey also lost the patronage of five men in Repps, one in Somerton, and Ulfkettel in Thurne. Was he perhaps the outlaw who returned to claim his land?[25] (See page 44)

25. Stenton, F.M. *St Benet of Holme and the Norman Conquest,* 1922, pp 227-8, 232, for details of Bigot's acquisition of St Benet's freemen. H.C.Darby, *Domesday England,* 1977, discusses the position of the many freemen in Eastern England at length.

The Freemen and Sokemen and their farms

Freemen and sokemen under different feudal lords are found in all the Flegg villages. Four small villages, Thrigby, Clippesby, Bastwick and Repps had no manors and were communities composed entirely of freemen and their families. At Repps, Count Alan was the lord of two freemen, Roger Bigot of seven, the Abbot of St Benet's of six, William de Ecouis of one, and another group of seven freemen, who had paid no taxes before the Conquest, were placed in the care of Roger Bigot. Other villages had patterns of lordship almost as complicated as that at Repps.[26]

Free tenants are often recorded as holding land in groups, but the size of the group varies enormously, and it is impossible to know how the land was divided among the tenants. The eighty sokemen at Ormesby and eighty freemen at Caister are exceptionally large groups. At Martham thirty-six freemen under the patronage of the Bishop held over five carucates of land and fifty acres of meadow, an estate larger than any Flegg manor. More usually the groups contained ten or fewer tenants. A small group may have all been members of one family. At Bastwick two free women, the only women mentioned in Flegg, held thirteen acres from Roger Bigot. They were surely sisters who had inherited the land on the death of their father.

Table 3.2. Numbers of Tenants in Groups

Group size	2 - 5 tenants	6 - 10	11 - 20	20 - 50	Over 50
No. of holdings	30	22	10	3	2

As well as tenants in groups Domesday also records many single tenants and the size of their holdings as shown by Table 2.7.

Table 3.3. Size of Holdings of Single Tenants

Acreage	Under 10 a.	10-19a.	20-29a.	30-39a.	Over 50
No. of holdings	6	7	7	5	1

26. The pattern of divided lordship survived into the sixteenth century. A survey of Fastolfs and Oby manors in Repps and Bastwick in 1572 shows eight manors in Repps with Bastwick. See NRO, EVL 485.

There was no standard size for a free holding. Tenants could sell and purchase land, and this tended to produce a wide variation in the size of holdings. They ranged from three acres, which a blind man held at Martham, to the hundred-acre mini-manor of a St Benet's sokeman in Winterton. Freemen and sokemen were found at all levels of society. Many had holdings, as small as five acres or even less, while others had holdings of about ten or twelve acres, quite adequate to support a peasant family in East Norfolk. A few had substantial farms of over twenty or thirty acres, often with other freemen, villeins and bordars under them. Such a freeman was Stanhard, the Deacon, a tenant of Roger Bigot. A mid-twelfth century document describes his estate in Clippesby. He held twenty-five acres of arable land and eight of marsh. Under him were five tenants with holdings of between five and eight acres and a few acres of marsh each. Stanhard's homestead lay near a copse, on a three-acre site, with a barn and other farm buildings in the courtyard, as well as a hall and a solar. The barn, the storehouse of the precious grain, probably dominated all the other buildings, including the hall, the only room with a fire, and the solar, which was Stanhard's private apartment. This is the earliest description of a domestic building that I have found in Flegg, and it may be the original Clippesby Hall. I doubt whether in the eleventh or twelfth centuries many freemen had as extensive an establishment as Stanhard.[27]

Roger Bigot's freeman at Ness in Mautby with his fifteen-acre holding was perhaps more typical of a self-sufficient free tenant. His holding lay on a spur of high land between the Bure estuary to the south, and the tongue of marshland to the north, now known as Mautby Decoy. His dwelling was probably on or near the present Decoy Farmhouse. He kept two oxen, which he could use for many operations about the farm and which would join those of other freemen to make up a full plough-team. He held an acre of meadow and a share in a salt-pan on the estuary. The value or rent of his holding was 16d. a year. He and his descendants appear to have preserved their independence into the twelfth century for in 1198 Adam de Ness was in possession of a fifteen acre holding in Mautby. Members of the de Ness family were active in the thirteenth and fourteenth centuries on various local government

27· F.M.Stenton 'St Benet's at Holme and the Norman Conquest' 1922, p.232, E.H.R. vol..27.

Decoy Farm, Mautby

Probable site of Freeman's Farm at the 'lost vill of Ness', Decoy Farm stands on a ridge overlooking the marshes and the River Bure.

commissions and by that time seem to have been regarded as members of the lesser gentry.[28]

In general, however, holdings in Norfolk were small compared with peasant holdings in other parts of England. Professor Darby asks whether 'large numbers in Norfolk and Lincolnshire were maintaining themselves as independent members of society on resources that can have been little more than adequate for bare subsistence?'[29]

Historians tend to use the evidence of the Midlands and Southern England to judge peasant agriculture. In those areas peasant holdings were usually fifteen or thirty acres. Farming was organised on a two or three field system, in which a half or a third of the arable land of the village remained unsown each year to rest the land and to provide summer grazing for livestock. There is no evidence that such a system existed in East Norfolk. The fertile and well-drained soil did not have to be rested every second or third year, nor, in a land of extensive meadow and marshland, was a large area of the arable needed for summer grazing. A Norfolk

28. Barbara Cornford 'Lost Vill at Ness' in *Norfolk Archaeology* 1998.

29. Darby H.C. 1977.

freeman could crop most of his holding each year. He and his neighbours had the animal power and equipment to cultivate the land, dung from their livestock to maintain the fertility of the soil and family labour to work the land intensively.

It is easy to forget that the holdings were mixed farms, where animal husbandry was almost as important as arable farming. Most farms included an acre or so of meadow, which would provide rough hay for winter feed and summer grazing for the cattle. The family cow provided the household with milk and cheese. Since pigs were found on even the smallest manors in Flegg it seems likely that many freemen kept a few pigs. Those freemen lucky enough to have saltpans would have another valuable product and a possible source of income. Free fishing in the rivers and all the resources of the marsh helped to sustain a viable standard of living. Professor Darby wonders whether the freemen augmented their livelihood by sheep farming, but sheep do not seem to have been kept extensively on peasant farms in Flegg until after the Black Death. I think it was the cattle that gave the freemen and sokemen an extra economic resource in the eleventh century.

Nearly three quarters of all the ploughs in Flegg were in the hands of the freemen and sokemen. (See Table 3.4) It seems probable that each freeman was expected to bring a pair of oxen to a plough; four free tenants frequently kept a full plough-team of eight oxen and two freemen often have half a plough. In Flegg and elsewhere in East Norfolk some tenants, including the two Bastwick ladies and Bigot's freeman at Ness, are said to plough with two oxen, which again suggests that two oxen may have been the customary number for a free holding to provide. Each plough-team would usually cultivate the land of a number of tenants.

Table 3.4 Number of Ploughs on the Manors, and on Free Holdings

	No. of ploughs on demesnes	No. of ploughs of unfree tenants	No. of ploughs of free tenants
East Flegg	14½ (11 manors)	7	98
West Flegg	18½ (12 manors)	19	69

Barbara Dodwell has calculated that in East Norfolk each 'free' plough with its team of eight oxen would keep about 20 to 40 acres of free land in cultivation. My calculations are similar, suggesting that in West Flegg each plough belonging to free tenants kept 32 acres in cultivation, and in East Flegg, 27 acres. This suggests that a freeman's land was probably ploughed more thoroughly and more frequently than the manor demesne.[30]

The imbalance between the number of plough-teams found on the manors and on the freemen's holdings is very striking. (Table 3.4) On a Flegg manor the number of plough-teams on the demesne is almost always identical with the number of carucates on the manor, that is one plough to 120 acres. Of course the lord could call on the ploughs of the villeins and bordars to work on the demesne, but they seldom provided more than one extra plough-team, even on the largest manors. (Hemsby is a notable exception. See p. 42-3) If the lord wanted to exploit his land as fully as the free tenants did their small holdings, he needed the freemen's ploughs to work the demesne intensively. On certain manors St Benet's Abbey expected their sokemen to provide ploughing services on the demesne. Earl Ralph and other landlords were eager to add freemen and sokemen with their numerous ploughs to their manors. We can only guess what inducement or pressure persuaded so many free tenants to become part of the manorial organisation after the Norman Conquest and to accept the imposition of ploughing services.

After the Norman Conquest

In many ways Flegg had not changed much in the twenty years between the Norman Conquest and the writing of Domesday Book. Unlike some parts of Norfolk, there is no indication that Flegg was involved in Earl Ralph's rebellion. In entry after entry the number of ploughs, men and livestock are the same for the two dates, and where there are variations, they are usually very slight. This continuity probably indicates a stable and generally prosperous economy. (The puzzling entry for Ormesby which records thirty-three ploughs at the Conquest, and twenty-three in 1086 may be a scribe's error. The lower figure is probably correct.)

30. B Dodwell, 'The Free Peasantry of East Anglia' in *Norfolk Archaeology* vol. 27, 1941.

The days of relative prosperity and independence for the free tenants were coming to an end under the régime of the Norman landlords. The new lords no longer sub-let their manors to Saxon or Danish freemen, but to their own clients. For example, at Somerton Count Alan replaced Harold's freeman, Aelfric, with his steward, Wymarc. Increased rents and heavy taxation meant that freemen and sokemen had to sell their land, their produce or their labour to find the money to satisfy the demands of landlords and the King. The value of most freemen's holdings increased between 1066 and 1086, indicating that the landlords raised the rents during those twenty years.

In the twelfth century the introduction of windmills gave the landlords other sources of income. By 1200 windmills at Herringby and Rollesby had been recorded and by 1300 windmills were common in all Flegg villages. At the same time the use of horses for ploughing meant that the lords were less dependent on the ox-drawn ploughs of their freemen and sokemen to cultivate the demesne. By 1245 ploughing was done by horses on the Abbot of St Benet's manor of Ashby and no doubt on most other manors. Throughout the twelfth and thirteenth centuries manorial lords in East Norfolk were curtailing the use of the common marshes and rivers by establishing private turbaries and fisheries, as is seen in the annals of St Benet's Abbey. In 1274 de Burgo claimed a private fishery from Burgh bridge to Stokesby Fleche which used to be common, and in 1284 William de Stalham and Walter de Burgo divided the fisheries in the remainder of the Muck Fleet between them. These political and economic circumstances left the free tenants at the mercy of their lords, and for many of them this meant complete integration into the manorial organisation.[31]

31. For windmills see Kealey. E 1984. Use of horses for ploughing , see NRO For de Burgo's private fishery see Blomefield vol.xi, and for the division of the Muck Fleet fishery in 1284, Ancient Deeds 11645.

Chapter 4. The Monastic Manors of Flegg in the Twelfth and Thirteenth Centuries

In England the twelfth and thirteenth centuries saw the continuing growth of population, increasing trade and a rise in prices particularly in the period 1180-1220. Landlords and farmers with a surplus of agricultural produce could find a ready market in the growing towns and ports, such as Norwich and Yarmouth. The measure of Yarmouth's prosperity is reflected in her 1334 assessment for taxation at £100, which was slightly higher than £97 for Norwich. Flegg shared in Yarmouth's prosperity, for Flegg farms fed the town and victualled her ships. It is no surprise that the Flegg taxation assessments, like those of Yarmouth, were among the highest in the kingdom.[32]

Monastic estates benefited most from the high grain prices and the low cost of labour at a time of an expanding population. Being permanent institutions, monasteries could not be subject to death duties. They could buy land on the open market and often received gifts from wealthy landowners in return for prayers to be said for the souls of the donors and their families. The monks did not concern themselves with the day-to-day business of their landed estates, for the monastery employed a steward with specialised training. He was responsible for keeping the records of the estates belonging to his institution, and that included the annual accounts that the manorial bailiffs presented each year. The records of the larger monasteries, such as the Cathedral Priory of Norwich, have usually survived much better than those of smaller monastic houses or of lay landlords.

The Estates of the Cathedral Priory in Flegg

When Bishop Losinga founded the Cathedral Priory monastery in 1101, he endowed it with extensive lands in Norfolk including the

32. R.E. Glasscock,1963, 'Distribution of Wealth in East Anglia' in *Institute of British Geographers; Trans. and Papers 1963.* P.D.A.Harvey 'English Inflation of 1180-1220' in *Peasants, Knights and Heretics* ed. R. Hilton. CUP. 1951.

manors of Hemsby and Martham. Hemsby was the most valuable manor in Flegg according to the Domesday record, and the only one with a plentiful supply of villein labour. Unfortunately its records have not survived as well as those of the Priory manor of Martham. At first the two manors were let for rent, but the price-rise at the beginning of the thirteenth century meant that fixed rents were a wasting asset. With the increase in the price of grain it made economic sense for the Priory to take the estates in hand and to enjoy the produce and profits. In 1257, when the rent was two years overdue, the Priory ended Sir Walter de Mautby's lease of the two manors. Sir Walter was compensated with the manor of Beckham in North Norfolk, and was paid the very large sum of two hundred marks (£126 6s. 8d.) for renouncing his claim to Hemsby and Martham. For the next two hundred years a Bailiff appointed by the Priory ran the two Flegg estates which were the most valuable corn manors in the Priory's possession. Arable land in Hemsby and Martham was valued at 3s. an acre, twice as much as on any other Priory estate. These figures alone explain why the Prior was prepared to pay a high price to end Walter de Mautby's lease.[33]

These two estates consistently maintained high yields of corn year after year in the late thirteenth and early fourteenth centuries. Campbell considers that the average yield of wheat per acre was comparable with that of late eighteenth century England. This high standard was achieved in a number of ways. Both Martham and Hemsby enjoyed a fertile, well-drained soil and, in the case of Martham, a compact demesne farm lying close to the manor farmyard. Spring-sown crops predominated leaving much of the land unsown during the autumn and winter to be prepared for sowing in the spring. A growing population meant a ready supply of cheap labour for such tasks as digging and spreading marl, dung-spreading, breaking up the ground, hoeing and weeding. The usual wage for this work was 1d. or 1½d. a day. More than three quarters of the demesne was cropped each year, and land that was left fallow was ploughed four or five times during the year to control the weeds. Peas were grown to improve the soil and to provide live-

33. See H.W.Saunders, *First Register of Norwich Cathedral Priory*, Norfolk Record Society vol xi, Saunders 1939, No 33. for the end of Sir Walter de Mautby's lease.

stock with a nutritious food that would ultimately be returned to the land as dung. Agricultural production must have been stimulated by the growing port of Yarmouth, which provided an expanding market for the produce of the manor. The thirteenth century was the period of so-called 'High Farming' when, with stable or high prices, low labour costs and a growing expertise in farming methods, large estates were very profitable concerns. Martham and Hemsby, rather like Holkham in the late eighteenth century, were prime examples of the intensive farming methods of their time.[34]

The two manors supplied much of the wheat and malt used in the Priory kitchens and brew-houses. Hemsby sent on average one hundred and eighty-three quarters of wheat (possibly as much as thirty-six tons) and double that amount of malt each year to the monastery, while the smaller manor of Martham provided about half that quantity of both grains. Livestock farming, although on a smaller scale, had an important function in providing draught animals for the ploughs and manure for the fields. Surplus grain and livestock was sold locally. Both manors made cash payments to the monastery, Hemsby providing an average of £42 a year and Martham £14 in the late thirteenth century. The manors also supplied the monastery with eels and pike, geese, swans and peacocks. More information about Martham manor will be found in Chapters 7, 8 and 9.[35]

The medieval manor house at Hemsby stood at the end of Hall Road. Little or no trace of it remains today, but an inventory of the house and farmyard taken in 1352 has survived. It provides a

34. The Charters of the Cathedral Priory shows that in the twelfth century in Hemsby the Prior on several occasions acquired small pieces of land next to existing demesne land through purchase, gift or exchange. Dodwell 1985. In this way, I think, he tried to build up a compact demesne.B.Campbell. 'Agriculural Progress etc.' 1983 for the efficiency of the agriculture of Hemsby and Martham manors. *Proficuum Maneriorum* in NRO DCN 40/13. This Account Book of the Priory lands puts a value on each acre sown with corn on the demesne land of its manors in the early fourteenth century. Hemsby and Martham were both valued at 3s.an acre, twice as much as any other manor.

35. N.R.O. DCN 60/23/1 onwards for Martham Manorial Accounts. DCN 60/15/1 1265-1335, for Hemsby Manorial Accounts.

picture of sparsely furnished living accommodation, adequately provided with kitchen and other service rooms. The house provided accommodation for the bailiff and for occasional visits by the steward and other Priory officials The inventory was taken only two years after the Black Death, so it is not surprising that some of the old and broken items had not been replaced.

The hall with its central hearth was the main room where meals were taken, business conducted and the manor court met. It contained six trestle tables, four benches, a broken basin, a broken set of fire irons and a wall-hanging. At one end of the hall were the buttery and the pantry from which drink and bread were served. Two chambers, each furnished with a bench, provided rooms for the bailiff and the steward on his visits to the manor. The kitchen, larder, dairy and bakehouse were separate buildings. There was also a chapel equipped with two altars, a painted panel above the altar, a bell, a cupboard and a bench.

In the farmyard the only building mentioned in the inventory was the granary. The barn at Hall Farm, Hemsby, contains some thirteenth century woodwork, which may have survived from the original granary. The bailiff's accounts show that other buildings included a stable, a bullock shed, and a malt-house and kiln, where half the barley harvested would be made into malt. The animals included ten plough horses, a herd of three bulls and twenty-six cows and the usual collection of pigs, geese, cocks and hens. A well provided water for the household and a newly-dug horse pond drink for the livestock. Farming equipment included ploughs, harrows, carts and tumbrels and a collection of forks, spades, shovels, scythes and a pack saddle. The usual clutter of a farmyard was obviously present. The accounts show that a pillory and a ducking stool were built in 1272, but I can find no record that they were ever used. The manor house and farmyard were probably typical of the larger manor houses in fourteenth century, although those lived in by a gentry family may have had a little more accommodation for the family and have been slightly more comfortably furnished.[36]

36. Inventory of Hemsby Manor in NRO DCN 3 /4 and David Yaxley *The Prior's Manor-houses*, Larks Press 1988, for translation and comment.

Smaller Priory Estates in Flegg

As well as Hemsby and Martham the monastery held small estates in Scratby and Ormesby. The Prior was the rector of All Saints in Scratby and held the advowson, that is the right to appoint a vicar and to receive the great tithes of corn and hay. The estate also included about fifty acres of glebe land. Twelve of the bailiff's accounts survive for the years 1295-1362. Unlike the manors at Martham and Hemsby, Scratby manor did not send any grain to the Priory, but sold its barley and malt locally, providing the Priory with £40 to £60 in cash each year. As rector, the Priory was responsible for the upkeep of the chancel of the parish church, and small expenses are recorded for the repair of the chancel windows. In the year 1297-8 a lead worker and a glass-maker were employed for six days at a cost of 15d. Nine iron bars and some nails were bought for their use at a cost of 8½d. Scratby church has vanished long ago.[37]

The Prior also held the advowson of the four churches in Ormesby; St Margaret, St Michael, St Peter and St Andrew. As at Scratby, the Priory held a small estate in Ormesby for which the bailiff's accounts survive for only four non-consecutive years. Their greatest interest lies in the information given in the 1337-8 account about the production of peat that must have come from the turbaries in what is now Ormesby Broad. In Norfolk peat was dug in long blocks called turves, about three and a half inches square and two to three feet in length. Ten thousand such turves made a last. In 1336-7 ten and a half lasts were produced at Ormesby, that is 105,000 turves, enough peat to fill a barn. The turves, cut from the water-logged ground in summer and stacked to dry out on the marsh, had to be removed before winter. In 1338 two lasts were used on the manor, five were sold and the rest was sent to the Priory by water. Eight men were employed for two days at a cost of 12d. to take forty-six thousand turves by horse and cart to Yarmouth where they were stacked on the quay to await the Priory boat. A heap of fuel the size of a small barn must have been a temptation for thieves, so a man was hired for 6d., that is two or three days' pay, to watch over the peat until it was taken safely to Norwich. Evidence from the Priory accounts suggests that the

37. For Scratby Accounts. NRO DCN 60/ 31/onwards.

number of turves cut was not exceptionally large that year. When we remember that other manors all over East Norfolk were producing peat on much the same scale, we can appreciate how the Broads were excavated over several hundred years.[38]

Estates of St. Benet's Abbey

The outstanding feature of the Map of St Benet's Abbey and South West Flegg is the extent of the marsh and wetland around the rivers Bure and Thurne. The Abbey stood surrounded by marsh, on the gravel ridge of Cow Holme, about two or three miles up the river Bure from Thurne. The Abbey dominated this area of Flegg, holding manors and free tenants in Repps, Rollesby, Ashby, Thurne, Oby, Burgh, Billockby and Clippesby. Notice also how the boundaries of six of the parishes converge on Stefne, the area of heath and woodland, which was the meeting place of the Hundred Court of West Flegg. (The word 'parish' was not used in the Middle Ages, but their boundaries seem to be more or less identical with those of the Domesday 'vills') By the thirteenth century two of the smaller vills seem to have been combined with larger neighbours, Ashby with Oby and Repps with Bastwick. There is no record of a church in Oby, and the inhabitants went to Ashby Church, which is no longer standing. I have found no recorded boundary between Bastwick and Repps, although Bastwick had its own church. (Map 4.1)

On the whole the St Benet's records have not survived as well as those of the Norwich Cathedral Priory, but they contain some of the earliest bailiff's accounts in Norfolk. The accounts for the manors of Ashby, Oby and Thurne in 1245 are very brief but they show that all three manors grew wheat, rye, barley, oats and peas. These were the typical crops grown in Norfolk throughout the Middle Ages, although progressively less rye was sown. On the St Benet's manors barley was the main crop and about two thirds was made into malt. All the wheat and most of the malt went to the

38. For Ormesby Accounts. NRO DCN 61/39,40,41. Lambert et al. 1960, *The Making of the Broads, R.G.S. Research Series No 3.*, 'Turf in Medieval Broadland' p. 82-91 for information on peat-digging.

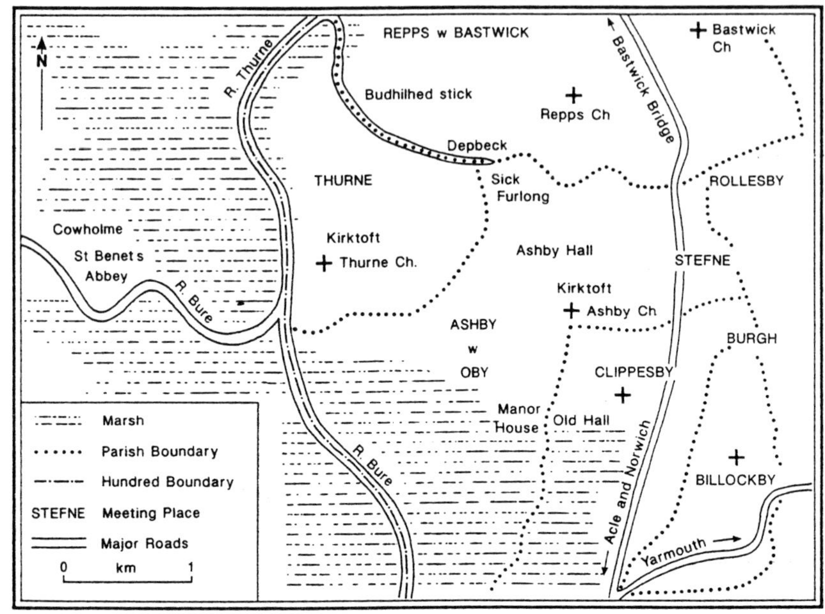

Map 4.1 St Benet's Abbey and South West Flegg in the early Thirteenth Century

Abbey by boat. Rye and barley were used as part payment for the workers on the manor.[39]

Livestock is only mentioned at Ashby in these brief accounts. By this time most of the ploughing was done by horses, not the big farm horses of the nineteenth century, but smaller animals called 'stotts'. Ashby kept four stotts, but also relied on the tenants, who may still have used oxen, to plough the demesne. In nearby Burgh, tenants could bring either two stotts or two oxen for their ploughing duties (See page 131). At Ashby there was a herd of eight oxen, a bull, four cows and their followers. Most of the milk was made into cheeses that were eaten at harvest by the farm workers. The farmyard also contained four breeding sows, sixty-two geese, a hundred and seventy-three doves and eight peacocks. Peacock meat was considered a great delicacy in the Middle Ages,

39. Bailiff's Accounts for Ashby, Oby and Thurne manors in 1245 only, NRO Diocesan EST 2/1.

but it seems the birds were difficult to rear, for they are only occasionally mentioned in Flegg.[40]

It must have been very inefficient to employ a different bailiff on each of three manors lying so close to each other. At some time between 1245 and 1341, which is the date of the next surviving account, Ashby and Thurne manors were combined to form 'Flegg manor'. The lands of this combined estate lay scattered in seven villages, Ashby, Thurne, Oby, Repps, Clippesby, Billockby and Burgh. There were manor houses and farm buildings to maintain at both Ashby and Thurne; in the later fourteenth century the manor courts were held alternately in the two places. The two hundred acres of the demesne did not form a compact farm as at Martham, but the lands were dispersed all over the estate in twenty-six pieces of varying sizes. The later bailiff's accounts name the demesne fields and give an indication of their area. I can identify Budhilhedstick, (3½ acres) in Repps, Ashby Kirktofts (three small tofts, 11 acres), Thurne Kirktofts (two small tofts, 8 acres), 'Sick furlong' on the Repps border (3 acres) and Stefne (17 acres) I suspect this last piece is land taken in from the heath. There were 12 acres near Ashby Hall and five other fairly large fields of 16 to 18 acres the whereabouts of which I cannot identify. The general picture is a of very dispersed demesne.

In 1341 the bulk of the wheat and malt from the demesne continued to go to the Abbey to feed the monastic household. The manor also supplied the Abbey with about twenty pigs each year, a hundred geese and about six hundred eels that had come as rent from the tenants who fished in the Thurne and Bure. The doves and peacocks seem to have disappeared.[41]

Like the demesne, the farms of the tenants lay in several villages. It cannot have been easy to manage so dispersed a

40. Peacocks in Flegg; Martham kept peacocks between 1300 and 1306, but in that year one died and the remaining seven were sent to Norwich. At Hemsby the peacocks were rather more successful. In 1300 there were seven, but by 1322 only two remained and in the next year one died leaving only one hen. In 1337 a single peacock was sold for 10d. at Mautby.

41. St Benet's manor of Flegg (Ashby and Thurne) Manorial Accounts, NRO. Diocesan Est 9/ onwards.

property or to organise tenant services on the scattered demesne. Flegg manor had many labour troubles throughout the fourteenth century, and, as we shall see, appears to have been the one manor in the area that really responded to the Peasant's Rising of 1381.

Abbey Property leased to Laymen

The Abbey leased out its other Flegg manors at Caister, Winterton, Filby and Rollesby. Probably they were too small and scattered to be worked directly from the Abbey, and were more profitable when let at a realistic rent. We know that the rent at Rollesby, which was 25s. at Domesday, had risen to 40s. in the mid-twelfth century.[42]

In the twelfth century, kinsfolk of the Abbot were rewarded with grants of monastic property. The first Norman Abbot, Richer, settled his family on lands at Winterton and Caister, which scandalised the Saxon monks. His niece, Mathilda, was granted land in Winterton on her marriage about 1157. Ten or more years later, when she was a widow, she was taken into the care of the Abbot and renounced her claim to the land at Winterton. She brought with her a hanging (that would be a curtain or wall-covering), a bench and three marks (£2) that her son Thomas had given her. She was granted what is described as a monk's pension for life, which must have been adequate for her keep, as well as 32d. yearly for clothes and three loaves weekly for her servant. Monasteries often took in a few paying guests; in Mathilda's case perhaps she was settled somewhere near the Abbey, maybe in the hospice at Horning or in the outer court of the Abbey and lived in reasonable comfort in the medieval equivalent of sheltered housing. It is possible that Mathilda was accommodated in the Abbey itself, for there are records of women living in the Abbeys of Bury St Edmunds, St Albans and Evesham.[43]

42. West S.G. 1932 page 274.

43. For Mathilda at St Benet's Abbey, see S.G.West, ' The First Register of the Abbey of St Benet's at Holm'. Norfolk Record Society Vols 2 & 3,1932, page 244. I would like to thank Dr Roberta Gilchrist for information about women living in abbeys.

Chapter 5. Two Lay Manors in the Thirteenth Century: Runham and Mautby

The history of these neighbouring manors, which were so similar in size and composition at Domesday, could hardly be more different. Runham, like many manors in Flegg, had an absentee landlord and a divided inheritance, while Mautby remained in the hands of one resident family for three hundred years. (See Map 2.3 for position of the two vills in East Flegg.)

The records of manors in the hands of laymen have not survived as well as those of monasteries. Land changed hands very frequently and new owners would see little point in keeping very old records. Landowners often sold their land to raise money to go on a crusade or a pilgrimage, or to maintain their life style in an age of rising material standards. Often they granted land to their relations or clients, or as dowries to their daughters. If a man died without a male heir, it was usual to divide his estate between his daughters, as happened at Runham, Winterton and Moregrove manor at Martham. Inquisitions Post Mortem are another source of information for lay manors. These were taken on the death of tenants-in-chief and give the names of the heirs and brief details of the estates. Runham manor will serve as one example of a lay manor for its history can be followed from eight Inquisitions, taken between 1272 and 1351.[44]

Runham

At Domesday Runham manor was a medium-sized estate of one and a half carucates with ten villein holdings, sixteen saltpans and a flock of a hundred sheep. The hand of its earlier owner, Earl

44. Inquisitions have been calendared and printed in volumes I.P.M. Inquisitions Mortem for Runham. PRO. 1272 C133/3/12, Printed vol 2 No 32; 1300 C133/93/20, vol 4 No. 368; 1306 C133/122/1, Vol 4 No. 368; 1316 C 134/48/ Vol5 608; 1327 C 135/3/14; 1340 C 135/59/17, Vol 8 215; 1351 C135/100/12.

Ralph, can be seen in the twenty-three free tenants with six ploughs who were attached to the manor. (See page 45) Henry I (1100-1135) granted the manor to the de Evermure family from Lincolnshire for a rent of two hundred pears and four hogsheads of pear wine. Nothing is known about the origin of this rent, which is not recorded in Domesday. Did the pear trees grow in the manor garden at Runham, or, what was more likely, did the de Evermures buy the pears and wine in London before delivering them to the Exchequer? Blomefield says, but does not quote his source, that the pears and the wine were still being paid in kind in 1319, but that in 1340 the manor paid a money rent of 6s. to the crown instead of fruit and wine.[45]

In 1272 the last male Evermure died and his estate was divided equally between his three daughters, Euphemia, Margery and Alice. The Inquisitions show that, on paper at least, each daughter had exactly a third share of each asset of the manor; that is a third of the site of the manor, a third of the arable lands, pasture and marsh, and a third of the income from the tenants' rents, the market tolls and the rents from the salt works. In fact the estate was probably let, and a lawyer collected the income and dispatched a third share to each heiress, or rather to her husband.

Further Inquisitions, taken on the death of the husbands and their heirs, help to build up the picture of Runham manor. The site of the manor lay, like so many Flegg manor houses, on the edge of the arable near the marsh at TG 460108. To the north of the manor grounds stood the church which, to judge by the early fourteenth century windows of the chancel, was possibly being extended at the time of the Inquisitions. The manor house has long since vanished, and the church, now closed for worship, looks abandoned and dilapidated. In 1272, when Walter de Evermure died, the manor house was described as a capital messuage valued at 7s. By 1316 the house site was valued only as pasture, and by

45. Runham Pears and Wine rent. IPMs and Blomefield, *History of Norfolk.* Vol xi page 241.

1327 the house had disappeared for the site is described as 'non edificata', 'not built on'.[46]

In 1272 the manor farm consisted of eighty-one acres of productive arable land valued at 2s. an acre and fourteen acres of slightly inferior land valued at 1s. 6d. The meadow, marsh and reed bed was worth £2 annually, and the enclosed pasture 5s. 4d. The rents from the free and customary tenants came to £4 0s.6d. Later Inquisitions show that there were about twenty free tenants, perhaps the descendants of Earl Ralph's freemen, fifty or sixty holders of customary land and three cottagers. The customary tenants had to do ploughing, weeding, harvesting and carting for the lord, but it is likely that the tenants did not perform the services, but paid an additional charge to cover their obligations.

The price of the services was ½d. for weeding and 1d. for each ploughing and harvesting duty. At least once a year a representative of the lord of the manor would come to Runham to collect the rents and hold a manor court. The lord was entitled to the fines imposed by the court, amounting to between 6s. and 10s. a year. A weekly market on Mondays had been granted to the Evermures in 1227 and in 1272 the tolls came to 9s. 6½d. The market does not seem to have flourished, for in 1300 its value was only 1s. 6d. and that is the last we hear of it. Perhaps that is not surprising because in 1271 a market had been granted on the same day of the week to the lord of Burgh, a village three miles away and on a major road, and Yarmouth with its greater opportunities for trade was only six miles from Runham.

Salt production was much more profitable, for the rents from the salt-pans of about £3 a year in 1272, increased in the early fourteenth century. The pans were probably on the detached part of Runham that lay five miles nearer the sea on the outskirts of Yarmouth. Although salt rents are mentioned at Winterton, Caister and Mautby in the thirteenth and fourteenth centuries,

46. IPM. Runham for 1272. In 1272 the estate was already divided between Walter de Evermure, who held two thirds, and his mother Alice de Evermure who held one third. Walter de Evermure's part was leased to Walter de Brues for de Evermure's life. I do not know whether his heirs continued to let the estate to de Brues. The Brues were a local family with other property in Flegg.

Runham seems to have been the only manor in Flegg that is known to have maintained productive salt-working into the fourteenth century.[47]

The manor was fairly profitable in the fifty years after the death of Sir Walter de Evermure, despite the failure of the market. The value of the land remained constant, rents increased and the profits of the salt-workings doubled. However the last two Inquisitions are very brief. In 1340 the value of the manor site had halved and the arable lands were only valued at 8d. an acre. No rents from either the tenants or the salt-pans were mentioned, and the profit of the manor court was only 12d. A windmill, which may well have been in existence for many years, was valued at 6s. 8d., but despite this new feature, the impression is of an estate in decline. Bad weather, poor harvests and epidemics among livestock marked the early years of the fourteenth century and these may have affected Runham. The divided lordship and the absence of a resident bailiff or tenant farmer probably meant that the manorial discipline was not maintained, probably to the advantage of the tenants. Before the next Inquisition was taken, an event occurred which had a devastating effect on lords and tenants alike, the Black Death of 1349. In 1351, when Thomas de Essex died, the value of the manor site was only 6d., the tenants' rents were 12s.4d. and the profits of the court were nil, because 'all the tenants are dead'. This last statement should not be taken too literally, but obviously Runham had been severely affected by the pestilence.[48]

47. That part of Yarmouth is still called Runham. In the eighteenth century a pleasure garden called Vauxhall was built there. In 1848, when the railway from Norwich reached Yarmouth, the terminus was at Vauxhall, which as 'Yarmouth Vauxhall' has remained the main station for the town. This area of Yarmouth has been administratively part of the borough for over a hundred year. A modern signpost on the A 47 points to 'Runham' along the southern bank of the Bure, but a traveller who hoped to get to Runham village that way, would end up on the wrong side of the river, five miles from a bridge in either direction.

48. There were other estates in Runham, and at least one other windmill. PRO C Inq. Misc. 29 (4): A Survey of the lands of Hugh de Nevile and Adam de E. in Runham in 1249 includes arable land, a windmill, a dovecote and rents of salt, all worth £21 19s. 7d.., PRO C Inq. Misc. 29 (4) and calendared as Misc. Inq. 813.

Mautby

Few manors in Flegg live up to the popular picture of a medieval estate, unchanging in its size and nature, and held, over the centuries, by one resident family who wielded local power and influence from generation to generation. Such a family was the de Mautbys of Mautby. The first mention I have found of the family is in 1198 when Simon de Mautby was confirmed in his possession by right of inheritance of fifteen acres in Mautby.[49] His surname, de Mautby, suggests that he was a major landowner and probably lord of Mautby manor. About sixty years later in 1257, Sir Walter de Mautby, perhaps finding it difficult in a time of inflation to maintain the standard of living expected of a knight, failed to pay the rent of the manors of Martham and Hemsby that he had leased from Norwich Priory, and had to relinquish those estates. (See Chapter 3, page 46).[50]

By the late thirteenth century the de Mautby family was of importance in the locality. In 1295 Robert de Mautby was appointed Custodian of the coast of East and West Flegg, and four years later he held the lucrative post of Collector of Customs at Yarmouth. One unusual aspect of the de Mautby estate was that it could not be divided between male heirs. In 1219 six brothers agreed that their eldest brother, Robert, should inherit the estate in its entirety. Nearly a hundred years later, in 1304, a jury confirmed that the de Mautby lands should never be divided. This ruling kept the estate intact for the next hundred and fifty years.[51]

At Michaelmas the bailiff of a manor would present the lord with a financial account of the running of the home farm and the management of the estate for the year. Three sheets of the accounts for Mautby have survived for the years 1335 to 1337, and from these it is possible to get some idea of the manor in the

49. Is there any significance in the fact that in 1086 Roger Bigot's freeman also held 15 acres in Mautby? See page 49. Was 15 acres perhaps the traditional size of a holding in Mautby ?

50. General Information on the Mautby family, see Barbara Cornford 'The de Mautby Family at Mautby' in *Yarmouth Archaeology 1991*.

51. Mautby estate not to be divided. See Blomefield Vol xi, page 226.

Table 5.1 Cropping at Mautby, and Martham

The size of the demesnes was roughly the same

Manor & date		Wheat	Barley	Peas	Oats	Rye
Mautby 1335	Harvest	84qrt	169qrt	37qrt	86qrt	12qrt
1336	Sown	30a.	90a.	53a.	40a.	4a.
Martham 1334	Harvest	110qrt	225qrt	40qrt	16qrt	nil
1335	Sown	38a.	124a.	47a.	4a.	nil

N.B. 'qrt.' = quarter, a measure of volume, about one fifth of a ton.

The Mautby figures are combined from two Accounts both taken in the year from Michaelmas 1335 to Michaelmas 1336. The figure of *90 acres of barley is taken from the post-Black Death Account as the 1336 figure is indecipherable.

half of the fourteenth century. A fragment of a later account taken after the Black Death adds to the picture.[52]

The home farm at Mautby was probably two hundred acres, about twice the size of the demesne of its neighbour, Runham. As on other manors in Flegg, wheat, barley, peas and oats were grown, with barley the main crop. Table 5.1 shows the cropping patterns at Mautby and Martham, manors which each had a demesne of roughly the same size. From these figures it is clear that Martham, under the very expert management of the Prior's Steward, was more productive than the home farm at Mautby under the bailiff, Walter de Wells. Most interestingly Mautby produced a much greater quantity of oats than the Prior's manor and sowed a correspondingly larger acreage. At Mautby, where a wealthy gentleman had a social position to maintain and business, military and political trips to undertake, there were more horses and so oats were a major crop. The plough beasts consumed ten quarters of oats, the riding horses twenty-one quarters and the owner's two war-horses had a particularly nutritious mixture of oats and peas, eating nearly three quarters in five weeks.

Most of the crops harvested were consumed at Mautby manor. Wheaten bread was eaten by the lord's household, while the farm

52. Mautby Account Rolls NRO Phillips Collection. Phi 489, 490 Martham Account Rolls DCN 60/23/ 23.

servants had bread made from a mixture of rye and barley. White peas were kept for the lord's table, but black or field peas were fed to the livestock, particularly to fatten the pigs. Barley was also fed to the livestock and to the lord's swans, but the largest single use for barley was, as usual, for malting. The wages of the farm servants were paid partly in barley and malt, and it is from a list of these 'liveries' of malt that we learn about these servants. Twelve workers were regularly employed, seven ploughmen, a carter, a harrower, a gardener, a gamekeeper, and a dairy maid called Rose, who was given two bushels of the prestigious wheat as well as her livery of malt and barley. A boy was employed for thirteen weeks in summer to look after the cattle on the marsh pastures. (Martham with no resident landlord only employed four or five ploughmen, a cowherd and a dairymaid as full time workers.)

As usual in Flegg, animal husbandry was less important than corn growing. The farm maintained a dozen stotts for ploughing and for riding. (Martham had on average six stotts on the manor in the early fourteenth century.) At Mautby the herd of cattle consisted of two bulls, thirteen bullocks and fifteen cows with their calves. The dairy provided the household with milk, butter and cheese. The pigsties contained a boar and two sows, nineteen pigs and thirty-one piglets. Fourteen fat pigs and nineteen piglets were sold. Other sales of stock included eleven calves, seven geese and a peacock for 10d., making a total livestock sale of £4 9s.11d. for that year.

Mautby Hall like so many Flegg manor houses, lay on the edge of the marsh (TG 489124) nearly a mile away from the church. The fourteenth century accounts are not very informative about the house, but describe a productive garden with apple and pear trees, nut trees, beehives, and plots of woad, hemp and flax, under the care of the gardener. From the marshes came peat for the fires, gorse faggots for kindling, rushes for floor-covering and roofing. Did the Mautby ladies and their servants spin and weave linen cloth made from their own flax and dyed with their own woad?

Farm surpluses were sold. In 1336 corn sales brought in £7 17s. 6½d., sale of livestock £4 9s. 11d., the tenants' rents and services about £7, but it was the rents from marsh lettings which made the largest contribution of £17. In 1336-7 the lord, Robert de Mautby, needed ready cash. His father's funeral at Mautby and the religious and social rites that took place a year later were expensive; his four-day stay at Mautby for the anniversary of his father's death cost £4 12s. His father's debts still had to be paid and £4 10s. was due to Alexander Fastolf of Yarmouth for a last of herrings.[53]

Robert de Mautby also appears to have been on the last Scottish expedition of Edward III to Scotland in 1337. One entry in the accounts reads, 'In wages to the boy of William Canely for four days before the retreat of the lord from Scotland with shoeing two horses. 12d.' The many horses at Mautby were a drain on his resources. The horse doctor or marshall came from Blofield, and tallow, oil, wax, pitch and bitumen had to be purchased for his use. The two war-horses required special attention. Thomas Stedman was paid 29s. for their care for the half year from December 23rd 1336 to June 22nd 1337. Then Thomas was paid 5s. to take the horses to Ipswich. It is not easy to piece together the sequence of these events, but the fragmented evidence of the bailiff's accounts demonstrates the financial demands made upon any member of the gentry whose interests and aspirations extended beyond his own estate and local community.

Despite their large estates and income from official positions the gentry were often seriously in debt. The de Mautbys continued to hold the estate until the middle of the fifteenth century when the heiress, Margaret de Mautby, married John Paston, bringing him Mautby and other estates in Norfolk.[54]

The picture of Runham manor from the Inquisitions Post Mortem is of an increasingly run-down enterprise, with a dilapidated manor house and a failing market, while Mautby manor, although suffering some financial problems, had an effective manorial administration and a well-maintained house and

53. White's Directory of Norfolk (1845) gives the acreage of Mautby parish as 1626 acres of which 450 are marsh. Much of this was across the River Bure.

54. Edward III Scottish Expedition. McKisack, May. The Fourteenth Century, O.U.P.196

garden. The comparison must not be pressed too far because the evidence for the two estates come from completely different sources. The Inquisitions are the work of an Exchequer Official, concerned to record the inheritance and wealth of one of the Crown's smaller manors, of which he is unlikely to have had any personal knowledge. Bailiff's Accounts at Mautby are concerned with the day-to-day running of an estate by the Bailiff, who is closely involved with the profitability of the manor. It is possible that the tenants at Runham may have appreciated the lax manorial control of the Crown, while some aspects of the regime at Mautby may have been a source of resentment among the tenants. The nature of historical evidence must always be evaluated before jumping to any conclusions.

Scaring birds with a sling
From the Gorleston Psalter

Chapter 6. Charitable Institutions

Although there were no monasteries in Flegg itself, a steady flow of lands and money went to monasteries and charitable institutions, usually with the stipulation that the inmates pray for the souls of the donors and their families. In 1269 Hugh de Caly gave a house at Repps, twenty-one acres of land and the advowson of the church to the Great Hospital in Norwich. The advowson, or right to appoint a priest to the church, was a very valuable part of such a gift for it provided a useful source of patronage or income. No thirteenth century records of the Great Hospital estate at Repps appear to have survived.

West Somerton Leper Hospital

Two small hospitals were founded in Flegg itself. In the twelfth century Ranulf de Glanville founded a Hospital for thirteen lepers at West Somerton and endowed it with the Somerton manor. The Prior of Butley Abbey in Suffolk, also founded by de Glanville, was to be guardian of the Hospital and was responsible for its administration. The site of the hospital lay near the church, just to the east of the manor house at TG 474169. There seems to have been no special reason to place the hospital at West Somerton, except that de Glanville owned the manor.

Indeed, very little is known about its history until a number of incidents came to light when the Prior was charged in 1291 with maladministration. The jurors in the case found that only eight lepers were living in the hospital instead of the stipulated thirteen and that before admission lepers had to swear never to leave the hospital or to complain in any way or to contact their friends. They might not even look over the walls or climb trees to talk to friends outside. A large strong dog was tied up at the gate to deter visitors. The court ordered the Prior to admit the correct number of needy and poor lepers and never to exact such an oath in the future.[55]

55. Richard Mortimer. 'The Prior of Butley and the Lepers of West Somerton' in *Bulletin of the Institute of Historical Research vol liii, No 127,* May 1980, for most of the information about the Leper Hospital.

It proved difficult to make the Prior obey the order, or to produce satisfactory financial accounts of the income he received from the manor. Further accusations were made against him. He had charged one leper for admission while allowing a protégé of the Bishop of Norwich to have a free place. He seems to have treated the hospital as his country residence, for it was alleged that he kept a house within the hospital where he entertained his friends, both clerical and lay, with their horses and greyhounds and held parties for men and women who stayed the night. This hospitality was paid for with money that should have been used to feed the inmates. After this the Prior had to accept strict supervision by the King's lawyers, but he retaliated in 1297 by accusing six lepers of colluding with a gang of thieves, led by the parson of Mutford, to rob the Hospital. They destroyed the chapel, and, not surprisingly, killed the guard dogs. The lepers and their friends carried off the wheat and barley from the store along with eight silver spoons, two wooden bowls, nine swans (presumably dead) and bread, beer, meat and fish. They took a chalice, a missal and vestments from the chapel and broke into a chest and removed charters and court rolls. It appeared that the parson and his brother had a grievance against the Prior and had incited the riot and looting.

Having gained a judgement against the rioters, the Prior was prepared to take no further action, but it is doubtful whether he or his successors improved the standards at the Hospital. In 1374 the place was said to be dilapidated and the Prior was accused of negligence. By 1399 the Prior seems to have washed his hands of the place, for the house is described as desolate. Although lepers were apparently still living there, they received no material or spiritual sustenance from the Prior or the chaplain. The Prior explained that the land in West Somerton had provided an annual income of £60 when the hospital was founded, but in 1399 it only produced ten marks (£6 13s. 4d.) a year. It is difficult to believe that, even after the Black Death, income from a manor in West Flegg could be so diminished. Nevertheless the Crown closed the Hospital in 1399 and the income from the manor was granted to Butley Priory to maintain two canons to celebrate mass regularly for the King and the Founder. The manor can hardly have been as unproductive as the Prior had maintained in 1399, for in 1444 it was let for a rent of £24 a year, the money going to the Abbey. It is of course quite probable that by the end of the fourteenth century there was no call for a leper hospital in a country village. The story of the Leper Hospital is a good illustration of the ineffective and haphazard nature of much medieval charity.[56]

God's House at Herringby

The other charitable institution in Flegg, 'God's Poor Almshouse' founded by Hugh atte Fen in 1475 in Herringby, has quite a different story. Hugh atte Fen was born in Yarmouth, probably about 1418. He rose to importance in his home town, being elected burgess to sit in Parliament for Yarmouth in 1450. By 1447 he had moved to London and had become an officer of the Exchequer, a lucrative and important post. He was a friend of Sir John Fastolf and of John Paston and used his influence in London on their behalf. He never lost his interest in Norfolk, and for some years before his death in 1476, his main concern was the foun-dation and endowment of an almshouse at Herringby, near the church where his mother was buried.

In his will, besides the usual elaborate arrangements for his burial at Herringby and innumerable bequests to churches and religious institutions in London, Suffolk and Norfolk, he made provision for the almshouse in Herringby. It provided accommodation for a master, three priests, eight poor folk and two servants, and was endowed with lands bringing in £44 a year. After eighty years the Almshouse surrendered to the Crown in 1545. It seems to have fulfilled the terms of its founder in every respect, although the ratio of three administrators and two servants to eight recipients may seem too high for modern critics of welfare provision.[57]

56. Lease for 7 years from William Boley Prior of Butley Abbey to Edmund Palmer of Wytton next Broomholm, of the Manor of West Somerton N.R.O NRS 16214 32B2.

57. Roger Virgoe. 'The Will of Hugh Atte Fenne 1476' in Norfolk Record Society Vol. LVI, 1991.

Map 7.1 Medieval Martham

Reconstructed from the Survey of 1292

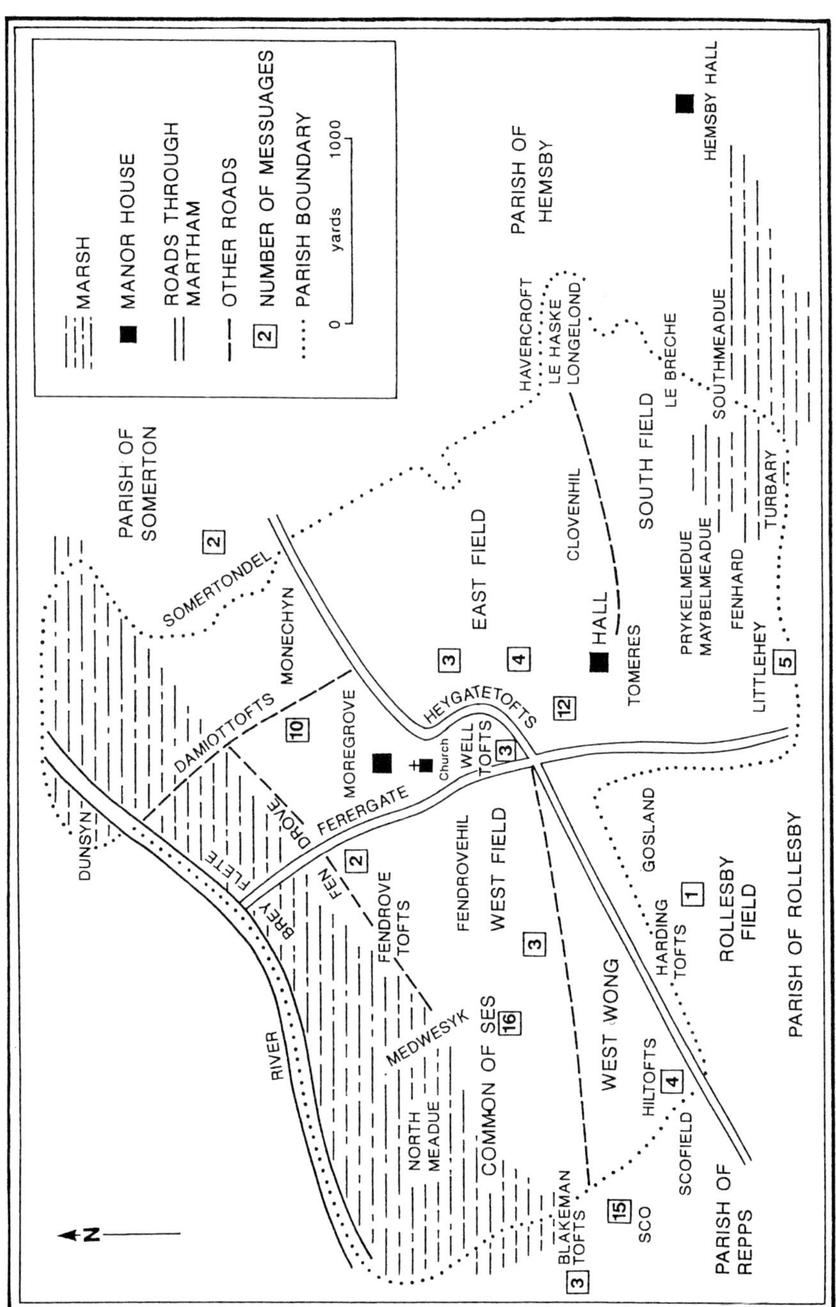

Chapter 7: A Survey of Martham in the Thirteenth Century

The next three chapters deal with the Prior's manor of Martham in the thirteenth century, using three quite different types of manorial documents, the Survey of the Manor of 1292, the Account rolls of the manor from 1261 onwards and the few surviving Manor Court rolls of the 1280s and 90s. It is very unusual for the medieval historian to find that three contemporary manorial archives have survived in this way. Together they give a very detailed picture of the history of the manor, the administration of the manor by the Bailiff and the ways in which the tenants tried to cope with the problems of the late thirteenth century.

The 1292 Survey of Martham, along with surveys of twelve other manors belonging to Norwich Priory, is bound in a book now in the British Library.[58] Its main purpose was to record the various assets of each manor, such as the area of the demesne lands, the land held by the tenants and the rents and services owed by them. On most manors, where the tenants' traditional holdings or tenements were still recognisable, sufficient information was provided by a list of the tenants, the size of their holdings in acres and a brief indication of their rents and services. At Martham the tenements had been so fragmented by the end of the thirteenth century that it was necessary to record every strip which each tenant held in the open fields. This explains why the entry for Martham covers eighty sheets of parchment, twice as many sheets as was required to deal with the eleven other manors in the book. From this detailed Survey, it is possible to draw a map of the village.

The Map of Medieval Martham (See Map 7.1)

The road pattern does not appear to have changed much over seven hundred years, although some roads, important enough to be called *via Regis*, 'the King's way', in 1292 are now non-existent,

58. British Library. Stowe 936 and Additional Ms 5795. A microfilm of the Stowe document is in the Norfolk Record Office, NRO, MF514

or no more than tracks or footpaths. In the Survey two roads are described as going through the middle of Martham, *'per medium Martham'*, one from west to east and the other from north to south. The first is the road from Repps that went through the village by Hilltofts, along Heygate and so to Somerton and Winterton, a route similar to the present B1152. The north-south road went from a river crossing over the Thurne, up Ferergate, along the west side of Welltofts, and so on to Rollesby. The name, 'Ferergate' comes from the Danish word *ferja*, meaning a ferry or some means of crossing water and suggests that the river could be crossed at that point as it still is today. The Green is not mentioned in the Survey, nor is a church or a graveyard, which is surprising in so very detailed a document.

Photo: Judy Rose

Martham Ferry

Ferry is a Danish word meaning a river crossing. The road to the ferry was called Ferergate and is now called Ferrygate. A swing ferry is in action today.

The two hamlets of Damgate, called Damiottofts in the survey, and Cess, always written Ses, were old settlements in the thirteenth century. Ses had a special importance to the whole community because the village common lay there. Livestock could be driven along 'the fen drove' which went by the edge of the marsh from Damgate and Ferergate and on to the Common at Cess. The 'drove' skirted the arable lands known as Fendrovehill, now called Thunderhill. To the west of Ses lay the populous hamlet of Sco, mentioned as a vill in the Domesday Book.

There were two manors in Martham, the Priory manor and the Gunton manor. The Hall, or manor house of the Priory manor, lay to the south of the village at the end of what is now Hall Road. From the Hall a road ran eastwards to le Haske on the village boundary with Hemsby. It is now a farm track and public footpath, known as the Hun Road. Most of the demesne lands of the manor lay to the south of this road. The Gunton manor house was in Moregrove Field in the north of the village. The strips of land belonging to the tenants of the two manors lay intermingled in the open fields of the village.

The map shows three main fields, West Field, East Field and South Field. However the Midland three-field system of one field of winter-sown corn, one of spring corn and the third left fallow, was never practised in Martham, which, like most of Norfolk, had a more flexible pattern of crop rotation. Green lanes, called 'meres', gave access to the arable land and many of these have become public footpaths, but not, unfortunately, the Fendrove which was closed by the Enclosure Act of 1807. There were other smaller fields; West Wong, lay between the roads to Repps and to Sco. Monechyn, north of the East Field, may mean the 'monks in', or 'intake'; the name survives today as Moonshine, calling up pictures of fairies and lovers rather than monks. Clovenhil or Clovenhoe may record the existence of twin tumuli. Le Breche is a name for marginal land that has been 'broken' or taken into cultivation, in this case on the edge of the marsh. The name is also found in Rollesby, Hemsby and Ormesby for land at the edge of Ormesby Broad, and sometimes appears as Brakenholm or Brakenham. Dr Sandred thinks that Tomeres in the South Field, may be 'tom (empty) ears (of corn)' a reference to poor land. Gosland in Rollesby Field may have some connection with geese for the rent of a cottage on nearby Littlehey was a goose.[59]

To the south of the Hall lay meadows and marshes. Osbert and Stephen Maybel each had an acre in Mabelesmedwe. Beyond the meadows were the turbaries or peat-diggings, which have since become part of Ormesby Broad. The villagers could lease half an

59. Sandred K.I. *Place Names of Norfolk. Part two, The Hundreds of East and West Flegg, etc.* English Place Name Society 1996.

Martham Tower

The church tower is a good place to see the layout of the village.

Photo: J.C.Barringer 2000

acre in the peat-diggings for an annual rent of 1d. On the other side of the village to the north lay more pasture and marsh as well as the common of Ses. Medwesyk was a low-lying area along which a stream ran to the river Thurne. Most of the demesne meadows lay in this strip of land. The stream is now part of the surface water drainage system. Breiflete and Dunsyn, along the river Thurne, were hay meadows in the thirteenth century. Breiflete is now drained marsh and Dunsyn is poor water-logged land invaded by scrub, but the name is still preserved as Dungeon Corner, a spot well known today to sailors and fishermen.

Many tenants held small plots of land called 'tofts' that contained their houses. The medieval word for a house is 'messuage'; 'half an acre in his toft with messuage' describes the house in its home field. Tofts were usually enclosed by hedges, which must have given variety to a landscape largely devoid of trees. Some tofts had no messuages, and no doubt were used for livestock or crops, but they were always potential building sites. In Martham tofts often lay side by side, adjacent to a road or to Ses common. Figure 7.1 on page 83 is an attempt to show the layout of some of the tofts. Note the way in which the homesteads of different members of the same family lay together. These rows of houses were a feature of thirteenth century Martham. Houses did not congregate in the centre of the village, but were usually in or near the field in which their occupants held most land.

Views from Martham Church Tower

East to Somerton, over Heygate and East Field, then as now arable land

South over Welltofts towards the Green, South Field and beyond to the meadows, Littlehey and Turbary

Photos: Courtesy E. Walker

Views from Martham Church Tower
West over West Field towards Cess

North over Moregrove Field, Fendrove Field and marshes towards Hickling

Photos: courtesy E. Walker

The word 'toft' is also applied in the plural to larger areas, often combined with the name of the family which held most land there, such as Hiltofts, Hardingtofts, Blakemantofts. Other 'tofts', such as Damiottofts, Fendrovetofts, Heygatetofts, and Welltofts reflect geographical position rather than family ownership. Welltofts is aptly named for it is a waterlogged area that in the past contained many ponds and a well. I think it was originally part of the common pasture, now called the Green, but by the thirteenth century even that ill-drained area had been occupied in an effort to feed a rapidly growing population.[60]

I have tried to place the houses that are recorded. In the west of the village this was not too difficult because most of the messuages abutted either on to roads or to the Common. It is not so easy to place the houses in the middle of Martham or in the East and South Fields. However, in the end there were only twelve instances where I had no clue as to the position of the house. About eighty messuages and cottages are recorded, and about the same number of tofts without buildings on them. No doubt the messuages do not represent the full count of homesteads in the village because others must have stood on the Gunton estate, and St Benet's Abbey had at least one holding with a messuage in Damgate, at a rent of 12d. a year.

Ses was a favoured site for tofts and messuages. Sixteen tofts lay with the arable lands of West Wong to the south and the common pasture to the north. (Fig 7.1) This edge-of-common settlement with its regular layout is found in other Norfolk villages. Only three or four of the sixteen homesteads now remain, although traces of house platforms can be seen along the southern edge of the old common. Four other messuages faced west towards the common, and here houses and cottages, mostly of nineteenth century date, stand today, possibly on the sites of earlier homes. In the thirteenth century Ses and Sco seem to have been more populous than the centre of Martham. Now the name 'Sco' is forgotten, although there is still a scatter of farms and cottages in the area. Cess survives as a hamlet and contains about twenty houses. Today they lie on or near the modern road which follows

60. Welltofts. Houses were not built on this area until the 1980s, when the developers had difficulties with the drainage. Until about 1970 there was a stone in the churchyard on which was written, 'THE WELL'. I could never find anyone who could give any explanation for this. The stone had disappeared by 1982.

Figure 7.1 Possible layout of Tofts and Messuages along Common Edge, Martham c.1292

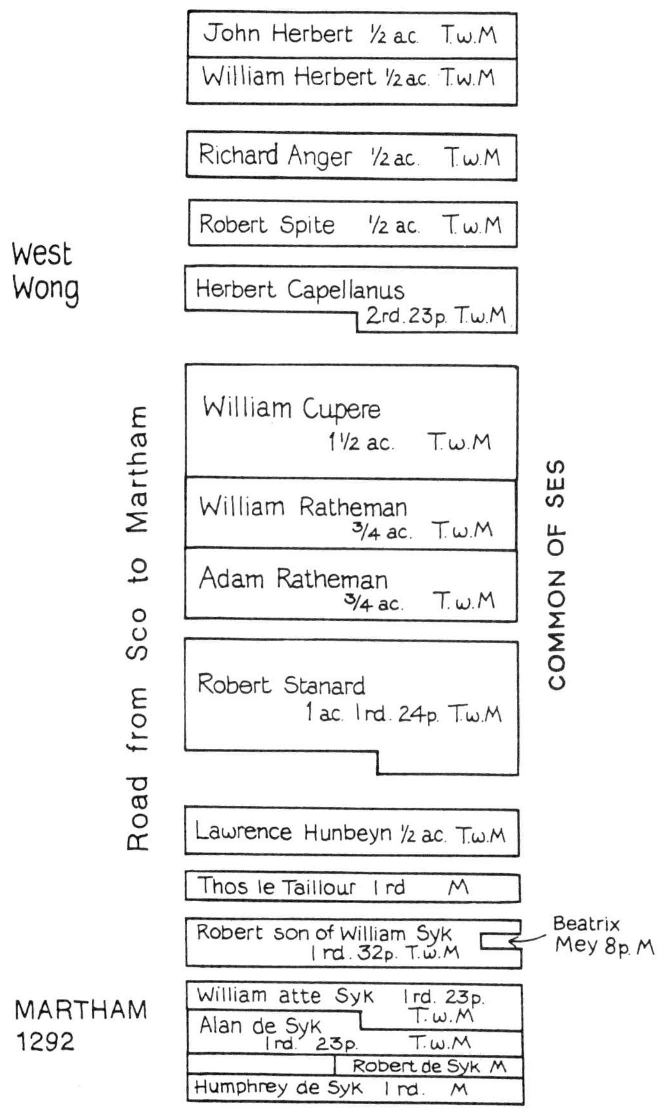

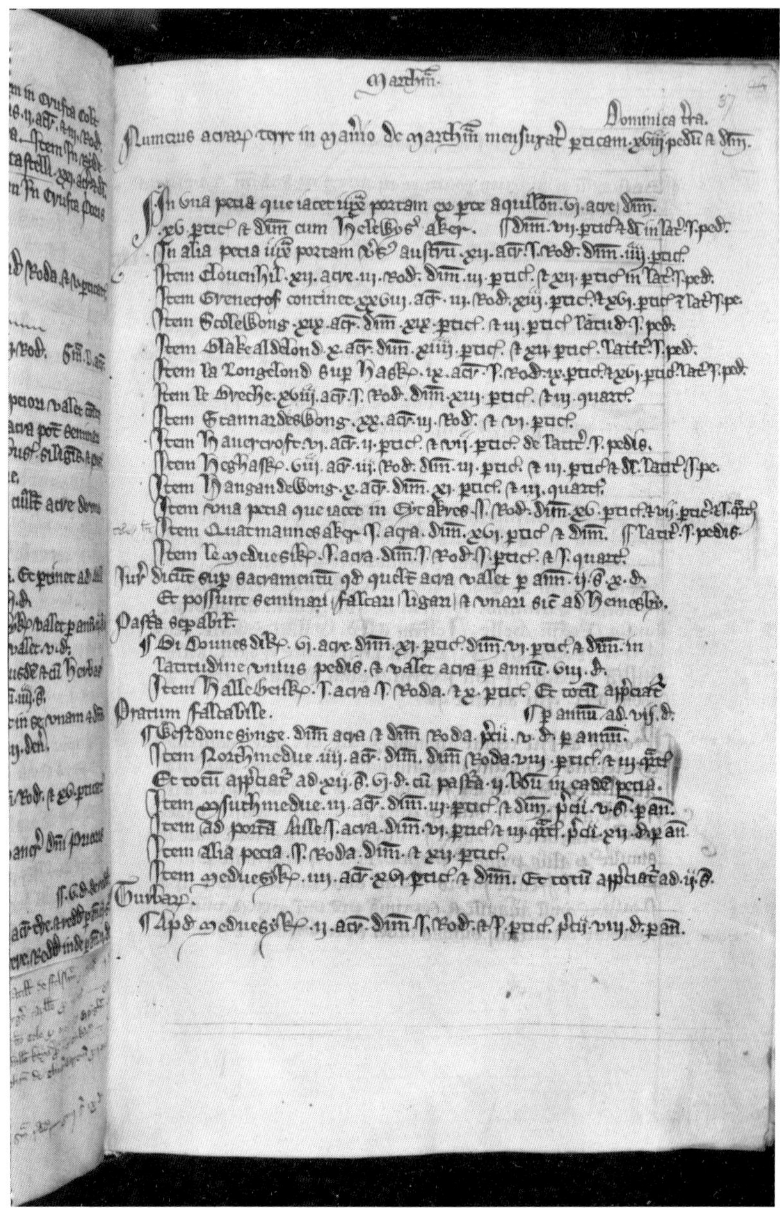

The first page of the 1292 Survey of Martham Manor, the Demesne Lands

Photo: British Library

Medwesyk to the river at Martham Boatyard (TG 439 192) A walk along the Cess footpaths will produce both admiration for the present cottage gardens and an understanding of the attraction which this warm and sheltered spot has always offered.[61]

A photograph of the first page of the Survey is on page 82 and gives a record of the demesne lands of the manor. It begins by listing 6½ acres of arable land to the north of the hall and 12½ to the south. The names of nine other blocks of land can be picked out. They are Clovenhil (11¾ acres), Grenecrof (27¾ acres), Scolewong (19 acres), Blakealdelond (10½ acres), le Longelond super Haske (17¼ acres), le Breche (18¼ acres) Stannardeswong (22 acres), Havercroft, which lay in Hemsby, (6 acres) Heghaske (8¾ acres) and Hangandewong (10½ acres). These are comparatively large blocks of land, but they were divided into strips to facilitate ploughing, and usually two or more types of crop were sown in each field. Only three or four of these fields can be placed on the map, but I am sure that most of the demesne lay in the eastern section of the South Field, forming a compact and manageable home farm near the manor house. Three other small pieces of demesne lay elsewhere in the open fields, making a total of 169 acres of arable valued at the very high sum of 2s. 10d. an acre.[62]

The demesne also included 5½ acres of hay meadow to the south of the manor and nine acres of meadow at Medwesyk and Dunsyng. Seven acres of demesne pasture lay at Breyflete by the river Thurne and three acres of demesne turbary at Medwesyk. On the whole this seems a rather small area of meadow, pasture and marsh for a manor the size and importance of Martham.

61. Fertility of Cess. For many years the Starkings family had a very productive small holding on the back gardens of two of the cottages facing the Dry Common. The Starkings sold their produce every week in Yarmouth Market, as no doubt Martham farmers had done for centuries.

62. Demesne in the South Field. Clovenhoe is the only field which contains both a block of demesne land and the tenants' strips. No tenant land is found in any other demesne fields recorded in the Survey. I conclude therefore that most of the demesne lay in discrete blocks in the South field, well away from the tenants' holdings.

The Demesne Pasture at Dunsyn
This was mowing meadow in 1292

Medwesyk Demesne
Pasture and Turbary

Martham at the beginning of the thirteenth century

In 1292 a jury of twenty villagers was called to give evidence about the lands, rents and services of a hundred and five 'former tenants' as well as detailed information about the contemporary pattern of land-holding. It is possible that there was in existence an earlier survey or rental naming the former tenants to which reference could be made. Internal evidence suggests that the 'former tenants' lived between 1175 and 1220, let us say at the beginning of the thirteenth century. The whole Survey is organised under the names of these tenants. Each entry gives the acreage of land that a 'former tenant' had held and the services he had owed, followed by the names of the tenants who held the same land in 1292. This section of Chapter 7 looks back to the beginning of the thirteenth century, at the 'former tenants' and their holdings, or 'tenements', as the Survey calls them.[63]

The first two entries in the Survey show that there were two types of regular tenement in Martham, one of ten acres and one of land called mulelond. Mulelond, often called socage land in the Survey, was land held by a 'mol' or money rent along with light services. Roger de Hil paid 4s. a year in rent and 11d. in aid. An aid was an occasional charge levied when a new Prior was appointed, or on other special occasions. It was a device to supplement the fixed rent and helped to bring the lord's remuneration in line with twelfth century inflation.

Then come details of Roger Hil's services. He had to work for three days at harvest (price 1½d.), and the lord provided him with a meal. The contents of the meal were laid down; it must consist of bread, soup and a plate of fish, meat, cheese or milk. He had to carry barley or malt to Norwich, and he had bread and beer when

63. Dating of 'former tenants'. The division of the old tenements suggest that about three generations, say seventy years, separates the former tenants from the tenants of 1292. The Survey mentions a grant of land by Prior Tankard (1172 - 1175) so it must have been written after that date. It seems reasonable to conclude the 'former tenants' lived sometime between 1175 and 1220. The end of the twelfth century, or early in the thirteenth, seems a fairly satisfactory date. It is interesting that the 1292 jury of twenty tenants contain seventeen jurors with the same family names as 'former tenants'.

he got there. If he did no carrying duty he paid 1½d. If he had a cart, he had to do a day's carting at harvest time; if he had no cart he had to come with his pitchfork, and again he had his meal provided. He had to thresh corn for half a day or pay ½d., and he had to make a fixed amount of malt or give 1d. He had to plough if he had his own plough with all his plough beasts, and for each ploughing he had three loaves of bread and nine herring. (Ploughing was boon work, which meant there was no fixed number of days for the service; and the tenant would work when the bailiff summoned him.) If he had no plough or plough-team, he did no ploughing. He harrowed for half a day with one horse or paid 1d. Finally he gave the lord a hen and five eggs. All tenants holding a ten-acre tenement had to do the same services as Roger de Hil. Any tenant who held only a part of a tenement had to do services in proportion to the size of his holding. These practical details about work in the fields, the harvest meal and the prospect of a supper of grilled red herrings after a chilly day's ploughing give us a little insight into the life of a medieval peasant. Herrings were bought by the manor for the ploughing boons until the Black Death in 1349, and details about the provisions for the harvest meal are given each year in the bailiff's annual account.

The next entry is that of Thomas Knight who held twelve acres of villein land sometimes called 'werklond' because a considerable part of the 'rent' was paid in work rather than in cash. Although the holding was larger than Roger de Hil's, the cash rent was only 16d. with 14d. as aid, but the services were considerably heavier. Thomas had to work sixteen days at harvest and, like Roger de Hil, he had a meal each day. He did ten days' weeding, price ½d. a day. He did six carrying duties to Norwich or he paid 9d. Like Roger de Hil he had bread and beer when he arrived at the Priory. He had to make about five times as much malt as Roger de Hil or pay 6d. He did twelve days threshing or paid 12d. He had to plough when required and received bread and herrings for each day's labour. He harrowed rye, oats and the fallow land whether he had a harrow or not. (No doubt the manor could provide a suitable implement if necessary.) He had dung-carrying and ditching services, valued at 12d. and 1d. Again those tenants who held part of a twelve-acre tenement had to do the appropriate services.

The services of the ten and twelve-acre tenements are typical of a system of unpaid labour intended for the cultivation of the manorial demesne. In the case of the Prior's manor of Martham the services were geared to the production and distribution of grain crops. No mention is made of haymaking or livestock farming. It is very clear that the services on the villein tenements were considerably heavier than those on the ten-acre socage holdings. Apart from ploughing boons, the socage tenants were only obliged to do six or seven days work in the whole year, while the tenants of 'werkland' had at least forty-four days work, as well as other services, such as dung-carrying and spreading, for which no times are given.

The origin of the ten and twelve-acre tenements may lie in the Anglo-Saxon period before the Norman Conquest. It would appear that the pattern of land-holding was changed after the Bishop endowed his new Priory with land in Martham and also granted an estate to the de Gunton family. It then became both necessary and possible to reorganise the land-holding pattern to the landlord's advantage. Campbell suggests that 'the regulation of holding layout and cropping and grazing practices may have been imposed by the manorial landlord, as at Martham'.[64] The Bishop's manor of two carucates at Martham, which at Domesday had been attached to the manor of Hemsby, (see page 42) became the nucleus of the Priory manor of Martham. The demesne was consolidated in the eastern half of the South Field, making a compact farm close to the Hall. The twenty-seven sokemen, who apparently held only thirty acres in 1086, were granted enlarged tenements of ten acres.

A manor with its demesne, the origin of the Manor of Moregrove, was created for the Gunton family from part of the five carucates held by the Bishop's thirty-six freemen. Making a manor was not unusual. Earl Ralph is reported in Domesday Book to have done just that from the lands of his eighty freemen in Caister. At the same time, perhaps following the example of the manor at Hemsby with its plentiful supply of villein labour, the freemen's holdings were transformed into villein tenements of twelve acres carrying most of the agricultural services on the manor. These villein tenements with their tenants seem to have been shared

64. B.M.S. Campbell *Economic Historical Review 2nd Series 1980.* 'Common Fields on a Norfolk Manor' p178. For history of Moregrove Manor see Chapter 10 on p. 122.

between the Priory and the Gunton manors. The new Norman landlords would have been in a strong enough position to impose the new arrangements. The ten and twelve-acre tenements described in the 1292 Survey were probably formalised in this way sometime in the twelfth century.[65]

These tenements, with the rent paid in a combination of cash payments and labour services, are typical of most manors at the time of the Norman Conquest, but other patterns of landholding existed by the end of the twelfth century. On the Priory manor the two standard holdings occupied about 500 acres of land. However by the thirteenth century another 330 acres of arable land was held by former tenants and described as socage land in the survey, but it was not divided in the traditional pattern. Much of it may have been gradually brought into cultivation after the two traditional tenements had been established. The size of the holdings on this miscellaneous socage land varied from half an acre to sixteen acres, and the rents are quite arbitrary, ranging from 2d. an acre to 8d. Each holding may represent a separate bargain made with the Prior when a new tenant took over the land. Although the rents varied considerably, the duties on these holdings were uniform and light, usually three harvest days, a hen at Christmas and five eggs at Easter.

Indeed some of the very small holdings have only rent and aid to pay and no services. A few holdings have duties, such as cutting turves or haymaking, which are not found on the standard holdings. Three tenants, who each held 1½ acres, had to drive pigs or carry hens to Norwich. The Cellarer of the Priory was due a gift of pigs each year at Christmas. At one time the tenants may have chased pigs to Wey Bridge at Acle and then up and over Mousehold Heath to Norwich Priory, but the Bailiff's Accounts show that, by 1265 if not earlier, the Cellarer preferred to receive 10s. 9d. in cash each year rather than take delivery of several squealing pigs. The relatively high rents and light duties attached to the miscellaneous socage land suggest that by the beginning of the thirteenth century the Prior, like the Cellarer, preferred a money rent to a series of varied services.

65. B. Dodwell. *Economic History Review* 1967 'Holdings and Inheritance'. Traditional holdings in the Norwich area are frequently 12 or 14 acres. As the population increased these holdings were divided between a number of tenants. See Campbell, B.M.S, 'Population Change and the Genesis of Common Fields' 1980, p.178 for the viability of 5 acre holdings.

The reader will notice that on the standard tenements many of the duties are given a cash value. If the tenant was not required for a day's work he had to pay the price of the service. In the bailiff's words, 'the work was sold' to the tenant for the stated sum. The earliest surviving bailiff's accounts from 1265 onwards, show that many services were transformed or 'commuted' into a cash payment in this way. The tenants of villein holdings no longer had to cart dung or dig ditches; instead they paid the lord of the manor 12d. for carting duties and 1d. for digging. Nor did the cottagers have to take the pigs or hens to the Cellarer. On Martham manor threshing corn and making malt was always done by paid labour, but the tenants had to pay a charge for the work they had not performed. Carrying to Norwich was usually commuted. Only ploughing, harrowing and harvesting, services that needed most labour and were vital to cereal production, were still worked by the tenants. In general the bailiff preferred to use paid labour which could be hired as and when necessary for many of the tasks on the manor.

At Martham, as was usual in East Norfolk, a tenant's holding was not a block of land, but a collection of strips in the open fields, usually in the fields nearest to the tenant's home, although some holdings were scattered more widely in the village. By the end of the thirteenth century many of the ten or twelve-acre tenements had been divided to provide farms for the increasing population. No effort seems to have been made either by the lord of the manor, or by the peasant holders themselves, to preserve the traditional tenements of ten or twelve-acre farms.

The actual size of the former tenants' holdings at the beginning of the thirteenth century varied considerably, from half an acre held by Wluina Bo to Richard Gemere's twenty-nine acres. Figure 7.2 on page 95, shows this pattern of landholding. Over two thirds of holdings were larger than the five acres that Campbell considers necessary for a viable peasant farm in East Norfolk In fact holdings were slightly larger than the figures suggest. A note at the top of the first page of the survey, (see page 82) tells us that the rod, pole or perch, by which land was measured, was not the standard 16½ feet, but was 18½ feet in length. This meant that every acre recorded at Martham is by the standard measurements 1¼ acres in size. So a four-acre holding would contain five acres, and an eight-acre holding, ten; 'former tenant', Richard Gemere's twenty-nine acres would contain thirty-six. In this book the sizes of holdings are given as they are recorded in the Survey, and no attempt is made to redefine them by the standard rod of 16½ feet.

Norman-French customs and culture seem to have spread quite quickly to Flegg, particularly, perhaps, after the Bishopric moved to Norwich and the Priory was founded. Surnames were formalised early in East Norfolk. At the end of the twelfth century, about a hundred years after Domesday Book was written, the majority of the 'former tenants' in Martham had recognisable surnames such as Knight, Chaplain and Pecke, all names still familiar in Flegg. Most had a Norman-French first name such as Roger, William, Alice or Mathilda. In the twelfth century, East Norfolk enjoyed a very active commercial economy based on the widespread use of money. It was a sign of the times that the Prior preferred a money rent and cash to the miscellaneous services of his tenants. With the continuing division of the traditional tenements to accommodate a growing population and the commutation of many agricultural services into money charges, the old manorial pattern was slowly eroding.

Martham in 1292

The thirteenth century saw considerable changes in land ownership and social patterns. The Survey names a hundred and five 'former tenants', but by 1292 the tenant numbers had risen over threefold to three hundred and seventy-six, yet they held the same area of land as the 'former tenants' had done about a hundred years earlier. It seems that there was no more land suitable for arable farming that could be taken into cultivation. Not surprisingly the average size of a peasant holding had been reduced from eight acres to just under three. This increase in the number of tenants cannot be explained by the natural increase in population alone, but by a new pattern of land-ownership. At the end of the twelfth century there were only ten families among the 'former tenants' who, judging by their surnames, may have had more than one member holding land on the manor. By 1292 seventy-five families had two or more members who were tenants of the manor, and the Rede and the Long families each had ten tenant members. Fathers and sons, brothers and sisters, uncles, aunts, widows and cousins all held land in the manor. Land-ownership had been spread much more widely in the community.

The Figures 7.2 and 7.3 on page 95 show patterns of land-holding on Martham manor at the end of the twelfth century and in 1292. As we have seen, the first model shows a fairly even distribution of the size of holdings with over two thirds of the tenants having more than five acres. By 1292 we see a massive base of small holdings of two acres or less, and then the shape narrows to a peak of one holding of thirteen acres and an other of seventeen. Only 48 holdings (11%) were 5 acres or more. Even taking into account Martham's slightly larger acre, many of the 1292 holdings were probably too small to support a peasant family without some additional source of income.

On many Norfolk manors it had become the custom during the thirteenth century for a man to leave his land divided equally among his male heirs. In many cases the actual strips of land were divided between two brothers. In this way, at a period of rising population and in a community with a limited area of arable land, the young men of each generation were provided with a share of the available land. Over the years this had resulted in the constant sub-division of holdings. Of course many tenants had only one male heir, and relatively few had more than two, so partible inheritance was not the only factor in the fragmentation of holdings. There was also a very active land market. Tenants, both bond and free, could dispose of their land as they wished, by gift, sale, or exchange so long as the transfer was registered at the manor court and a fine paid. The pieces of land involved were small, usually half an acre or less, but Campbell has counted ninety-seven transfers of land amounting to about sixteen acres each year in the twelve manor courts held between 1289 and 1298.[66]

This redistribution of land was in part a response to the hard times of the thirteenth century. Increasing manorial charges, rising prices, the steady growth in population, a deteriorating climate and a series of bad harvests made it necessary for tenants to sell small pieces of land from time to time to raise money to pay rent or to buy food. The land market was particularly active after years of bad harvests and high prices, when tenants had to sell small plots of land. Dr Campbell and Dr R. M. Smith have drawn attention to

66. Land Transactions in Martham Manor Court Rolls show frequent transfers of small pieces of land. Twelve to sixteen acres may have changed hands each year, B.M.S. Campbell 1980, p.186.

the same frantic selling in bad years at Coltishall and Redgrave, which was followed, after a spell of good harvests, by an attempt to buy land again.[67] In Martham land was frequently transferred among members of the family, which may have been a deliberate attempt to ensure that, as far as possible, all the members of a family had a share of land, the only economic asset that held its value and was easily negotiable.

Not all communities dealt with the problem of an expanding population in the same way. On the Duke of Norfolk's manor in Forncett in south Norfolk, the surplus population left the village. Between 1272 and 1306 a hundred tenants paid chevage, which is the annual fine allowing a villein to live outside the manor.[68] Some men from Forncett migrated to the Flegg villages of Martham, Somerton, Hemsby and Scratby as well as Eccles in Happing Hundred, Yarmouth and Lowestoft. The attractions of this area were probably the opportunities for employment in fishing and trade and possibly in casual work on the prosperous manors of Flegg. In contrast, at Martham there is no evidence that many tenants left the village in the late thirteenth century. According to the bailiff's accounts chevage raised only a few pence each year and never more than 2s; the few manor court rolls that have survived show only one instance of the actual payment of chevage.

As a result of partible inheritance and the active land market, the old tenements at Martham, some of which had already been divided by the end of the twelfth century, became even more fragmented. The old tenements had little relevance to the layout of tenant holdings in 1292, but still they were recorded in great detail. In theory at least a tenant would have to pay his share of the rent and do his share of the services in each traditional tenement in which he held land. There is no explanation in the Survey or in the manorial documents of how the rents and charges were actually collected or the services allocated. The system must have worked in some rough and ready way for the manor court rolls record relatively few cases of failure to pay rent or other charges, or to do

67. Bruce M.S.Campbell, 'Population pressure, inheritance and the land market in a fourteenth-century peasant community'; Richard M. Smith 'Families and their land in an area of partible inheritance: Redgrave, Suffolk. In *Land, Kinship and Life-cycle'* ed. R.M.Smith. C.U.P. 1984.

68. Davenport, F. 1906.

Figure 7.2 Size and number of holdings in Martham 1192 (n=107)

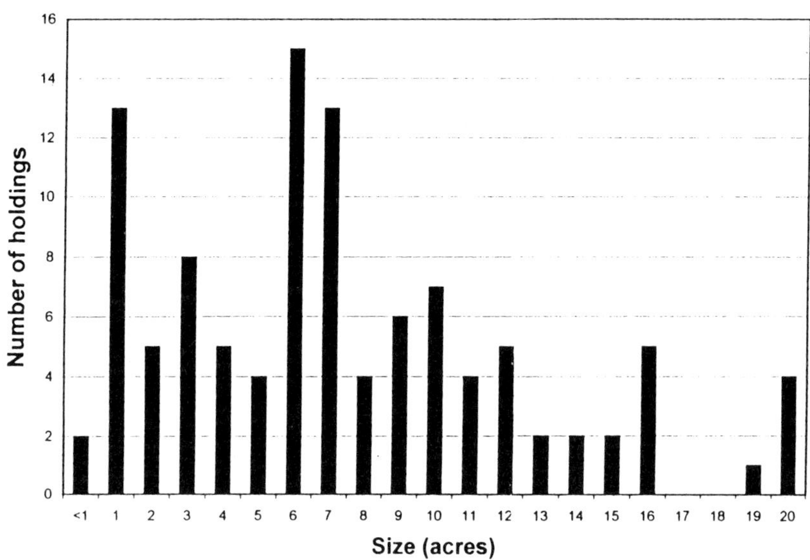

Figure 7.3 Size and number of holdings in Martham 1292 (n=375)

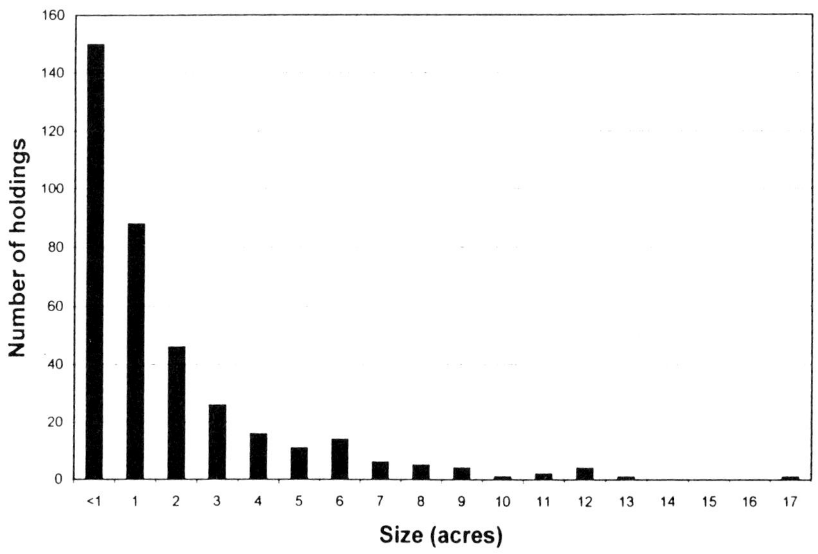

services. It was nearly a hundred years before a more rational system of rents and services was adopted in 1386.[69](See page159)

We must not imagine that the very small holdings of under two or three acres were all individual farms. The Survey records the ownership of land and so emphasises the fragmentation of the old tenements as land passed by inheritance or other forms of transfer to an increasing number of tenants. It was not concerned with the use that was made of the land. In many cases the actual farms on the ground must have been larger than the Survey suggests. If, during his lifetime, a father transferred a few acres to his son it is unlikely that the family farm was immediately split into two farming units. Brothers, who held adjacent strips in the open fields, may well have co-operated to run a family farm.

Tenants might hold an acre or so in other manors. We know that some villein tenants held land in both the Priory and the Gunton manor, and were called upon to do villein services for both lords.[70] It was not unusual for tenants to hold an acre or two on a manor in a neighbouring village. At the other end of the social scale a few members of the gentry and substantial freeholders are recorded as holding a little bondland in the Priory manor which would be only a very small part of their total estates.

Leasing was as common as purchase and enabled many tenants to vary the size of their farms according to their immediate needs. Manorial records show that John de Flegg was an old man without heirs in 1289 when he leased all of his holding to Robert ffellawe for three combs of barley a year. Galfrid le Greyve may have been a young man with a growing family in 1290 when he expanded his holding by renting two separate half acres from two different tenants. These frequent short-term leases meant that the amount of land that an individual tenant cultivated sometimes bore little relation to the size of his holding as recorded in the Survey. By

69. Some record of the old tenements must have been preserved, for they were still used to elect manorial officials, such as the reeve and the collector, right into the 15th cent. Usually the tenant with most land in the tenement was appointed, but he could pay to be excused. See Glossary for manorial officials.

70. B.Dodwell 1985, Agreement between the Prior of Norwich and Laurence de Huntingfield, who held the Gunton Manor. The document states that some villeins held land in two manors and had to do services for both lords, 'which was against justice and reason'. Henceforth villeins were to do services for one lord only.

sale, purchase, or lease of small plots of land, usually no larger than half an acre, the individual tenant could adjust the size of his holding to his needs.[71]

Yet many tenants must have held holdings too small to provide for their families' needs. Society, then as now, was composed of people with different economic requirements. Some tenants had paid employment. The manor provided a good deal of work, even if much of it was casual and ill paid. For the craftsmen of the village, an acre of land would supplement the income they gained from their trade. The Survey records such names as Carpenter, Cupere (Cooper), Scynere (Skinner), Sutor (shoemaker) le Taillour, le Webbestere (weaver) and Faber (smith). The average size of the holdings of these tenants was 1¼ acres. The cultivation of an acre or so would have provided welcome food for the craftsman's family. The Long family may have specialised in the production and sale of peat. Whereas most tenants rented an acre or half an acre of turbary in the South Fen, the heirs of Nicholas Long held two acres and a meadow. Another member of the Long family, Simon, was employed as the swanherd at Martham and Hemsby manors. There are so many ways a countryman can make a living, especially if he owns his own home and a little land.[72]

The village also had its share of traders with names like Mercator (merchant), Chapman and Rathman. Richard Mercator had a substantial holding of 7½ acres, but the other tenants in this group had much smaller holdings. The name 'Rathman' may be puzzling. Men were described as 'rathmen' or 'raffmen' throughout the Middle Ages, and the nature of their trade is not clear. In the thirteenth century they were usually timber merchants, while in the fifteenth century they also dealt in tallow and candles. In 1289

71. P.D.A.Harvey, *Peasant Land Market in Medieval England,* Oxford 1984, 'Norfolk in the Thirteenth Century' by Janet Williamson.

72. Countrymen have always been able to make a living with very few resources. I was told of a man who lived in Martham early in the twentieth century who had his own cottage with a small field. It was matters of pride to him and of respect from his neighbours that he had no regular work and was not beholden to any employer. His two cows were tethered and grazed on the grass verges of the lanes and fields. He took farm work when it pleased him and always at harvest. He went to Yarmouth for the fishing in the autumn. In the winter there was reed-cutting and work on the drainage dykes and cutting thorns for the sea defences. Fishing for eels, wild fowling and all the other resources of the marshes and the hedgerows provided him with food and extra money.

Adam Rathman was fined for being absent from the manor court which suggests that he may have been a travelling craftsmen or a peddler. According to the Survey, he held under two acres. Perhaps he, or his son, prospered, for a man of the same name from Martham was able, ten years later, to pay £2 to buy his freedom. Free status must have been very desirable for an itinerant trader, who could then travel outside the village without manorial restrictions.[73]

Women had always held land in the Middle Ages. In the late twelfth century fifteen women appear among the 'former tenants', about 14% of all tenants; by 1292 nearly a quarter of the tenants were women, 93 out of a total of 376. Women generally had very small holdings; sixty-one had less than an acre. On marriage her father usually gave a daughter half an acre of land. The land was legally hers and reverted to her when her husband died. This gave her economic standing in the community and made her eligible for remarriage. Unmarried daughters appear also to have held small pieces of land. These were in the nature of a piggy bank for the tenant, for the land could be let annually for the rent of a few shillings or for a measure of barley, or, if necessary, sold. A few women held sizeable holdings; Margareta Kilderous was a minor when she inherited 4½ acres on the death of her father in 1290. Her mother managed her land until she became of age and the holding had increased to 5½ acres by the time of the Survey two years later.

Land might form an annuity for old age. In 1289 the Court Rolls record that John Cope granted to Thomas Godknape 1¼ acres of land on condition that Thomas gave John and his wife two quarters of barley each year for their joint lives and one mark (13s. 4d.) yearly, until 40s. was spent. John Cope was still living when the Survey was taken three years later. These examples show that the possession of even a small piece of the very fertile Flegg land could give a measure of economic security.

What sort of a picture do we get of Martham at the end of the thirteenth century? It is not possible to calculate the population of the village from the number of the Priory tenants, because they do not include all the households in Martham. However, taxation

73. Adam Ratheman's manumission. N.R.O. Magister Camera Rolls DCN 1/1/16; Wallace, May 1992 for Raffmen.

records for 1332 show that Martham had 124 taxpayers (they would be the relatively well-to-do inhabitants) while Winterton and Hemsby had 92 taxpayers and Ormesby 90.[74] Martham, with 1000 to 1500 inhabitants, may well have been the most populous village in Flegg at the end of the thirteenth century.[75]

Derelict cottage with productive garden on the edge of the Common at Cess

Old cottage in the row of tofts on Common Edge. The garden is used as a market garden by the Starkings family (see note 61 page 85).

Martham was a complex society of peasant farmers, craftsmen, merchants, manorial officials, churchmen, and members of the gentry. At the other end of the social scale were families who, in a period of high prices and poor harvests, scraped a living from an acre or so of land augmented by ill-paid casual work and the products of the commons and the marshes. In Martham the need for economic security through the possession of land had led to the fragmentation of the traditional land-holding pattern.

In some ways the social pattern of the community seems surprisingly like ours. Modern medieval historians have remarked that the typical peasant landholder of East Norfolk was an individualist. Partible inheritance, along with purchases and gifts of

74. PRO. Subsidy Roll 1332. E 179/149/9.

75. As large as many present villages. See 1991 Census.

land meant that men often came into their property while they were still young. It was possible for a man to set up a home in his own messuage as soon as he acquired any land. His household would consist of himself, his wife and children, a pattern similar to our traditional nuclear family. Neither manorial authorities nor the tenants themselves seem to have tried to preserve the traditional tenements or the patriachal family farm. The typical tenant was not bound by many manorial constraints. He could chose which crops to grow and what animals he wished to put on the common. In a large community like Martham there were opportunities for employment or the acquisition of a trade. He could sell or lease his land as he wished, but every transaction in the manor court meant the payment of a fee. The commutation of most of his manorial services into a money charge meant he was freed from many manorial duties, but it was in effect a rise in his rent. He was trying to survive in difficult economic circumstances, in a society as much dominated by the value of money as by the value of land. It is not surprising that while some men prospered many fell into poverty.

Acorns for the pig
From the Gorleston Psalter

Chapter 8: The Manor Farm: the Bailiff's Task

The thirteenth century saw important economic and social changes. The increase in population and in food prices made the direct exploitation of the demesne farm very attractive to landlords. The key figure in the management of the demesne of any manor was the bailiff, appointed by the lord and answerable to him. The first surviving Bailiff's Account for Martham is for the year 1261-2, that is three years after the end of Sir Walter de Mautby's lease of the two manors of Martham and Hemsby in 1257, described in Chapter 4 page 55. The twenty-nine annual Bailiffs' Accounts which have survived for the manor of Martham between 1261 and 1340 give a detailed picture of the methods of intensive farming practised on one of the most profitable manors in Norfolk during this period of 'high farming'.

The bailiff's task was a formidable one. At Martham he had to run a two-hundred-acre mixed farm, maintain the manor house and farm buildings, including a malt kiln and a windmill, manage a very diverse, and sometimes reluctant, labour force and produce an annual set of very detailed accounts. For at least twenty-six years, from 1287 to 1313, Adam de Bawdeswell was the bailiff of both Martham and the larger manor of Hemsby. He must have received some training from the steward of the Monastery, and have had a method of keeping records of the income and expenses of the manor. With this task two other officials helped him, the keeper of the grange and the beadle. The beadle was one of the tenants, chosen by the manor court, but the bailiff and the keeper of the grange were appointed by the Priory and were probably members of the lesser gentry. The actual writing of the account was the work of a monastic scribe, who visited the manor to take the account from the bailiff. (See Glossary, Manorial Officials, page 196.)[76]

The Martham account nearest in date to the Survey of 1292 is that from Michaelmas 1294 to Michaelmas 1295 and it will do very well as a typical year to study. By the end of September 1294 the corn was stored in the granary under the eye of Thomas de Eton, the keeper of the grange. Grain in Norfolk was stored in the

76. For General Information, Campbell 1983a.

Photograph of Martham Hall in the late nineteenth century

This is an eighteenth century building. The building to the right is on the site of the medieval Hall. The farm buildings and the horse pond give an idea of the medieval farmyard.

traditional coomb sacks, each containing four bushels. Two coomb sacks made a 'quarter', the measure by which corn was always sold. In the nineteenth century a quarter of barley was reckoned to weigh about 4 cwt, but medieval grain may have weighed a little lighter because the grain was not so thoroughly threshed. The very large comb sacks were still in use on Norfolk farms at the beginning of the twentieth century. [77]

Table 8.1: Harvest 1294 compared with other years

	Wheat	Barley	Peas	Oats
Product of 1294 harvest in quarters	47½	247	39	19
Average of 5 harvests between 1287 and 1299	81	270	33	26*

* The figure for oats is rather high as the result of a crop of 42 quarters in 1287 due to special circumstances. In 1287 a new granary was being built, and on many occasions horse-drawn carts were used to collect building materials from Yarmouth. It is possible that extra oats were sown in 1286 to provide oats for the horses or bullocks engaged in this work.

The 1294 harvest does not look particularly good, especially for wheat. The late thirteenth and early fourteenth centuries saw many years of poor harvests and high prices. In such years the manor may have had less corn to sell, but at the enhanced prices income from corn sales were usually no lower than in normal years. In 1295 the sale of peas brought in £7 6. 2d., and the sale of barley £6 9s. 11d. The accounts show how the price of barley rose, exceeding the usual level of 3s. to 4s. a quarter. The first recorded sale was at 6s. 2d. a quarter, then the price rose to 8s. and finally to 9s. 4d., before falling at the last sale to 4s. a quarter. The Priory had obviously been able to hold back some of its grain until the price was high. That year's sale of corn brought in £16 17s. 4 d., about twice the income usually received from corn sales. (See Appendix 9.1)

Barley was the universal grain used for both bread and beer.

77. The Bailiff's Accounts for the Priory manor of Martham are in the NRO, but in two separate Collections, the Dean and Chapter Records (Ref DCN 60/23/ 1 onwards), and for some years in the fourteenth and fifteenth centuries, in the Record Society Collection. (Ref NRS 20 D1 5889 onwards.) Reference for accounts for 1294-5, NRO DCN/60/23/7.

Barley bread was the general fare at the manor house; sacks of barley and malt formed the major part of the farm servants' wages, and barley was also fed to horses, pigs, dogs, geese and hens. Barley was sown on about a hundred acres each year at Martham, that is half the arable demesne land. Wheat occupied about twenty acres, peas thirty and oats ten. Half the barley crop was malted on the farm and most of that was sent to the Priory. In 1294, 36½ quarters of wheat and 136 quarters of malt (possibly seven tons of wheat and twenty-seven tons of malt) were taken from Martham to Norwich at a cost of 26s. 5d., but the accounts do not record whether by road or by water .

As at Mautby, horses, not oxen, were used for ploughing. Horses were more efficient, worked more quickly and for longer hours. Much of the ploughing on the demesne was done by the services of the tenants. Each year two hundred herrings were bought for the ploughing boons as explained in the 1292 Survey. (See page 88) A smith from Winterton, William Faber, was retained to shoe the horses regularly and maintain the ploughs and carts.

The manor herd of cattle consisted of two bulls, fifteen cows, eleven bullocks and the young stock. As well as providing milk, the herd produced valuable dung. In most years some animals were sold, usually a cow, one or two bullocks and about twelve calves. Then cows were bought to replenish the herd and to introduce new stock. Only at harvest time was a beast slaughtered for food. The bulk of the milk was made into cheeses, many of which were sold. Each cheese weighed about 3¾ lbs (1¾ kilograms) and cost 2¼d., a day's wage for a skilled man. In the summer of 1295 forty- two cheeses were sold, weighing in all 11 stone. I have no information about where the produce and livestock was sold, but I imagine it was at Yarmouth market, although the cheese may have been sold more locally.

The manor did not have a flock of sheep of its own, although a ewe and a lamb appear in some years among the manor livestock. The lord of the manor had the right of faldage, that is he could compel his villein tenants to fold their sheep on the demesne after harvest each year. There is no record of the number of tenants owing this service, nor of the number sheep involved, and after 1272 I can find no mention of faldage in the annual accounts until after the Black Death. More important than the tenants' sheep was the Priory flock from Fulholm, a marsh near Yarmouth. The Fulholm flock was brought to Martham to be folded on the demesne stubbles for a couple of months after harvest. The manor paid the shepherd's wages during this period. [78]

The manor farmyard contained the usual assortment of domestic animals, including pigs, geese and poultry. In the autumn the manor always bought a large number of goslings at 1½d. each, probably from local men who had trapped the young wild birds on the marshes. The goslings were fed on the stubbles and then sold very profitably at 4d. each. The manor had its own flock of poultry but also received over 100 hens and nearly 500 eggs as rent. Thirty hens were sent to the Priory and 118 eggs were used at harvest time, but many of the hens and eggs were sold.

More than a thousand eels came from the rents of the two fisheries on the River Thurne. Most eels were sold, but some went to the Priory.[79] The manor kept a small number of breeding swans, looked after by the swanherd, Simon Long. In the cold winter of 1295-6 he received an allowance of one quarter of oats to feed them. Occasionally one or two swans were sent to Norwich for the Prior's table, but the breeding of swans does not seem to have been very successful. Doves and peacocks are recorded in some years. In general livestock husbandry was of a good standard in the thirteenth century, for animal numbers are constant year after year, natural wastage accounting for the deaths recorded.

The bailiff lived at the manor house, and the maintenance of the buildings was one of his responsibilities. We have no inventory

78. In the mid-13th century an agreement between Roger de Burgo and the Prior allowed the shepherd of two Priory flocks from Fulholm to water the sheep in de Burgo's marsh. This document is in the Martham section of the Priory Charters and must relate to Martham manor. (Dodwell, B.1974) I expect the shepherd took his flock from Fulholm along the south bank of the river Bure, swum them across the river at a convenient place, and then walked them over de Burgo's land in the Muck Fleet valley land to spend the time of shack after harvest on the Martham demesne lands

79. Before 1272 the manor had a stock of over a thousand eels, and employed a fisherman. It is not clear whether the manor had its own fishpond, or whether the eels lived in the river. The numbers declined as years went by, and after an outbreak of disease in 1272-3 no more eels are recorded as stock, but the manor let two fisheries on the river and recorded the rents in eels or cash.

for Martham manor but from the record of the repairs it seems that the manor house was very similar to the house at Hemsby, with a hall, two chambers and a solar. (See page 56) There is no mention of a ducking stool or a pillory at Martham.

The windmill called for constant attention and new grind-stones, costing about 25s. each, had to be bought every five or six years. The transport of the heavy stones from Yarmouth, whether by land or water, was always a costly item. From 1312 until at least 1340 Martham had two postmills working. The need for another mill, with all its expense, indicates the productivity of both the demesne and the tenants' farms. We do not know where the mills were in the fourteenth century, but in 1429 a new mill was built near le Ask on the Hemsby boundary (TG41 474 178); un-fortunately it is impossible to say whether this was on the site of one of the older mills. The farm track along the parish boundary from the Somerton Road to the Hemsby Road is still called Mill Lane.[80]

It is clear that the manor gave employment to many people. Six farm labourers, a dairymaid and a cowherd were employed throughout the year and were collectively called *famuli,* the servants. They did not live in the manor house, but took some of their meals there to judge by the use of oats or peas for their pottage. Their combined pay in the thirteenth century was only 5s. 4d. a year, with a separate payment for work at harvest, but they each had a 'livery' (delivery) of a quarter of barley every ten or twelve weeks. Extra ploughmen were employed in the winter months, and a swineherd and a gooseherd in the summer when the livestock was taken from the farmyard and fields to the meadows and marshes. Specialists such as the smith, the rat-catcher and the swanherd were retained during the year. Simon Long, the swan-herd, who was also responsible for the swans at Hemsby, earned 8s. a year. Craftsmen, such as daubers, carpenters, roofers and thatchers were constantly needed for the repair of the buildings. Casual labour was employed for many jobs on the farm such as breaking up the ground, spreading dung and marl, ditching, peat-digging, mowing and haymaking. Threshing was always done by paid labour, costing the manor £2 l0s. 2d. in 1294-5. It must have provided many men with a small but welcome addition to their income in the winter months.

80. For the mill built in 1429 at le Ask, see NRO 20D3 5920.

The manor would be busiest at harvest time. The accounts always give a detailed entry of harvest expenses. In 1296 harvest started on the 12th August, which was rather late, since the usual date was August 1st, and lasted five weeks to the 16th September. There were nineteen workers, who, as the accounts say, 'were resident at the lord's table' for the whole of the harvest. They were Thomas Eton, the keeper of the grange, Nicholas, the 'beadell', six carters, three stackers, three reapers, the cowherd, the swine-herd, the gooseherd, the dairymaid and her girl. Workers employed for the whole harvest were paid a special harvest rate. In 1296 the wage bill came to £1 12s. 7d., but no information is given about individual pay packets. In 1313 the regular workers received 2s. 6d. each, the cowherd 1s. and the swineherd and the gooseherd 6d. each. This seems to have been the usual rate for the harvest up to the Black Death of 1349. In the nineteenth century it was still the custom for farm labourers to agree with their employer to bring in the harvest for a fixed sum, however long that might take.[81]

The manor provided a harvest meal each day for the regular workers and for the tenants working on the demesne. Although numbers may have fluctuated, the manor must have had to provide fifty meals on some days. The details and cost of the food consumed were recorded. For bread the manor provided a little wheat and mixed corn (wheat and rye), some wheat chaff and a great deal of barley. Beer was brewed from five and a half quarters of malt. The manor farm slaughtered a cow and also provided four 'perne', literally bones but more rationally 'limbs or hams', eight geese, ten chickens, forty-five cheeses and all the milk in the dairy during harvest. In addition two pennyworth of bread, eleven pennyworth of beer and meat costing 2s. 9d. was purchased. For the fish meal on Fridays a hundred and two mullet were bought costing £1 2s. 8d. The meal must usually have taken place in the evening, for in some years candles were bought as well as cloths, dishes and spoons. It may have taken place in the hall of the manor, or perhaps in an empty barn or farm building, and the cooking was probably done out of doors. The bailiff's accounts were kept meticulously in the same form year after year. They recorded the management of a complicated agricultural enterprise, which maintained a very high level of productivity. Not only did the manor supply the Priory with food and drink but it also made money payments to the monastery. The amount varied consid-

81. 1296 Harvest. NRO DCN/60/23/8

Bailiff's Account Roll 1333-4

N.R.O. heading and the 'minute' (small expenses)

erably each year. In 1294-5 and 95-6, when corn prices were high and the manor received a good price for its sale of corn, the Priory received £23 and £27. In other years in the late thirteenth century the payment varied from £6 to £16. The neighbouring manor of Hemsby contributed £50 in 1294-5 and £69 in 1295-6, but more often about £20. The extract from the accounts for 1334-5 on page 106 opposite shows the detailed care with which the bailiff kept the records of the manor.

The Annual Account Rolls of Martham Manor usually appear under the names of two manorial afficers. For 1334-5 these were Roger Orger, the Collector, and Peter Ockle, the Custodian of the Grange. The accounts were written by a monastic scribe, who probably visited the manor several times in the year to collect the information. Accounts were presented in the same format each year, and followed a similar pattern on every manor. They begin with the income for the year, recording money received from Rents, Sale of Grains and Livestock, and from other other products of the manor, such as straw, cheese, and fines from the Manor Court. For the year 1334-5, income at Martham amounted to £49 19s. 11d.

The expenditure section, always the most detailed, included thirteen sections in 1334-5, of which seven are shown, *Caruc* (ploughs 21s. 2d.), *Carect* (carts 11s. 5d.), *Stipend* (wages 8s. 4d.), *Doms* (buildings 16s. 2d.), *Dairy* (4s.10d.), *Molend* (mill 3s. 10d.) and *Minute* (minor expenses).

The *Minute* (small or miscellaneous expenses) is often the most interesting section, because it illustrates such varied activities on the manor. The first line of this account reads, 'Castrating 16 Pigs, 8d. *Item,* spreading dung *(fumi)* 10 days by one hired man, 10d. *Item* 1 seed basket or seedlip (*sementino*) bought 2d. It would be tedious, and sometimes difficult, to interpret the whole section, but purchases of many farm implements were made, including two spades, two shovels and two forks. One of the most expensive purchases was 336 herrings for 44 ploughing boons, 3s. 7d. (13d. per 100). The manor made its own grain sacks and spent 7s. 5d. on 60 ells of sack cloth, 4d. on rope and string and 1d. for 'reeding' (the red dye, reddle) to mark them. Other assorted expenses included pasturing 10 bullocks, 10s., ferrying 2 lasts of peat (*mora*) 7s. 6d., and making turves from the peat. The Mickle-medwe was mowed, cost 8d., and mowing Medeswykes cost 10d. In all, 65s.1d. was spent on these items. The total of expenses for the year was £45 8s. 8d., but the Collector was still owed £4 11s. 2d.

Chapter 9: Tenants of Martham Manor and the Manor Court in the late Thirteenth Century

Information from the records of the manor court can help to build up a picture of some of the tenants and their families. The only surviving Court Rolls for Martham before the Black Death are those for 1289 to 1291 and for the year 1298. This is lucky because they are more or less contemporary with the 1292 Survey. There are many problems with the interpretation of manor court rolls. They tend to give indirect rather than direct evidence; we only learn of farming or social customs when individuals transgress them and are brought before the manor court. Customs and rules of the manor are not usually written down until they are in danger of becoming outdated or forgotten, so it is often not until the fifteenth and sixteenth century that formal statements of manorial regulations are recorded.[82] You may want to consult the map of Martham on page 75 when reading this chapter.

Only six acres of free land, held by two tenants, were recorded in the Survey, a very small acreage of free land compared with most Norfolk manors. The ten-acre and twelve-acre tenements and the miscellaneous socage land covered 830 acres in the village fields and was bondland, subject to the manor court, although not every tenant was necessarily a villein. The manor court recorded all transfers of land, whether by inheritance, gift, lease, or sale, showing how the tenements of the 'former tenants' were split up to supply smaller holdings for the growing population of the thirteenth century.

Peasant Families in Martham at the end of the Thirteenth Century

The fortunes of two families show how by the end of the thirteenth century the holdings of 'former tenants' had often become divided not only between their descendants, but also among tenants who had no apparent relationship with the original owner. At the end of the twelfth century 'former tenant', Roger de Hil, had held a traditional ten-acre holding and his rents and services were described in full at the beginning of Chapter 7. Three acres of his

82. Martham Court Rolls are in NRO DCN 60/22/1 for 1288-90; DCN 60/22/2.

land was in Hiltofts, the small field that was known by his name. Three and three-quarter acres lay in neighbouring Sco Field, while the remaining three and a quarter acres were in Hardingtofts, Rollesby Field and West Field, all quite near his messuage in Hiltofts. He also had a quarter of an acre in the East Field. In Martham it was usual, but not universal, for a tenant to have most of his holding in the fields near his home.

By 1292 his three male descendants, John, Robert senior and Robert junior each held only 1½ acres in the ancestral tenement. Their messuages lay in half-acre tofts lying side by side in the usual Martham fashion, and abutted on the road from Repps to Martham. Eight other tenants, apparently unrelated, held land in the remaining 5½ acres of the family tenement. Only John Hil had added any significant amount of land in other tenements, bringing his total holding to 4½ acres, which, given Martham's long measuring rod of 18½ ft, might have been a holding large enough to support a peasant household. Another member of the family, Cecilia Hil, a widow, held half an acre in West Wong, which was probably her dowry. In 1298, she transferred her holding to her son, Robert Hil senior, with the proviso that she should have the use of the land until her death. The 2s. fine he should have paid for the transfer, was reduced to 1s. 9d. because 'he keeps his mother', *'custodiet matrem suam'*, an example of care in the community in the thirteenth century. Apart from this transfer, the Hil family does not appear in the manor court records of the thirteenth or fourteenth centuries.

At the end of the twelfth century 'former tenant' John le Rede had held a ten-acre tenement of miscellaneous socage land; by the end of that century it had become divided between fifteen tenants, ten of whom have the name le Rede, seven men and three women. In 1292 the le Rede holdings ranged from 10 perches held by James le Rede to nearly three acres held by Roger le Rede. Only Roger had any land outside the ancestral tenement, and that was only an eighth of an acre. The Rede land lay in the Sco area to the west of the village. Their messuages, each in its toft, lay side by side, facing the road from Sco to Martham. The court records show that, like so many other Martham families, they transferred small pieces of land among themselves. All the Rede holdings seem pitifully small and the family may have been sinking into destitution. The word '*pauper*', poor, was written against Reginald's name when he failed to pay a fine of 2s. for one of these transactions. It appears from the histories of the Hill and the le Rede families that, as the holdings of the 'former tenants' fragmented over the thirteenth century, tenants who were unable to acquire any land outside their ancestor's tenement, were facing a bleak future, unless, of course, they had another source of income. It may also be relevant to the apparent decline in prosperity of both the Hil and the Rede families that they held almost all their land in Sco, away from the main village and on the edge of Stefne Heath where the soil may not have been as fertile as the land of the West and East Fields.

It was however possible by inheritance or purchase to build up sizeable holdings. In 1292 the brothers Robert and Eustace Stanard held seventeen and twelve acres respectively in fourteen of the old tenements, including three acres in the Hil tenement. (Their ancestor, Mathilda Stanard, had held only six acres.) Robert's holding was the largest on the manor and over half of his land lay to the west of the village in West Field and West Wong. Thomas Godknape was another tenant who held more land in 1292 than the five acres which 'former tenant', John Godknape, had at the end of the twelfth century. Thomas' holding of 11½ acres lay scattered all over the common fields in thirteen tenements. Unlike Robert Stanard, he does not seem to have tried to acquire land in one area of the village. We can get some idea of the ways in which he built up his holding from his acquisition of 1½ acres from John Cope in exchange for an annuity to John, as described on page 98. It is clear that some men could buy up land and prosper.

The Knight family are perhaps more typical of the thirteenth century peasant farmers in Martham. Their ancestor, 'former tenant', Thomas Knight, had held a traditional twelve-acre villein tenement and also four acres of miscellaneous socage land, sixteen acres in all. His land was concentrated in the East Field. In 1292 the brothers, Matthew and John Knight, each held six acres, while Andrew, the son of John Knight, had 2¾ acres. The Knight family seems to have been rather unruly and quarrelsome. John was apparently involved in a brawl in 1289, for he was accused in the manor court of assaulting three different people. Andrew was convicted in 1289 of stealing turf valued at 3d.; but he was excused the fine because of poverty. Beatrice Knight, a widow, held an acre in the Knight tenement, and was also described as poor in 1298, when she failed to pay a fine. She had a lengthy dispute with the Long family about her dowry. She seems to have been a lively character for she broke into the lord's pound and took away a cow, for which she was fined 2d. (No doubt the cow was hers and had been impounded as a stray). Like many other tenants, members of the Knight family engaged in sale, purchase or exchange of small pieces of land with other tenants.

Another member of the family, James, does not appear in the Survey, but the court records show he was a chaplain and had absented himself from the Manor Court without permission. In July 1289 his lands and crops were confiscated. He also had a dispute with his mother Margaret and his brother Andrew. In May 1290 he returned and paid a fine to excuse himself from attendance at Court and settled his affairs with his relations. Matthew had the confiscated 3½ acres, and Andrew received 40s., while the errant chaplain had to pay the court the unusually high fine of half a mark, that is 6s. 8d.

Three men, Robert Elsy, James Knight and Robert le Longe, all of them from villein families, are described as *capellanus* in the Court Rolls. It was not unusual for the vicar of a large village like Martham to have one or more chaplains to work for him. Robert Elsy was probably the village chaplain for there is no record of him leaving the village, but Robert Long, like James Knight, paid to be excused attendance at the Manor Court, possibly to pursue a career in the Church. It is interesting that three men of villein status from one village were able to become priests. The standard may not have been very high but a cursory knowledge of Latin and the service book was surely necessary. Blomefield says that in the early fourteenth century a priest was licensed to hold a school in Martham, but unfortunately gives no reference for this. Possibly the school was already in existence at the end of the thirteenth century. At such a school, boys from peasant families would have access to sufficient education to take Holy Orders and might then make a career in the Church.[83]

83. Blomefield, vol.xi p. 166 &173.

Unfortunately the court rolls do not give lists of free and villein tenants; however, chance references in the court records and other documents sometimes reveal the status of tenants. For example in 1289 the brothers Richer and Robert de Martham, members of the Gunton family, granted to the Prior, 'Warin, son of William Horn, our bondman with all his offspring and his goods and chattels'. Warin was described as *'nativus'*, 'bondman by birth', his children by the word *'sequela'*, a word usually used for the brood of animals. The Prior gave the De Martham brothers 10s., and Warin got nothing but a change of landlord, which probably meant very little to him.[84] Three years later, in the 1292 Survey, Warin is recorded as holding 1½ roods of land and two other male members of the Horn family had holdings of less than one acre.

From other thirteenth and fourteenth century records I have found the names of fifty-seven villein families and forty-three free families in Martham. In the late thirteenth century some villein families, such as the Elsys, the Longs and the Knights had substantial holdings and seemed to be doing well in the community, while others such as the Horns and the Redes had little land and may have found it difficult to survive. The free families are more difficult to trace. Being freemen they were more mobile, and could leave the village without seeking permission of the manor court. Both the de Syks and the Erl families seem to have had both free and bond members. The heiress, Margaret Kilderous, also came from a free family. However since most tenants on Martham manor, whether bond or free in status, held bond land, they would all have to attend the manor court and have to fulfil the services attached to their land. In most aspects of life the legal status of a man probably made little difference to his position in village society.

Matthew Knight's Farm

Matthew Knight with his six-acre holding may be taken as a fairly typical Martham tenant. His messuage lay in a toft of nearly half an acre abutting on to Ferergate, probably next door to his brother John's messuage in Fendrovetofts. Matthew's house would be a

84. B.Dodwell, *Charters of Norwich Cathedral Priory, Pipe Roll Society,* 1985.

one or two-roomed dwelling, with mud walls and roofed with turf or rushes, which he had built himself with help from friends and family. The toft, enclosed with hedge or fence, would contain a barn and other outbuildings, and would also provide an area where animals could be penned and various household and farming tasks be performed.

Some idea of his household possessions may be gained from Blomefield's record of the items which a villein in Hemsby could retain on the death of his father. In theory all the other moveables in the house and toft reverted to the lord when the tenant died. At Hemsby the heir could keep a cart, a plough with its equipment, a ladder (perhaps a wide ladder to fit on the end of the cart at harvest time), a table with cloth, a basin, a washing bowl, dishes, plates, a cask and a vat, a hair mattress, a spade and a fork and what Blomefield calls a grindstone; surely a hand quern to grind corn would be more likely. You can see that the heir was left with essential farming implements and household goods. They are not so very different from the possessions recorded in the probate inventories of poorer husbandmen in the sixteenth century. Of course not every villein tenant would possess all these items. [85]

Most of Matthew Knight's arable land lay half a mile away from his messuage. He held 3 acres in nine strips in the East Field and Monechyn. (See map of Martham on page 75.) Nearer to home he had half an acre in both Damiottofts and Fendrovetofts and an eighth of an acre in both the West Field and in Moregrove. Then, right over in the south side of the village, he held two quarter acre strips in Tomeres. It seems amazing that Matthew knew where his strips lay in each field. In Martham, as in many open fields all over the country, each strip was separated from the next by an unploughed furrow. I could not believe that this was adequate to mark one man's land from another's until I saw Braunton Great Field (Devon) in July. A narrow ridge had been left between the strips, and even a week or two before harvest, a

85. Information about peasant housing from Barbara A.Hanawalt, *Ties that Bind* OUP, 1986, chap 2. Peter Wade-Martin & Lawrence Butler 'The Deserted medieval Village of Thruxton' in *East Anglian Archaeology No 46,* shows plans of deserted toft at Thruxton with discussion of the buildings. For the implements an heir could retain, see Blomefield, *History of Norfolk,* vol xi. NRO have no records of the Court Rolls of Hemsby manor, so I am not able to check this reference.

sinuous line of lowered vegetation could be seen stretching through the corn and dividing one strip from the next. (See page 109) However, in Martham with its innumerable divisions the single furrow was not always adequate to prevent disputes over boundaries. [86]

One would think that a farm which consisted of small strips of land scattered all over the village would be a very inefficient one, but perhaps it did not seem so to Matthew Knight. Some of the cultivation of his land, such as ploughing, was probably done in co-operation with his neighbours, while at other times he would work alone with his spade and hoe preparing the soil and dealing with the weeds like any modern allotment-holder. Campbell suggests that, with the constant tending of the land and the labour provided by members of his family, the productivity of the small peasant holdings was as good as that on the demesne.[87]

Few clues exist about the rotation of crops on the arable lands in Martham. In theory, at least, Matthew could grow what he wished on his land. In fact, like everyone else, he grew barley on most of his holding with an acre or so of peas and perhaps a little wheat or rye. An example from Coltishall may provide some relevant information about the crops on a peasant's farm. In 1315 Ralf Lif grew barley on just over half of his five-acre holding, as well as a little rye, oats and peas. [88]

With so many mouths to fill, the major consideration of the medieval peasant was to grow enough corn to feed his family, to save some seed for the following year and to sell some of his produce to pay his rent. Animal husbandry took second place to arable farming. Some tenants may have kept sheep, but they do not figure in the Martham records. Chickens, possibly a pig, and certainly the family cow were found on most farms. The cow gave milk and manure, while bullocks provided pulling power for plough and cart. Traditionally the cow and the dairy were the women's responsibility, so it is not surprising that women were sometimes brought before the manor court for allowing their cows to stray.

86. See Manor Court Rolls, 1506, NRO NRS 20D5 5952.

87. See Campbell 1983a 'Agricultural Progress' page 39. In a period of rising population most peasant farmers had an abundant supply of unpaid labour, and the skill and equipment to use it proficiently.

88. For Ralf Lif's farm See Campbell 1983a, 'Agricultural Progress' page 40.

Agnes atte Syk probably had a small herd of cows for she was accused of overstocking the lord's pasture in July 1290; she may have added to her family's income by selling her milk and cheese.[89]

Grazing regulations on the open fields and on the common were simple. The time of 'shack', when all animals could be turned on to the stubble fields, lasted from the end of harvest until mid-November. Between then and early May, animals might graze on the open fields and green meres, but they had to be tethered or kept under control, usually, I imagine, by the oldest or youngest working member of the family. After May 3rd all animals were banished from the open fields to the common or marsh pastures. Martham had so much marsh grazing that it was not necessary to impose strict limits on the number of animals turned on to the common. After haymaking, the meadows, even those in private ownership, were opened to the livestock of the community. The common at Cess, called the 'dry common' to distinguish it from the marshy 'wet common', could be used at any time of the year for grazing, so long as the animals did no damage. [90]

Moger's Meadow

The common with its varied vegetation was vital to the tenants of Martham. This meadow was originally part of the common

89. Owners of sheep were usually the wealthier farmers. In 1315 John Wyre of Dilham was arrested for stealing forty sheep from Geoffrey of Somerton who held the smaller Somerton manor. In 1309 John Morwen stole ten sheep from Alice, widow of Robert de Runham. Both examples from Hannawalt. B. 1976.

90. Information about the regulations grazing on the fields and meres are from 16th century court rolls when tenants flagrantly flouted the traditional regulations.

After November the rank grasses on the stubbles and the common would not have contained much nourishment for the animals. In winter the cow could be kept on its owner's toft and fed barley straw and fodder gathered from the marshes. Then dung could be collected and spread on the fields. It is incorrect to think that the medieval peasant did not understand the value of manure or marl. When Matthew Knight was accused of digging a hole in the highway he may have been hoping to find marl to spread on his land. Digging holes on the common or the roads is a frequent charge brought against tenants in the manor court.

The Role of the Manor Court

In many ways the manor court dominated the social and economic life of the tenant. There was heriot to pay when he inherited his father's holding and merchet when his son or daughter married. If he sold, exchanged or leased a piece of land he had to register the transaction and pay a fine. (In this way his ownership of the land was recorded in the court rolls and could be consulted in cases of dispute.) Tenants were fined for breaches of the customs of the manor, particularly in the use of the common and the control of livestock. A good deal of the court's time was taken up with cases of assault, bad debts and disputes over land. Family disputes frequently occurred over the land that a widow should inherit as her dowry after her husband's death. Pleas of assault or drawing blood are very common. Settlement always involved the payment of a fine to the court. Serious cases, or those that involved tenants of other manors, were referred to the hundred court. Manor courts were held about four times a year, usually in February, May, June and November under the supervision of the Priory steward. For the lord of the manor the court was a lucrative source of income, but for the tenant many of its orders must have been irksome and the constant imposition of fines a serious drain on his very limited financial resources.[91]

There were relatively few complaints about failure to pay rent or to do manorial services. The offenders were usually tenants from wealthy peasant families or members of the gentry who held a few

91. Merchet, the marriage fine, was usually charged simply on the marriage of daughters, but at Martham it was charged for both sons and daughters.

acres of bond land. By 1290 Roger Bavant, who had married a Gunton heiress, had not paid his rent of 1¾d. for fourteen years, and two members of the Erl family had not done a harvest duty for fifteen years. However in 1298, when Robert Erl died, the death duty on his messuage and 10 acres of land was raised from 10s. to 30s., possibly in compensation for his unpaid rent.

An interesting case in 1298 concerns five men who came from humble village families and were presented for 'contradicting and concealing their customary services', but as they were away in Yarmouth the fines could not be levied. Since the date of the court was October, I suspect that the men went to Yarmouth to earn money in the herring fishing, as villagers so often did for the next six hundred years. The great majority of tenants seem to have done their ploughing, harrowing and harvest works to the satisfaction of the bailiff. However so few Martham court rolls have survived for this period that it would be unwise to think that duties were always conscientiously performed. On the small manor of Boyes at Rollesby, one or two tenants were presented at almost every court in the early fourteenth century for failing to do their services. [92]

At Martham the obligation to grind corn at the lord's mill was regularly flouted. In 1290 and 1291 fifteen men and women were presented in court for this offence, most of them tenants with very small holdings. The offenders were each fined 3d., and this sum is so regular that I wonder whether the fine had become a licence to be excused from using the lord's mill. For a small farmer the regular use of a quern at home would be much more convenient than having to store a large quantity of flour from the mill.[93]

Certainly the fine for breaking the Assize of Ale was a sort of excise tax. Eighteen women were presented for this offence and fined 3d. or 6d. Their surnames are familiar ones, Alicia Knight, Alicia le Long and Margaret Godknape among others. The money that the wife earned from the sale of her product must have been a useful contribution to the income of many a peasant family. The village had only one baker, Robert Orger, who was fined 6d. for

92. Martham Court Rolls 1298 NRO DCN 60/23/ 2; Rollesby Court Rolls 1328-70 NRO Lucas and Willis 5/8/71. (R 188D).

93. The son of a Polish farmer told me that before Second World War his father always spent one day each week grinding corn on a hand quern to provide flour for bread for the family for a week.

breaking the Assize of Bread, another example of a fine that was in fact a regular licence; the court records contain no other mention of him.

Many presentments in the court show pressure to use every inch of land for growing corn. Some men were presented for encroaching on their neighbour's land, or for moving the boundary marks that stood at the head of the strips. Others extended their land by ploughing up the paths and roads. In July 1291 five men, including the Vicar of Martham, were accused of illegally cultivating a strip of land a foot wide along the highway. The Vicar was fined 3s., while the other culprits were only fined 3d. Was the Vicar the ringleader, or did the jurors consider a high fine appropriate for a man in his position in the community?

How did the tenants of these small farms survive? There was certainly poverty and hunger, especially as harvest approached and the family's stock of corn came to an end. In 1291 Alice Goggere, whose husband Robert had a 2½-acre holding, stole sheaves of corn from the harvest field. She was noted as '*pauper*' and did not pay the fine. Fourteen other tenants are recorded as 'poor' in the court rolls. Where we can link their names with the size of their holdings we see that most of them held under four acres, five of them holding an acre or less. Yet there is some ambiguity about these 'poor' tenants. Andrew and Beatrice Knight, and Eustace le Long, were each recorded as poor when they failed to pay a fine; they may each have held less than three acres, but other members of their families had holdings of six acres or more. Mathilda Littlegood and the brothers Roger and Nicholas Keneman had '*valde pauper*', 'truly poor', written against their names. These words suggest that they were really destitute, and that there was little chance of collecting their fines. The list of alms given by the manor indicates that poverty and hunger were prevalent in the years of high prices. (See Appendix 9.1)

The impression given by the bailiff's accounts and the manor court rolls is of a smoothly-running business and a relatively prosperous community. In Martham in the late thirteenth century marriages outnumbered deaths, fines were generally paid and no arrears were recorded in the accounts. Even allowing for the fact that both the court records and the bailiff's accounts were written by Priory officials and must have reflected the landlord's point of view, these thirteenth century records do not give the impression of a society on the point of economic collapse.

Appendix 9.1 Corn Prices and Alms

The chart shows the price of barley sold by Martham manor as given in the bailiff's accounts from 1261 to 1420. Prices are recorded for forty-three years out of one hundred and fifty-nine from 1261 to 1420. No other Flegg manor has a comparable sequence of prices. I have added some figures from the small manor of Scratby which record prices for the years of the Great Famine, years which are missing from Martham. Corn was sold by the quarter, a measure of volume, which held eight bushels. A quarter of barley probably weighed nearly a fifth of a ton.

I chose barley prices rather than wheat prices because barley was the chief corn grown on all Flegg manors, and all manors sold their surplus crop locally. Barley was also the chief bread corn for the rural population. In the year after a poor harvest the price of barley rose sharply, and this must have caused hardship for many peasants living near subsistence level. The manors always managed to sell a good deal of barley in years of bad harvests, even in the Great Famine. With higher prices they often had a better cash return than in normal years, even if they sold less grain. The starred dates are years in which the price of barley rose above 4s. a quarter. The years and figures in bold are years when the price rose above 6s. a quarter, a price which many peasant families could hardly afford.

The earliest record of the price of corn is from the accounts of the St Benet's manor of Ashby in 1245 when it sold for 3s.4d. This seems to have been the usual price for most of the thirteenth century. The late thirteenth and the early fourteenth century was a period of unsettled weather with many poor harvests and high prices. During the second quarter of the fourteenth century barley prices were steady at about 3s.-4s. a quarter, and on the whole remained so after the Black Death, with higher prices in some years. The fifteenth century saw a gradual fall in the price of barley to 2s.4d. However, the lack of figures at Martham for many years after the Black Death has probably distorted the over-all picture.

Table 9.1 Prices of Barley in Flegg 1261 to 1420

Date	Martham barley	Scratby wheat	Scratby barley
1261-2	3s. 6d.		
1263-4	3s.		
1265-6*	4s. 6d.		
1272-3*	5s.		
1273-4*	4s. 7½d.		
1287-8	3s.		
1294-5*	**6s. – 8s.**		
1295-6	3s. – 4s.		
1297-8	3s. – 5s.		
1299-1300	**3s.5d. – 8s.**		
1304-5	3s.8d. – 4s.		
1305-6*	4s.8d. – 5s.		
1309-10*	**4s.8d. – 6s.8d.**		
1311-12*	**4s.6d. – 4s.8d.**		
1312-13	4s.		
1314-15*		**7s.2d. – 14s.**	**8s. – 11s.**
1315-16*		**24s.**	**8s.6d. – 16s.**
1317-18*	**7s. – 8s.**		
1318-19*	4s.4d.		
1319-20	3s.2d.		
1320-21*	4s.2½d.		
1322-23*	**7s.2d. – 10s.**		
1323-24*	4s. – 5s.11d.		
1324-25*	4s.10d.		
1325-26*	4s. – 4s.8d.		
1326-27	3s. - 3s.4d.		
1327-28	2s.9d.		
1333-34	3s.4d. – 3s.10½d.		
1334-35	3s.4d. – 3s.10d.		
1337-38	3s. – 3s.9d.		
1340-41	3s.8d.		
1349-50	3s. – 4s.		
1359-60*	4s. – 4s.2d.		
1377-78	4s.		
1379-80	3s.4d.		
1390-91*	**6s.8d. – 8s.**		
1392-93	3s.6d.		
1400-01	3s.4d.		
1406-7	2s.4d.		
1407-8*	5s.		
1412-13	2s.4d.		
1414-15	3s.4d.		
1415-16*	**4s. – 6s.**		
1418-19	2s.4d.		
1419-20	2s.8d.		

Table 9.2 Alms at Martham, Hemsby and Scratby

Date	At Martham	At Hemsby	At Scratby
1265-66		4 qrts barley	
1272-73		Milk to poor	
1287-88	13s.4d. in mid-Lent	8 qrts barley, ½qrt rye	
1294-95	4 bus. peas	4½ qrts peas, 5 qrts barley	
1295-96	1 qrt peas	£2 3s. 4d.	
1297-98			2½ qrts peas
1299-1300	£1 + ½ qrt peas	1 qrt peas	
1305-06	1 qrt 2 bus. Peas	2 qrts peas	
1309-10	13s. 4d.		
1314-15			1 qrt peas
1315-16			3 qrts peas
1317-18		10 qrts peas	
1322-23		9 qrts barley	
1324-25	5s. 5d. + 1½ qrts barley, 6 bus. peas		

Comparison with the chart of the price of barley shows that alms were given by the Priory in the years of high prices, as in 1265-6, 1294-5 and 1311-12 at Martham and Hemsby, and at Scratby in the years 1314-16, and 1317-8 at Martham at the time of the Great Famine. This chart also shows that alms-giving was far more generous at Hemsby than at Martham. Hemsby was the larger manor, but did not necessarily have more tenants.

After 1324 there is no record of alms at Martham, except in 1392 when alms of 5s. was allowed by the Master of the Cellar. Individual tenants are sometimes excused their fines in the manor court because of poverty, but there is no record of general alms-giving. In one or two years in the early fifteenth century Ormesby manor bought a barrel of herring for the poor.

Chapter 10: The Moregrove Manor at Martham, the Clere Lands and the Nature of Lordship in Flegg

The last three chapters were dominated by the Prior's manor of Martham for which there is far more documentary material than for any other Flegg manor. Although Moregrove manor in Martham has no such consistent documentary evidence, its history makes an interesting contrast with the Priory manor.

The Manor of Moregrove in Martham[94]

The second manor in Martham is an example of a small manor with a complicated history involving the inheritance of heiresses, the transfer of ownership to a College of Priests in Kent, and the final return to the lordship of the Norwich Cathedral Priory. In the early twelfth century Bishop Losinga granted land to the de Gunton family in a number of Flegg villages including Martham. (See Chapter 7 page 89) There is no record of the size of the Gunton estate in Martham, but it was not as large as the Priory manor. However, the Gunton lands included the church and were important enough for some members of the family to take the surname, 'de Martham'. Robert de Martham appears in various charters in the late thirteenth century, and in the 1292 Survey he is recorded as living in a house in Moregrove Field, most probably the manor house. His descendant, another Robert de Martham, was lord of the manor in the early fourteenth century.

In the twelfth century many landlords granted their private churches to ecclesiastical institutions, both as a pious act and in expectation of prayers for the health of their souls, and in some cases, for financial return or favour. In the mid-twelfth century Roger de Gunton gave Martham church to the Priory, and Adam de Walsingham was appointed vicar. He was not the typical poor priest, who lived a life very similar to his village flock, but a

94. The only manorial record for Moregrove manor is an early 16th century Field Book called *The Buttles of land and pasture longing to the manor of Moregrove in Martham. Anno sexto Henry 8th. !514* NRO Dunston T168A. It contains copies of fourteenth century leases of marshes in Horsey.

dignitary of the church, who had other lucrative appointments and was in constant attendance on the Bishop, no doubt leaving his pastoral work in Martham to paid chaplains. About a hundred years later, in 1246, Matthew de Gunton endowed the church with a vicarage and twelve acres of land, the traditional size of a villein tenement in Martham. It seems probable that the vicarage stood on the site of Rectory Farm in Cess (TG 441 176). Both the 1292 Survey of the Prior's manor and the 1514 Field Book of Moregrove manor record the rectory in The West Field.[95]

There is no written record of the site of the early church, but in 1999, when work was done on the tower floor, the footings of a round tower were exposed. This suggests that the early church was on the same site as the present one.[96] Martham church was probably the home of an anchorite, Olivia de Raveningham, who is said to have been enclosed in or near Martham in the thirteenth century. Another reference to the Church is found in the Yarmouth Records of 1309 and 1310, which mention timber provided for Martham Church and for the Chapel of St Blide.[97]

In 1276 Matthew de Gunton died, leaving no male heir and the history of Moregrove manor becomes rather confused. The manor seems to have come to a Gunton grand-daughter, the wife of Roger Bavant, and later to Lawrence de Huntingfield. The bond-land of both the Gunton manor and the Prior's manor lay intermingled in the open fields, and some tenants were obliged to do ploughing and harvest services on both manors, a situation which even the lords agreed was 'irrational and without justice'. In 1322 the Prior and Lawrence de Huntingfield agreed that villeins holding land from both lords should, by agreement, work for one only.[98]

95. See note 94 above for reference to Martham parsonage.

96. Information from Anne Meakin of Martham, 3.5.99.

97. For donation of Martham church to the Priory see B. Dodwell, 1974. For anchorite at Martham see Clay R.M. *The Hermits and Anchorites of England* 1914 pp 232-3. I would like to thank Dr Roberta Gilchrist for this information. Paul Rutledge drew my attention to the mention of timber for Martham Church in the Yarmouth Borough Court Rolls, NRO Y/C4/32 and Y/C4/33.

98. Agreement between Lawrence de Huntingfield and the Prior 1337, see Dodwell, B. *Charters of Norwich Cathedral Priory vol. 2.*

Moregrove Farmyard

The Old Hall (demolished 1970) stood to the left of this picture

Moregrove manor held extensive marshes in the North Fen on both sides of the river Thurne, including Cowesgress, Sheepesgress and Seggehilles on the Martham bank and Styrkesgrass, now Starchgrass Nature Reserve, on the Horsey side. In the early fourteenth century Robert de Martham acquired marshes in Horsey, including pasture for one bullock and fifteen heifers in ffrythfen in Horsey. Unlike the Prior it seems that he had a serious interest in the economic value of his marshes.[99]

The estate in Martham changed hands fairly rapidly in the middle of the fourteenth century, and by 1351 was held by Bartholomew de Burlee, the husband of a Gunton grand-daughter. His son granted it to a College of priests in Cobham, Kent. This may have been a pious gift from de Burlee, but it seems that the priests at Cobham found the administration of a small estate a hundred and fifty miles away rather irksome. In 1380 an exchange was arranged by which the Prior of Norwich acquired the Cobham manor in Martham and gave to the College the church of Chalke in Kent which was in the possession of the Cathedral Priory. So

99. NRO. Copies of fourteenth century leases of marshes are found in *Buttles of Moregrove manor 1514,* Dunston 168 A .

Moregrove, or Cobham manor, came to the Priory. Particularly valuable was Cobham's Weir, a fishery on the river Thurne, near the present Martham Development Company's boatyard (TG 439191). In 1404 the fishery was let for an annual rent of £5 6s.8d. An area of marsh nearby is still known as Cobham's Furrow, which may refer to a medieval drainage ditch.

Although in the possession of the Priory, the Cobham lands seem to have maintained their identity, although somewhat reduced in size. In the early sixteenth century the Cobham estate was granted to William Knightly, as the manor of Moregrove and Knightlys. The demesne of sixty acres lay in Moregrove Field and thirty tenants held land in the village fields. The manor house lay to the north of the church in the middle of Moregrove Field overlooking the vast tract of marsh and reed-bed that stretches from Martham to Horsey and Hickling. The medieval manor house was replaced in the seventeenth or early eighteenth century. That house in its turn was demolished about 1970, but the pond and farm buildings still remain, and from the farmyard a network of footpaths and tracks leads to the church in one direction and to the marshes and river in the other. (See page 126)

The Clere Lands in Flegg in the Fourteenth Century

The only surviving manorial surveys contemporary with the 1292 Survey of Martham are those for the Clere Estates. The Clere family held the smaller manor in Burgh and leased the manor of Ormesby Kingshall from the absentee landlord, Roger de Ormesby. In the early fourteenth century several surveys and rentals were taken of the Burgh and Ormesby lands in the hands of the Clere family. (Later in the fourteenth century the Clere family became tenants in chief of Ormesby manor.)[100]

In two important respects the Clere estates and the Priory manor at Martham were similar, they both used the long rod of 18½ feet for the measurement of land, which may have been the traditional length of the measuring pole in Flegg. Another similarity is the size of the socage tenements. On both Martham manor and the Clere estate, socage tenements of about ten acres are found

100. PRO *Rentals and Surveys of Clere Lands in Burgh and elsewhere. T. Ed 1.* Sc 11/468 is the main source. Further information, much of it a repeat of the last document, is in *Rollesby Rental of Customary Receipts of Lord Roger de Ormesby 7 Ed III* (1333-34) Sc. 12/22/3.

are found with very similar services, even to the bread and herring provided after a full day's ploughing. (Table 10.1) A tenement of about ten acres measured by the long rod was perhaps established in Flegg by the twelfth century, or even earlier.[101] (See page 84)

However, in other important ways the Clere estates differed from the Martham manor. At Martham both the demesne and the tenants' lands were concentrated in the village itself, with only a few acres in the neighbouring fields of Repps, Rollesby and Somerton, and a couple of cottages in Winterton. Virtually all the labour force at Martham lived within easy distance of the manor demesne. In contrast the Clere lands were scattered in many Flegg villages. The manor of Ormesby Kingshall included tenants in Somerton, Winterton and Caister. Burgh manor had lands and tenants in Clippesby, Billockby, Rollesby and Repps. It is not possible to tell whether this had come about by inheritance, purchase, or through some old pattern of land-holding, or by piecemeal accumulation of land and tenants. The organisation of the tenant services must have presented problems on a manor where many tenants lived several miles away from the demesne, and most services were probably commuted for a money charge.

Nor did the demesnes of Burgh and Ormesby manors lie in a compact area, as at Martham. The ninety acres of arable demesne of the manor Ormesby Kingshall were scattered in twenty-one pieces, none larger than five acres, in Ormesby's open fields, and Burgh's fifty-four-acre demesne lay in forty-one pieces. A similarly dispersed demesne is found on the St Benet's manor of Ashby and Thurne. (See page 59)[102]

Unlike Martham, the Clere manors contained large areas of demesne meadow, pasture, turbary and marsh, the size and value of which were carefully recorded. At Burgh the demesne included sixteen acres of mowing meadow, nearly ten acres of pasture, fifteen acres of fishing or turbary, two acres of rush grounds, and nearly fourteen acres of whins (gorse), a total area as large as the

101. A rental of Hemsby manor dated 1422 states the rod there was sixteen and a half feet, the standard length. I do not know whether the long rod of 18½ ft was ever used at Hemsby.

102. Martham may have been the only manor in Flegg with a compact demesne. The Prior's demesne in Hemsby was also scattered in the open fields, although in the late thirteenth century the Prior appears to have tried to consolidate the demesne through a number of exchanges and acquisitions of land from his tenants. See Dodwell, B. *Charters of Norwich Cathedral Priory, vol 2.*

arable demesne. It was valued at £3 9s. 10d. a year. Fleggburgh is the only village that has preserved its common. At Ormesby Kingshall the demesne contained fifteen acres of meadow, pasture and turbary, as well as a fifty-acre marsh at Caymflete worth 16s. a year.

Chapter 5 has shown how valuable the marshes and meadows could be for the lord of a manor, in that case at Mautby. The manor of Moregrove in Martham also had a special interest in marsh pastures in the fourteenth century. (See page 126) The extent and variety of wetland belonging to these manors contrasts with the rather meagre allowance of twenty-four acres of meadow, pasture and turbary recorded on the Prior's larger manor at Martham. In the fourteenth century there is some evidence that pasture was in short supply. Scratby, on the coast and with little wetland in its bounds, always had to hire pasture on the Priory marsh of Fulholm for its animals at a cost of about 5s. a year. In a number of years between 1295 and 1327 the Priory manors of Hemsby and Martham also had to pasture their cows and horses at Fulholm, and pay for the privilege. In years of drought, landlords with plenty of marsh could increase their income by leasing their pasture to other manors. The surprisingly high economic value of marsh products is borne out by the Cathedral Priory's policy of hiring marshes along the river Yare each year to provide rushes for the monastery, at a cost of between twenty and thirty pounds a year. [103]

The Clere surveys list about twenty free tenants that include two members of the Fastolf family, the Prior of Butley and Peter Buxkin, a member of a gentry family. He enfranchised a bond holding of six and a half acres in Clippesby. As a result his rent was raised from 5s. to 7s. In future he would hold his land by charter. The extra rent may have seemed little to pay to be free from the manorial services attached to the property, and also from regular attendance at the manor court. This is the only example of the enfranchisement of a bond holding that I have found.

Customary tenants on the Clere estates, included tenants in Caister, Ormesby, Burgh, Rollesby, Repps, Bastwick and Winterton. A group of tenants in Caister, Rollesby and Burgh are

103. The Magister Camera Rolls of the Priory show that the monastery spent up to £20 or more a year on the hire of marshes and the cost of cutting and transporting rushes to the Priory each year in the late 13th century. NRO Magister Camera Rolls DCN 1/1/2-10 12 72-1299.

described as sokemen (*'franklendus'* in Norman-French) in Burgh. The model for a socage tenement at Burgh is a ten-acre holding with a low rent and light services, except for the harvest duty. (Table 10.1 page 131) You will notice that a socage tenement included allotments of meadow, turbary, rushes and whynns (gorse), each of which made a different contribution to the livelihood of the tenant and his family. This diversity of land may well have enabled tenants to deal with the environmental and economic problems of the late thirteenth and early fourteenth centuries more successfully than at Martham, where, if the tenants wanted meadow or marsh land, they had to rent it for cash. On other Flegg manors it was quite usual for tenant holdings to include allotments of different types of land, for example on the St Benet's manor of Ashby and Thurne.[104] A tenement which included a variety of land may have been the original pattern for a peasant holding in Flegg.

Mud block cottage on the edge of Fleggburgh Common 1973

104. Court Roll of Manor of Ashby and Thurne August 10 1381, the first Court after the burning of the rolls gives list of peasants' claims. Many holdings contain allotments of pasture, turbary etc. NRO Diocesan EST 8/1.

Table 10.1 Services on Socage holdings at Martham and Burgh

Price in brackets is the price the tenant had to pay if his services were not needed, or were commuted.

Martham 10 acre socage tenement c. 1200	Burgh Sokemen 10 acre tenement
	With lac meadow, 2½ a. turbary, 14a. rushes & 2½ a. whins (gorse)
Rent 4s., Aid 11d., a hen at Christmas	Rent 1s. 6d. Aid at Lord's will. A mallard at Christmas
Ploughing with his own plough & all his plough beasts, has 3 loaves & 9 herring for each ploughing	Ploughing from sunrise to 3 p.m., with 2 horses or two bullocks, has 3 loaves & 9 herring for each ploughing
Harrowing. Half a day with a horse (1d.)	Weeding. Half a day (1½d.), if a whole day he has food
Harvest 3 days with a meal (1½d.)	Harvest. Finds a man for all harvest or pays (2s. 2d.). Meal provided
Carting at harvest, 1 day if he has a cart.	Carting at harvest 2 loads of corn
Threshing half a day	Threshing sunrise to 3 p.m. (½d.)
Carrying to Norwich 1 day (1½d.)	Carrying 6 leagues (2d.)
Making malt, a specified amount (1½d.)	Mowing rushes or hay 1 day (1d.)
	Carting a load of rushes (1d.)
	Digging peat for half a day

Of course there are differences between the obligations of a socage tenant at Burgh and at Martham. The rent of only 1s. 6d. at Burgh was low, compared with 4s. at Martham. I suspect the hand of a powerful monastic landlord at Martham. On the other hand the Martham three-day harvest duty seems very light compared with the obligation of the Clere tenants to provide a man with a cart for all harvest or pay 2s. 2d. At Martham the main burden of the harvest services was borne by the tenants of the twelve acre villein tenements. It seems that on the Clere lands the socage tenements had to provide much of the labour, or its cost, at harvest time.

Feudal obligations on other Clere manors were not always exactly the same as at Burgh. Rent and duties were higher at Rollesby, where a sokeman paid a rent of 3s.1d. for his nine-acre holding and also had additional harrowing, digging and ditching services to perform. He was taxable on the marriage of his son or daughter at the lord's will. This was a typical villein service, but he does not seem to have been regarded as a villein tenant. In these surveys I can find no definite indication of villeins on the Clere estates.

As at Martham the effect of the growth of population was felt at Burgh and Rollesby. The socage holdings on these manors were in multiple occupation by the early fourteenth century and were divided between four or five tenants, some with similar surnames. No information is given about the location of the tenements in the open fields, nor of how the land and services were shared among the tenants, but in communities much smaller than Martham, collective memory would probably serve to locate the land of each tenement and to allot the services among its tenants. In many ways the organisation of the manors of Ormesby and Burgh seem to have preserved an older and less precise system of land use than that at Martham. The socage tenements and the absence of reference to villeinage are reminiscent of the freer society seen in the Domesday Book. No dominant landlord seems to have reorganised the Clere estates as the Prior had done on his manor at Martham. (See p. 89)

Size and Value of Flegg Manors and the Nature of Lordship

The final section of this chapter looks, wherever suitable evidence is available, at the relative size of demesnes, the value of arable land and the nature of lordship in Flegg.

Table 10.2 Size of Manorial Demesnes in Flegg

(These figures are taken from different sources and may not be exactly comparable.)

Manor	Lord	Size of demesne	Source
Hemsby	Priory	Over 200 acres	Manorial records
Ashby & Thurne	St Benet's	196	1341 Account
Martham	Priory	169 + 35	1292 Survey
Ormesby	King's	101	1304 IPM
Runham	de Evermure	94	1272 IPM
Scratby	de Acquilon	60	1216 IPM
Burgh	Clere	54	Ed. I Survey
Ormesby	Priory	50	14th C. Accounts
Scratby	Priory	40	13th & 14th C. Acc.
Rollesby	Boys	40	Blomefield vol. XI

The monastic manors of the Priory and St Benet's Abbey had the largest manorial demesnes in Flegg. They were very efficient estates whose success depended largely on the agricultural expertise of their stewards, an adequate labour force and a policy of maximising agricultural production. Most manors were quite small and had demesnes of less than a hundred acres, indeed many of less than fifty. The size of lay manors tended to decrease. They often split into separate estates, especially when there was no male heir and daughters inherited the manor, as at Runham. Land was sometimes sold to finance an expedition on a Crusade, or to maintain the ever-rising standard of living expected of a landlord. In most villages there were at least two manors and tenants often had holdings in more than one manor.

Table 10.3 Value of arable land in Flegg in 13th and 14th centuries

Date	Manor	Demesne size	Value per acre	Source
1272	Runham	80 acres 14	2s. 1s.6d.	IPM
1286	Scratby	60	2s.6d.	IPM
1290	Caister	90	1s.6d.	IPM
1292	Martham	196 (b)	2s. 6d.	1292 Survey
1295	Hemsby	291 (b)	3s.	Proficuum
1295 & 1341	Martham	180 (b)	3s.	Maneriorum
1323	6 vills	30 (c)	1s. 4d.	IPM
1325	Filby	80	2s.	IPM
1340	Runham	30 (a)	8d.	IPM
1343	Ormesby	102	1s.	IPM

Notes: (a) - a third of Runham demesne. (b) - the Prior's estimates of land in his own manors may be higher than an IPM. (c) - land in Mautby, Herringby, Filby, Stokesby, Runham and Martham.

The value of land in Flegg was uniformly high as you can see from Table 10.3. In 1295 the value per acre at Martham and Hemsby, 3s. an acre, was remarkable and probably the highest in Norfolk. The Priory estimate of the profit per acre of arable land on its other Norfolk manors ranged from 8d. at Sedgeford to 18d. at Thornham. In Flegg even small manors in lay hands gave returns higher than the usual value in Norfolk of 8d. or 12d. an acre. Only in the second quarter of the fourteenth century is there any indication that the value of land was falling. The IPM for Ormesby for 1343 includes a statement that the land could be cropped each year. Such intensive agriculture, if practised every year may account for the fall in value, while at Runham the divided lordship may be a contributory cause.[105] In general, however, even a small manor in Flegg gave both its owner and his tenants a good return in crops or cash before the middle of the fourteenth century.

The dominant landlords in Flegg were the Abbot of St Benet's and the Prior of Norwich Cathedral Priory. I can only think of two examples of their authority outside their own estates, the Abbot and the Prior shared the right to ships wrecked on the Flegg coast, and on several occasions the Abbot tried to control the right of passage on the Flegg rivers. At times lay landlords infringed established common rights, as in the late thirteenth century when Walter de Burgo and William de Stalham converted the common fishing along the Muckfleet to private fisheries. However the multiplicity of manors and landlords tended to minimise the power of the individual lords. The flexible pattern of tenant agriculture in Flegg meant that the landlord played little part in directing the rotation of crops or controlling the use of pasture through the manor court. Manorial services were attached to the holding and not to the tenant, and as land changed hands frequently and easily, this must have tended to loosen the personal ties between tenant and lord. Lordship was never as powerful in East Norfolk as it was in the traditional three-field village.

It is often difficult to be certain of the legal status of particular tenants. It is clear that on most manors there were both men of villein status, '*nativi*', or 'bondmen of blood', as the lawyers called them, and also a few freemen who held their land by charter and could use the King's Courts. However an indeterminate group of tenants held bondland and performed manorial services, but were not described as '*nativi*', nor yet as 'freemen'. In the charters of the Cathedral Priory they are described simply as 'men with their services'. In the inquisitions and surveys all holders of bondland

105. Unfortunately I can find no evidence for the value that the Abbot of St Benet's put upon his manorial lands .

are increasingly called customary tenants owing customary services.[106] On many manors villein tenants held some of the larger tenements and fulfilled manorial positions such as reeve or capital pledge. Their life-style can have been little different from that of other holders of bondland. In the rather meagre manorial records of the thirteenth and early fourteenth century I can find no example of any dispute in Flegg between villein and landlord about the status of the individual tenant and his duties in the thirteenth and early fourteenth century.

Braunton Great Field, Devon, July 1985

Still divided as an open field, an unploughed furrow marks the division between strips. See page 115.

106. Ray Lock The Court Rolls of Walsham le Willows 1303-50. Suffolk Record Society vol. xli.

11: The Fourteenth Century: The Great Famine and the Black Death.

The Great Famine and its Results

The late thirteenth and early fourteenth centuries were times of high prices and unsettled weather. In particular two wet seasons in 1315 and 1316 resulted in very poor harvests and soaring prices. The bailiff's accounts for Martham and Hemsby manors have not survived for those years, but those of the small Priory manor at Scratby have, and they show a dramatic rise in the price of corn. In the year Michaelmas 1314 to Michaelmas 1315, wheat, which usually sold for about 6s. a quarter, rose in price from 7s. 2d. to14s. It was the same with other corn. Barley, the peasant's staple food, which in most years could be bought for 3s.-4s. a quarter, was sold at the beginning of that year for 5s.4d. and rose to 6s. 8d. a quarter. After another disastrous harvest in 1315, the prices must have seemed horrendous. In 1316 wheat reached 24s. a quarter and barley 16s., more than four times the usual price. Wheat chaff, which was added to other flour to bulk out the bread and usually cost 2s. 6d. or 3s. a quarter, sold for 12s. a quarter that year. No wonder the years 1315 and 1316 are sometimes called the years of the Great Famine.[107] Prices remained high in the following years. Then, after a good harvest in 1319, the price of barley dropped right down to 3s. at both Martham and Hemsby. (See Appendix 9.1, page 122)

The poor harvests and high prices did not affect manorial finances as they did peasant households. The harvest may have been poor and less corn may have been sold, but the high prices meant that as much, or even more, money came to the manor as in normal years. Indeed it seems to have been policy on the Priory

107. Ian Kershaw, 'The Agrarian Crisis in England 1315-17' in *Peasants, Knights and Heretics,* ed. R.Hilton. Extremes of weather are recorded in the accounts; in 1322 rain spoilt the malt in Hemsby, in 1325 a great drought made it difficult to find pasture for the manorial cattle at Martham. Drought was recorded in 1335 when no rent came in from the manorial fishery. For information about the Great Famine see Scratby Account Rolls. NRO DCN 60/30/4-7.

estates to sell as much grain as possible in years of high prices and so increase cash income. As prices increased steadily with each sale, it would seem that the manor was playing the market and holding corn back until the price rose.[108]

In 1319 murrain, probably rinderpest, struck the cattle at Martham. Half the oxen on the manorial farm died and a third of the cows. All the calves and young stock succumbed to the disease, except one bullock. The seriousness of the murrain is emphasised by the sale in that year of hides, carcasses and tallow from the dead animals, which brought in £2 5s. 8d. Sickly animals were sold, including two bullocks for 9s. and twelve cows for 21s. 10d., far below their normal prices. It took about five years to replenish the herd with animals born and bred on the manor. Disease struck again in 1323-4 and 1325-6, not so virulently this time, but the numbers of cattle did not return to normal until 1333-4. One of the probable results of the murrain was the decision in 1327 to let the dairy on a franchise. The dairyman (or maid) leased the milking herd for £4 5s. a year and sold its products for his or her advantage, while the manor continued to provide the livestock. Strangely the bailiff's accounts for the neighbouring manor at Hemsby show no sign of disease among the cattle over these years.[109]

In the absence of any Court Rolls for the first half of the fourteenth century it is difficult to say how the Great Famine affected the tenants on the Flegg manors. The intensive nature of peasant agriculture required a high input of family labour. When the harvest failed the peasant farmer still had the same number of mouths to feed. Any produce he could spare had to be sold to pay his rent, and he could not afford to buy extra food at the enhanced prices of the famine years. He might sell a small portion of his land to raise money, but that could not be done too often. At Martham the cattle murrain must have been another bitter blow for the farmer, depriving him of his plough beast, dung for the land, and milk and cheese for his family.

108. Martham Account Rolls NRO. DCN 60/23/11-24; Hemsby Account Rolls NRO. DCN 60/15/1-16 for food prices. For Scratby NRO. DCN 60/30/4,5,6,7 for high prices.

109. Martham Account Rolls NRO. DCN 60/23/16,17,18. for the murrain.

Increased alms were given in the years of high prices, often at the order of the Prior. Medieval charity was haphazard, but the frequency with which food or money was distributed in the years of high prices is an indication of the sufferings of the tenants. (Table 9.1) Barbara Hanawalt has shown in her study of crime in East Anglia in the fourteenth century that the level of crime escalated in 1315, 1316 and in other years of high prices.[110] It has been suggested that the crisis of the Great Famine years under-mined the stability of peasant agriculture and that malnourishment on a large scale diminished resistance to the Black Death.[111] The poor ploughman portrayed by Langland must have been a familiar sight in the first half of the fourteenth century.

'As I went by the way, weeping for sorrow, I saw a poor man hanging on to the plough. His hood was full of holes and his hair stuck out of it. As he trod the soil his toes peered out of his worn shoes with their thick soles and he was all bedaubed with mud as he followed the plough. He drove four heifers that had become so feeble that you might count their every rib. His wife walked beside him with a long goad. She went barefoot on the ice so that the blood flowed. At the end of the furrow lay a little crumb-bowl, and therin a little child covered with rags, and two two-year-olds on the other side. They all cried the same cry, a miserable note. The poor man sighed sorely, and said "Children be still".'[112]

Black Death in Flegg

The Black Death arrived in Norfolk in the spring of 1349 and spread up the river valleys from Yarmouth. It was particularly severe in South Norfolk, along the Yare and the Bure valleys and on the coast. In the 1350s taxes were reduced for communities which had suffered most from the plague. Caister, Hemsby, East Somerton and Winterton, all villages on or near the coast, benefited from this relief. Unfortunately there are no manorial records

110. Hanawalt, Barbara, *Crime in East Anglia 1307-1316* . NRS vol. xliv.

111. Campbell, B.C.M., *Reinterpreting Medieval Agrarian History: the contribution of recent research on East Anglia.* Lecture given at the University of East Anglia in February 1993, which dealt with the effect of the Great Famine on peasant agriculture.

112. 'Pierce the Plowman's Crede' Modern version by H.S.Bennet *Life on the English Manor,* Cambridge University Press, 1971 edition, p.185.

for these villages in the mid-fourteenth century. However there are other indications that Flegg was severely affected by the plague. The Inquisition Post Mortem taken after the death of Thomas de Essex in 1351 for his manor of Runham states that all the tenants were dead. (See page 66) Blomefield's lists of rectors and vicars show how frequently new incumbents were appointed in the year 1349. Scratby had four vicars, Ashby, Burgh St Margaret, Martham and Ormesby St Margaret three, and Burgh St Mary, Rollesby, Herringby, Mautby and Runham had one change of incumbent in that year. Not all these appointments were necessarily the result of death from the plague, but the frequency with which they had to be made suggests that many of the clergy, like their parishioners, succumbed to the disease.[113]

Manor of Rollesby Boyes 1328–1350

A more detailed picture of the impact of the Black Death on a community can be found in the Court Rolls of the small manor of Rollesby held by Robert de Rollesby. In the twenty years before the plague one or two deaths are recorded in most years, but in 1349 and 1350 at least thirty-eight bond tenants died. In September 1349 twelve or more free tenants paid relief, the fine paid on the death of a free tenant, which suggests further mortality from the disease. (The figures are not precise because, not only has the writing faded, but also the pages of the court rolls are in a confused order and some information is definitely lost) Perhaps as many as forty or fifty tenants of this small Rollesby manor died in 1349. Of course this is not the full number of deaths in the village because the court only records the deaths of land-holders and from only one manor. It is possible to guess at the population of Rollesby. In 1332 fifty-three people were assessed for taxation, which may suggest a population of about four or five hundred of whom perhaps half had died of the Black Death.[114]

Sometimes whole families died. John and Lettice Gering and their son Thomas all died, leaving no heirs. Three members of another branch of the Gering family died and four other families

113. PRO Subsidy Roll 25 Ed lll E179/149/34 Tax Relief after the Black Death.

114. NRO Rollesby Court rolls 1328-70 Lucas and Wyllys 5/8/71 188D. PRO Subsidy Roll E179/149/9 for 1334 tax payers.

lost two or more members. Sometimes it was difficult to trace the heirs; in five cases there were either no heirs or they were unknown, and in three other cases the known heirs did not come forward to claim the land. In the confused conditions of the epidemic they may have been pleased to leave the manor and all its obligations and restrictions.

It is remarkable that the manorial organisation functioned at all during those years. By 1352 authority was being re-imposed. In July 1352 all bond tenants were ordered to come to the next court and show in writing, '*in scriptis*', the amount of land they held, where it lay and next to whom. It is clear that fourteenth century peasants were expected to have something in writing to identify their land. They may not have been able to read their documents, but at least they were expected to keep them safe. However, I found no evidence that any one had ever complied with this order and brought his parchment to court.

In 1354 twelve bondmen left the manor, the first time such emigration had been recorded. No steps seem to have been taken to recover them or to collect their chevage. Presentments of tenants who did not perform their customary services increased in number after the Black Death, although there had always been a few of these reluctant workers in Rollesby. The severe shortage of agricultural labour may lie behind the permission given to Isabell Skinner in 1358 to receive a certain Gerard fflemyng with his wife and family to live in her 'insett house' for a year from August 1st (the traditional date for the beginning of harvest) [115]

Manor of Martham 1349-1363

The Cathedral Priory's manor of Martham was a much larger and better organised estate than the Rollesby manor. It is eerie to read the manorial accounts for the year Michaelmas 1349 to Michaelmas 1350 knowing that the scribe was writing in the middle of the greatest catastrophe of the Middle Ages. There is none of the confusion found in the Rollesby court rolls. The Martham document is beautifully written and arranged under the usual headings and gives no sense of stress or turmoil. I wonder whether

115. Insett house was probably a small house between two buildings, that we should call an annexe.

either the bailiff or the Priory steward understood how long it would take to bring Martham manor back to its pre-1349 productivity? The 1349 harvest brought in less than half the usual amount of corn. With the high death toll many tenant holdings reverted to the lord, but the land could not be let that year and was left unploughed. No rushes or peat were sold and tenants could not be found for many of the marsh pastures. No money for the shepherd or the sheep-fold was recorded. Eleven tenants were excused the payment of rents and fines.

Yet the bailiff tried to run the manor as usual. Very unusually, no corn had been sent to the Priory that year, but about half the crop had been sold, bringing in £14 8s. Money was needed to pay for extra labour on the demesne farm. A useful contribution was made from the very high profit of £26 16s. 4d. from the manor court, partly the result, no doubt, of the heriots (death duties) of tenants who had died in the Black Death.[116]

The main problem for the manorial authorities was the shortage of labour. In 1350 less than half the usual hoeing and harvesting services were performed and extra labour had to be found. In the winter of 1349-50 four men were employed to thrash the corn for a hundred and one days at 2½d. a day with board and lodging. A carpenter was employed for five days at 5d. a day to make beds in the stable for the workers. Twelve extra men were employed on a more or less regular basis during the spring of 1350. One man earned £1 and three others over 10s., quite considerable sums in the fourteenth century. A man and his wife were hired to make meals for the workers from February to May, the time for the ploughing and preparation of the land for spring corn. The enlarged household had to be fed. The manor farm provided wheat, malt, beef and pork, and in addition 8s. 10d. was spent on extra meat, £1 19s. 11d. on herrings and fish and 3s. 5d. on cheese and butter. It was very unusual for workers to be fed at the manor in this way, except at harvest time.

It was Priory policy to bring the land back into cultivation and productivity as quickly as possible and at almost any expense. With extra labour, forty acres was sown with wheat as usual in the winter of 1349, and eighty acres of barley in the spring of 1350, about

116. NRO Martham Account Rolls 1349-50 DCN 60/23/25. For 1355 onwards NRS 5891 in 20 D1.

three quarters the normal acreage. However, livestock seems to have suffered from the disruption. The number of cows (twenty) and plough-horses (seven) were maintained, but the oxen had been reduced from eight to two with only two heifers left, and the four pigs had no young. More meat than usual had been eaten by the household and more stock sold to raise money for the wages bill. It is also possible that the shortage of labour had meant less care and attention for the animals.

The 1350 harvest was long, lasting seven weeks and three days. Only 368 out of a possible 617 harvest services were worked. Many tenants were dead, but others, perhaps, took advantage of the unusual situation to ignore the bailiff's summons. Twenty-eight men had to be employed for the whole of the harvest and were each paid 4s. Earlier in the century the harvest wage would have been 2s. 6d. Finally on Michaelmas day, the 29th September 1350, the corn was in after the longest harvest recorded at Martham in the fourteenth century. Unfortunately the account for the year 1350-51, which would have recorded the amount of corn received, has been lost. There are no more bailiff's accounts until 1355.

However, the manor court records help to fill the gap. They begin in December 1350 and continue, with a gap in 1352, until 1357. The death rate was high in Martham throughout the 1350s. In 1351 sixteen deaths were recorded, eight in 1355 and then the number fell to around five a year. Often there was no direct heir to inherit a father's land. In only fifteen out of the forty-seven deaths recorded between 1350 and 1357 did direct heirs inherit. In other cases the nearest heirs were brothers, sisters, uncles, nephews or nieces, or the land was taken into the lord's hand because heirs could not be found. Some men inherited land from more than one relative. Nicholas, son of William Christmas, inherited two acres from his father, three and a half acres from his uncle and two acres from his sister, along with two cottages and two messuages. He was described as '*pauper*', and was excused payment of heriot, but his inheritance must have changed his circumstances considerably.[117]

Although the business of the manor went on as usual during the 1350s, some evidence suggests a degree of social disorder. In 1353

117. Martham Court Rolls 1350-51 NRS 220B3, 1352 onwards DCN 60/22/3,4,5,6.

nine men and women broke into the manor farmyard and were each fined 3d. for doing damage there. Cases of assault were more frequent than usual; fifteen were recorded in 1351, fourteen in 1353, and then the number gradually declined to the usual six or seven a year. Other cases reflect the conditions of the times. Four tenants had their fines excused because of poverty, and occasionally there is the bald statement, 'could not be levied'. Some fines were surprisingly high. In December 1350 John Lawes, a freemen, was fined 20s. because his daughter married without licence. There was an attempt to maintain the population of the village by imposing higher fines on bondmen who married outside the manor. For example in 1351 two men paid the usual 1s. for permission to marry, but this was to be increased to 3s. 4d. if they did not marry 'within the soil of the manor'. As at Rollesby tenants were leaving the manor with or without the lord's permission, and little effort was made to restrain them or to charge chevage.

Shortage of manpower may lie behind many of the presentments in the manor court. Livestock was not under proper control. Nineteen stray sheep are noted in the bailiff's accounts for 1349-50, and at a manor court held in September 1351 sixteen men and one woman, owners of eighty-one cows were accused of allowing their animals to stray into the open fields. Tenants neglected their property and their communal responsibilities. About thirty tenants were presented for not maintaining their banks and ditches. Men also refused to do their manorial services. In 1353 all tenants were presented for not doing their harvest services, and in 1355 and the following year many harvest and ploughing services were not performed. In 1354 seven men were presented for not carrying wheat and malt to Norwich 'as custom required'. This was an attempt to revive an old manorial service which had been commuted for a money charge of 17s. 3d. for about a hundred years. No mention of this custom was made in any subsequent year and it seems that the service was not successfully re-imposed.[118]

The effort of the Priory to restore productivity at Martham was not immediately successful. The bailiff's account for 1355 runs only from 20 July 1355 to 29 September, and gives the impression

118. Details of the carrying services are given in the Survey of 1292 in B.M. Stowe 936. See Chapter 6. In every 14th century Account Roll until 1350 the carrying service had been commuted for 17s.3d.

of a poor run-down farm. The state of the open fields is most vividly illustrated by the entry '1 mower hired to mow the thistles before ploughing, 4d.' Only 240 harvest services were worked that year and in the manor court the jurors were fined for concealing the names of those who did not come to the bailiff's summons. Eighty-four extra workers were hired, including one Fleming. At harvest time the Priory had to subsidise the manor by paying the wages of twenty-four workers and supplementing the food for the harvest meals. In no other year for which accounts survive did Martham have to call on the Priory for help in this way. Again the harvest was very long, lasting six weeks and three days, but it brought in nearly as much corn as in pre-1349 years. Luckily the accounts for the next year (1355-56) have survived and show how the corn was used; forty-nine acres of wheat were sown, twenty-three of peas and ninety-six of barley, only a little less than in the pre-1349 years. Only a note at the end of the account that twenty-six fines from the manor court could not be levied strikes a less happy note.[119]

The next account to survive, for 1359-60, shows the estate again in trouble. Most of the corn was sold that year producing £49 8s. 8d., of which £37 6s. 8d. went in payment to the Priory. Did the Priory have a special need for cash that year? The sale of so much corn led to a shortage of seed corn and only thirty-one acres was sown. The harvest was spoilt by heavy rain (no help from the Priory with labour or food costs that year) and the livestock was depleted. Only three horses remained and there is no record of cows. No accounts survive to show how the estate managed in the next three years, but by 1363-4 the manor seems to have returned to its usual standards.[120]

Use of Fleming Labour in East Norfolk

It is surprising that Flemings left the Low Countries to work in England after the Black Death. Flemings were employed in many places in East Norfolk in the 1350s. In 1355 a Fleming was hired to cut and harvest five acres of wheat in Martham for which he was

119. Bailiff's Account for July 20 -Sept. 29 1355. NRO NRS 20 D1 5891. For 1355-1356 NRS 20 D1 5892.

120. Bailiff's Account 1359-60 NRO NRS 20 D1 5893.

paid 3s. 4d. This separate entry suggests that perhaps he worked away from the other harvesters. The next year a Fleming was employed for eleven days to thresh seven quarters of wheat at 3d. a quarter, which was considerably less than the usual rate of 5d. a quarter. I have found Flemings mentioned at Rollesby, Ashby and Scottow. St Benet's Abbey employed twelve Flemings for the harvest of 1356. Perhaps these men went round in a gang hiring themselves wherever they were needed. It is difficult to understand why they came across the North Sea to seek farm work. It has been suggested that the Black Death did not claim so many lives in the Low Countries where the standard of living was higher and resistance to the disease greater than in most of Europe. Perhaps there was a surplus of labour there and England offered more opportunity for work, even at low rates of pay. This argument does not seem very convincing unless there was an underclass of poor labourers who did not share in the general prosperity of the Netherlands.[121]

From the manor court records at Martham we can see how two Fleming families gradually settled into their new homes. In 1356 Henry Fleming was excused paying suit of court because he held no land, but in the same year he leased half an acre from the lord. The next year he acquired five small pieces of land making a holding of 5½ acres. Then he became a tenant of the manor and was placed in a tithing. However the Flemings do not seem to have settled easily into the community. In 1356 Alice, wife of John ffrendevene, a Fleming, stole beans from the house of Richard le Fishere, and in the next year Henry Flemyng set fire to two houses. Were the Flemings really such anti-social neighbours, or are these instances of xenophobia on the part of the jurors who presented the miscreants to the manor court? In the rising of 1381 Flemings were attacked in Yarmouth and Lynn for no apparent reason, unless perhaps they were regarded as scab labour who under-cut the wages of English labourers.[122]

Many Norfolk villages must have experienced the Black Death

121. *Employment of Flemings* N.R.O St Benet's Almoners Roll Diocesan EST 13, Scottow Account Rolls, Diocesan EST 11, Ashby and Thurne Account Rolls Diocesan EST 9.

122. For attacks on Flemings in Yarmouth and Kings Lynn in1381, see Powell 1896 & PRO KB9 166/1 Presentments of Hundred Juries, June to July 1381.

in much the same way as Rollesby and Martham. It is impossible to comprehend the suffering and misery of communities that lost up to half their population. Both peasant farms and manorial demesnes suffered neglect through lack of manpower and the countryside must have presented a dismal picture. Yet Martham, like most other Norfolk villages, weathered the disasters of the Black Death. By the 1360s and 70s economic activity had regained its momentum and communities their vitality. No place in Flegg appears in the 1423 list of communities with fewer than ten households. The Black Death does not appear to have created any deserted villages in Flegg.[123]

123. See Feudal Aids No.111 for vills with less than ten inhabitants in 1423.

Chapter 12: The Peasants' Revolt in Flegg

The period between the Black Death and the Peasants' Revolt of 1381 were years of tension between landlord and tenant. When Martham manor regained its normal productivity in the 1360s, the Prior and his steward expected a return to traditional management. The usual 180 acres of demesne land was sown with wheat, barley, peas and oats. The manor continued to send wheat and malt to the Priory while surplus corn and livestock were sold. The tenants, through their obligatory services, continued to plough the demesne and harvest the crops. Services, such as carting and dung-spreading, which had been commuted for money in the early fourteenth century, had to be worked again, although no further attempt was made to insist on the carrying service to Norwich.[124] (See page 143).

At this period, when the Priory was trying to re-establish manorial rule on its manors, the status of tenants is more often recorded, especially in the case of marriages. A bondman by blood had to pay a heavier marriage fine, or 'merchet', usually of a few shillings, while any tenant who was not known to be a villein was regarded as free, and would only have to pay pennies. From these and other records it is possible to estimate the number of bondmen and freemen in Martham. Fifty-seven bond and forty-one free surnames are found among the diverse thirteenth and fourteenth century documents. Among the familiar bond surnames are Knight, Elsy, Horn, Long, and Syk, and the free names include Chapman, Faber, Sutere (shoemaker) and Taillour, all craftsmen or traders. Some families appear to have had both free and bond members such as the Erl family.

After the Black Death at Martham

However long-term problems remained for the bailiff and the steward of the Priory. The price of corn, which was the main

124. Only three Account Rolls for Martham have survived for this period; 1363-4, 1377-8 and 1379-80. NRO, NRS 20 D1, Nos. 5894, 5895,5896. However eighteen court rolls have survived for the period between 1361/2 and 1380/81 in NRO DCN 60/22/8-32. And Court Rolls 1383-1399 in NRO NRS 20 D3 5924 – 5930.

source of cash income for the manor, continued at its pre-plague level, while wages, which had risen in the years of acute labour shortage immediately after the Black Death, remained high. A few examples will show the seriousness of the situation for the manorial authorities. Before the Black Death, 8s. 4d. paid the wages of all six regular farm labourers on the manor each year, but by 1378 the cost had more than trebled and had risen to £1 11s. The total cost of labour at harvest time rose from less than £2 in the years before the Black Death to about £5 or £6 for the harvests of the 1360s and 70s. The wage for a man who worked for the whole harvest (2s. 6d. in the 1330s) rose from 4s. in 1356 to 7s. in 1379. Craftsmen were also paid more, taking 5d. a day, or 7d. if they had a labourer with them; before the plague their daily wage would have been 2d. or 3d.

The lord's need for more money to pay his wages bill led to increased fines in the manor court, particularly for any offence where a tenant had concealed his action. Heavy fines were imposed on bondmen who broke their obligations. In 1362 William Smith was fined 6s. 8d. because he did not come when summoned by the bailiff to the harvest field. Tenants who married without a licence and those who sold bondland by charter as if it were free land faced heavy fines. Fines were imposed on tenants of bondland who sold their corn outside the manor. An unusual case was that of John Bill, a bondman, who paid 2s. 6d. for a licence to marry in 1379, but faced an increase to 40s. if he married a woman over thirty-three. Perhaps a woman over thirty was considered too old to bear children. In a time of labour shortage, an unfruitful marriage would deprive the lord of future workers. From year to year tenants were jointly ordered to make a rental which would record the size of their holdings and the rents they paid, on pain of a £20 fine. This large sum appears in the total fines for 1379, but it is clear from the yearly accounts that it was never collected. In fact arrears of rents and the non-payment of court fines were a regular feature of the 1360s and 70s.

Only in 1364 however is there evidence of serious friction between lord and tenants, when a group of tenants failed to do their harvest works. The usual price, that is the fine for not doing a harvest service, was 1½d., but that year tenants were charged 4d. for the duty they had failed to perform, because, as the bailiff explained, he had to employ others in their place. The charge for a harvest work remained at 4d. for the rest of the century, but there is no record of further concerted trouble over services.

Despite the efforts of the Priory to re-impose manorial obligations and restrictions, and in some cases to increase them, tenants found many advantages in the economic conditions of the 1360s and 70s. The government's efforts to control labour costs were not successful and wages never returned to the low pre-Black Death levels. As a result of the plague a considerable amount of bondland reverted to the landlords in cases where no heirs could be found, or where tenants had disappeared. Lords had spare land which they were willing to sell, or more frequently to let, to their tenants. At Martham it was possible to rent an acre of land on a five-year lease for four bushels of barley a year. The account rolls for 1377 and 78 record twenty-seven such leases, most for only one or two acres, but the land totalled 36 acres. Holdings were increasing in size, but it was a slow process for an ordinary tenant to accumulate land.

Tenants could and did leave the manor, some with permission and some without. Each year the court records the names of bondmen who had left Martham and lived in Yarmouth or elsewhere. They are described as 'anlepimen because they hold nothing of the lord and leave the village and do not pay chevage'. If they came back chevage was charged, but the authorities made very little effort to collect it. Tenants who lived away from the village, but owned property in Martham, usually liked to regularise their position. In 1367 Thomas Momme paid 5s. for a licence to remain in Yarmouth. In 1371 Thomas Erl paid 6s. 8d. to live in Potter Heigham for a year and in 1379 William Goode paid 3s. 4d. to be in South Walsham, where his family had been settled for twenty years. Other bond tenants lived in Ludham, Hemsby, Bastwick and Lynn, but most were in Yarmouth. The ease with which bond tenants were able to leave the village provided some escape from the tensions and frustrations of manorial rule.[125]

Tenants were developing new agricultural enterprises. Although arable farming always remained the main task for peasant families, livestock played an increasing part in their lives. Pigs,

125. At Hemsby, the 'anlipemen', that is 'bondmen holding no land from the lord and living in Yarmouth', were expected to come back to the village to work in the harvest and were then charged chevage. I think they would be paid a wage for their harvest work.

seldom if ever mentioned in the earlier court rolls, had become a real nuisance in the village by the 1350s. Hardly a manor court went by without some complaint about pigs trampling the corn or digging up the ground. The number of animals in each incident was always small which suggests that they were kept to provide meat for the family and not for sale commercially. In 1388, at the request of the villagers, the Prior approved an order that all pigs that wandered in the fields should be ringed between10th November one year and 7th September the next, that is for the whole year except the time of shack after harvest. Despite a fine of 4d. a pig, complaints about unringed pigs were made at most manor courts.[126]

Some animals were kept as commercial ventures. In 1366 William Ech overcharged the common with 500 geese and John Erl with 200. The large flocks must have been destined for the market, but it is doubtful whether these enterprises were successful. The market price of geese had fallen from 5d. a bird in 1363 to 4d. in 1380. The manor ceased to fatten geese and the tenants also stopped rearing geese in large numbers. There were no more complaints about flocks of geese on the common after 1366, although it is clear that tenants continued to keep a few geese for their own use.

Some tenants kept sheep. The manor revived the old custom of faldage whereby tenants' sheep had to 'lie in the lord's fold' from Michaelmas to December. The manor employed a shepherd to look after this 'cullet' or collected flock, which fed on the stubbles and manured the demesne arable. In 1367 Robert de Faldegate was fined 12d. for keeping twenty-eight sheep outside the lord's fold and Robert Folpe 6d. for his twelve sheep. In 1377 five men were fined for not sending their sheep to the lord's flock. I have found no mention of faldage after this date, although tenants continued to keep sheep. Some flocks were quite large. In 1372 Robert Elward was accused of overcharging the common with 200 sheep and was fined 2s.

Martham had a large area of common fishing, which attracted men from other villages. Men from Somerton and Winterton were fined for fishing in Martham waters. It was a great temptation to

126. Court held 18 February 1388 for regulation about ringing pigs. NRO. NRS 20D3 5927.

fish in the private fishery of the lord, and several men were fined for this offence. Over-fishing in the river and dykes was always a problem. In 1377 John Lokere fished with steel nets in the common waters and destroyed 'the little fishes to the damage of all the village'. (Steel nets or stakes were staked or stretched across the river or stream to catch all sizes of fish including small and immature fish.) He was fined 40s. That was a particularly heavy fine, but fines of 3s. 4d. and 10s. were not unusual for fishing offences. In the late fourteenth century the tenants of the manor found that the common and marshes could be exploited for animal husbandry, and the river and waterways for an important source of food.

Tenants no longer felt bound by the custom of partible inheritance; they exercised more choice in disposing of their land upon their death. For example in 1379 Robert Peye died leaving 2 acres to his sons, but he had already granted 2½ acres with a messuage to his wife, and made four other gifts totalling five acres. These grants included 3½ acres to Robert Wough and Robert Elsy who were to sell the land and put the money in 'alms for his soul and the souls of others'. I have found two other instances of men who left money or land for this purpose. Robert Erl, who died in 1369, is very specific about this. He granted ½ acre of land to his brothers to sell and then to spend 13s. 4d. on masses for his soul to be celebrated in the house of the Fathers of Mount Carmel in Yarmouth. This concern with the health of the testator's soul had always been a feature of gentry wills, but is not found before in the wills of tenants. By the late fourteenth century some men in Martham were sufficiently well-to-do to leave land or money for the welfare of their souls in a way that was customary among their social superiors. To be able to dispose of assets for religious purposes is surely a token of growing economic and cultural confidence.[127]

127. As at Hemsby there were many links between Martham and Yarmouth. Yarmouth men owned property in Martham, notably William Mustard, who may have given his name to Mustard Hyrne in Cess. Martham inhabitants dealt with traders from Yarmouth .The records of the manor court for July 1377 show that John Baker had bought a piece of woollen cloth costing 9s. from Warin Lucas of Yarmouth and had failed to pay for it. About a dozen Martham men lived in Yarmouth permanently.

St Benet's Manor of Ashby and Thurne

The St Benet's manor of Ashby and Thurne also had problems with labour services in the years before 1381. As at Martham the 'price' of a day's work in harvest was increased. In 1351 the fine for not doing a harvest service was 3¼d. By 1355 it had risen to 5d. and by 1364 to 6d., 'because the tenants were summoned and did not come and others were hired in their place'. This was a punitive increase for a medieval peasant. By 1369 the men must have returned to the harvest field, for the cost of a harvest service was reduced to 4d. because 'the men worked well that year', '*fec bene hoc anno*'.[128]

The regime on the St Benet's manor seems to have been more oppressive than that at Martham. In many ways the two manors were very similar; both had demesnes of about two hundred acres and on both manors most of the tenant's holdings were bondland owing villein services to the lord. The services were heavier at Ashby and Thurne both in number and in type than at Martham. The Abbey was only three miles up the river Bure, and the authority of the Abbot and his steward may well have seemed oppressive. At Ashby and Thurne 841 winter works were due from the tenants, while at Martham the tenants worked only 309 days. At Ashby and Thurne, with more labour at his disposal, the bailiff used the tenants' winter services for work such as weeding and ditching, jobs that at Martham would have been done by paid labour. Even so about a quarter of the winter works were not used on the Abbey manor and were sold back to the tenants, generally raising about £6. At Martham the sale of works produced only £3 in most years. The lack of opportunity for paid employment and the need to find cash for services not required by the bailiff, may well have been a continual source of resentment on the St Benet's manor.

At Martham it was relatively easy for a bondman to leave the manor. All through the 1370s and 80s tenants left the village to settle in Yarmouth or neighbouring villages. Seasonal absence on the fishing boats was an accepted custom. The destruction of the St Benet's court rolls during the Revolt means that there is no information about migration from Ashby or Thurne before 1381,

128. Ashby and Thurne, (St Benet's) Manor Bailiff's Account Rolls, N.R.O. DN EST 9/4 1351, 9/4 1351, 9/8 1364, 9/10 1369.

but between 1381 and 1388 only two men are recorded as leaving the manor, whereas a steady trickle of bondmen left Martham in the last quarter of the fourteenth century. It seems that the bond tenants at Ashby and Thurne did not, or could not, leave their homes to look for a new life in Yarmouth or elsewhere. The Flegg manor of Ashby and Thurne was the only manor to have serious disturbances during 1381.

The Course of the Peasants Revolt in Flegg

The immediate cause of the Peasants' Revolt of 1381 was the imposition of an unpopular poll tax, but that was not the only reason for widespread discontent. There was opposition to landlords who continued to impose manorial obligations and restrictions, and resentment against lawyers who enforced the action of feudal lords and the central government. On 13th June 1381, men from Kent and Essex, under the leadership of Wat Tyler entered London, and the next day won concessions from King Richard II. On June 15th, at a further meeting with the King at Smithfield, Wat Tyler was killed and, leaderless, the rebels dispersed and returned to their homes.

News of these events spread to East Anglia. By 14th June a group from Bury St Edmunds arrived in Thetford and the rebellion spread to south-west Norfolk. Meanwhile in the north-east of the county, John Litster of Felmingham sent his followers from village to village to urge men to gather on Mousehold Heath. On 17th June the rebels established their camp on Mousehold, entered Norwich and took control of the town. On June 18th Sir Roger Bacon, a member of the gentry who supported the rebels, with a group of men from Suffolk and south Norfolk took Yarmouth and destroyed its charter. In north-east Norfolk, Litster's men went to the manor houses of unpopular landlords and burnt the court rolls with their records of serfdom and manorial obligations. On 20th June a large group gathered at St Benet's Abbey and demanded the court rolls of the Abbey manors. These were surrendered by the monks and burnt by the rebels.

The rebellion had met with very little resistance until Bishop Despenser returned to Norfolk about 22nd June, rallied the gentry, and finally put the rebels to flight after a confrontation near North

Walsham. By July, order had been restored and the King's Justices were gathering details about the Rising, and in particular about its ringleaders. The presentments, which the Hundred juries made to the Justices shortly after the rebellion, are the main source of information about the events in the Norfolk towns and villages.[129]

The incitement to rebellion in Flegg came from two directions, from Yarmouth in the south and from Litster's men from the north. The day after taking Yarmouth, Sir Roger Bacon rode the ten miles north to Winterton, threatened John Curteys and extracted ten marks from him. We know little about John Curteys, except that he was a bailiff in some capacity, and the attack may have been a settling of old scores between him and Sir Roger. The next day Bacon and his men captured William Clere of Ormesby, a man who epitomised all the rebels hated. Not only was he one of the largest landowners in Flegg, but he was also a Sergeant-at-Law and a Justice of the Peace. He had twice been Sheriff of Norfolk, and had lent the King ninety marks (£60) for the war against France, money which ultimately must have come from his tenants. The rebels took William Clere to Caister Sands, a lonelier place in those days than it is today, where under threat of his life, he agreed to give Sir Roger Bacon his manor of Antingham, near North Walsham. Three members of the gentry were summoned, Sir John de Mautby, William Winter, vicar, and Robert Howard, who gave surety for the handing over of the manor. These men were in no way molested. William Clere returned a free man to Ormesby to find that his wife, Dionysia, had been imprisoned in the house by their bailiff, Richard Bray, and only released when she paid him twenty shillings. Three days later Roger Bacon, no doubt preferring money in his pocket to a property that might later be confiscated, sold the Antingham manor to its original owner, William de Witchingham.

Litster's men also came to Flegg to encourage rebellion. On June 18th three men from North Walsham and Buxton spoke at Billockby and Caister, villages which were probably chosen because of their association with unpopular landlords. Billockby was the

129. Indictments by the Hundred Juries, PRO KB/166/1 is the main original source for the Rising. For general reading: *The Rising in East Anglia* E.Powell, 1896, Norwich.*Studies towards a History of the Rising of 1381 in Norfolk*, ed. B.Cornford 1984. Norwich; *An Historical Atlas of Norfolk.* ed. P.Wade Martins 1993.

home of Reginald de Eccles who was killed at Norwich, one of the few men executed by the rebels. John Fastolf's house in Caister was sacked by Robert Stronghobbe, a former servant of Fastolf. The rebels took lead from the chapel roof and the gutters, as well as other goods worth forty shillings. The Fastolf family was influential in East Flegg and Yarmouth where Hugh Fastolf was one of the collectors of customs.

The jurors reported no other disturbances in Flegg until June 25th, although tenants from the St Benet's manors of Ashby and Thurne were known to have been present at the burning of the manorial rolls at the Abbey on June 20th. Then on June 25th and 26th, according to the presentment of the West Flegg jury, John Boys, a smith from Rollesby, and Thomas Taillor joined a demonstration against the King and the Bishop of Norwich at Rollesby. On June 26th three men from Martham were at a similar gathering at Potter Heigham. By this time the Bishop was confronting the rebel forces near North Walsham and the rebellion was virtually over. In Flegg there was not the same vigorous response to the rebellion as took place in other parts of north-east Norfolk

Blacksmith and assistant at work
From the Gorleston Psalter

A twentieth century Rollesby blacksmith
Photo: Norfolk Local Studies Library

where groups of rebels destroyed the court rolls on the manors of unpopular landlords.[130]

Manorial records provide further information about the men who played a part in the Rising. The record of the manor court held on 10th August 1381 at St Benet's manor of Thurne begins with the statement that 'all the rolls and custumals touching the lordship had been burnt by the lord's serfs and those holding bond land'.[131] (Notice that it was not only serfs, but also free tenants holding bond land who are accused of destroying the manorial documents.) After the collapse of the insurrection the land was taken back into the lord's hand, and, at the court in August, all the tenants of bond land did homage to the lord and received their land again on payment of a fine. The court roll gives the names of a hundred and three tenants who held bond land, and is in effect a rental of the manor. Among the tenants were John Boys senior and John Boys junior. The older John Boys held half an acre and a cottage at Oby and was probably the father of the John Boys

130. Presentments of hundred juries established under a commission headed by William de Ufford, Earl of Suffolk, June-July 1381. P.R.O. KB9 166/1. Court rolls were burnt on the manors belonging the Duke of Suffolk, the Sacrist of Bury Abbey, the Duke of Lancaster and other landlords.

131. Court held 10 August 1381, NRO Diocesan EST/8/1.

junior, whom the court rolls reported 'was killed because of treason caused by his rising against the peace of the lord King'. There is no indication how John Boys was killed, whether he was involved in the fighting at North Walsham or whether he was apprehended and summarily executed. His holding was very small, three quarters of an acre sown with peas, but as a craftsman he would not have been totally dependent on his land for his livelihood. His crop of peas was bought by Adam Waryn for eight pence. [132]

His companion, Thomas Taillour, whose surname suggests he may also have been a craftsman, was another tenant of Ashby manor who failed to claim his quarter acre of land at the court of August 10th. At the next court on October 18th his wife, Catrina, was granted her husband's land, so presumably her husband was either dead or had disappeared. Fourteen other men did not claim their land in August 1381. Eight came back at some time over the next year, but six, all men with very small holdings, never reappeared. Perhaps the confusion of the times gave them an opportunity to leave the constraints of the manor and start a new life elsewhere.[133]

Although only two men are known to have taken part in the rebellion, the tenants at Ashby and Thurne had reacted strongly to the events of 1381. The court held in August recorded that the whole homage, that is all the tenants of the court, were jointly fined 20s. because they did not come to make hay at the manor or at the monastery in the year of the rebellion, and a further 20s. because they refused to hoe the lord's corn. It seems that there was a general refusal to work on the Abbey lands in the summer of 1381 and at least two men continued this action into the autumn. Thomas Waryn was fined the large sum of 10s. at the court on October 18th because he had not come when summoned to work in the harvest field. His brother, Adam Waryn, was fined 3s. 4d.

132. The use of words *'interfectus est'* suggests that he was killed in battle or skirmish. Had he been captured and hanged after trial the words would be *'decollatus'* or *'suspensus est'*. See Herbert Eiden, 'Joint Action against Bad Lordship': The Peasants' Revolt in Essex and Norfolk' in *History, The Journal of the Historical Association Vol 83. No 269. January 1998.*

133. Ashby and Thurne (St Benet's) Manor Court Rolls for 1381. NRO. Diocesan EST 8/1. 1381-88.

for the same offence. Were they perhaps the leaders of the discontent? Two other members of the Waryn family, William and John, may also have been involved because they absented themselves from the manor for a year, and when they reappeared refused to take up their joint holding of 7½ acres. The Waryn family all had sizeable holdings of 10½, 9½ and 7½ acres, and held responsible offices in the organisation of the village. Christopher Dyer has pointed out that not all the rebels were impoverished peasants living off inadequate holdings. Many were artisans, such as John Boys, the smith from Rollesby, and Thomas Taillour, men who made essential economic contributions to their communities, as well as tenants with substantial holdings, such as the members of the Waryn family, who had held responsible offices in the manor court. They were often the local leaders.[134]

Martham,[135] although experiencing labour difficulties in the 1360s, saw none of the unrest that was so marked at Ashby and Thurne in the summer of 1381. The court held at Martham on August 1st in that year was quite uneventful. No mention of the rising was made then or in any later manorial record. Yet three men, Robert Bene, John Tubbes and John Durrant went to Potter Heigham on June 26th to join a demonstration against the Bishop. These tenants appear in the manor court records both before and after 1381, but seem to have been unexceptional members of the community. John Durrant was the messor (a position similar to reeve) in 1379 and 80. Only John Tubbes had any record of unruly behaviour for in 1381 he joined in an attack on a newly-erected fish weir at Somerton belonging to the Duke of Ufford. (The Duke was an unpopular landlord whose court rolls at Hickling and Oxnead were destroyed by Litster's followers.) Whatever the Martham men did in 1381, it did not apparently have a lasting affect on their lives in the years after the rising.[136]

134. Herbert Eiden in article quoted above in note 132, points out that many of the active supporters of the revolt had held office in the manor courts.

135. Ashby and Thurne, (St Benet's) Manor Bailiff's Account Rolls, N.R.O. DN EST 9/4 1351, EST 9/8 1364, EST 9/10 1369.

136. Martham Manor Court Rolls, 1377-81. NRO. DCN 60/22/29-32. Attack on the Duke of Ufford's fish weir. P.R.O. CP40/484.

The style of management on the St Benet's manors appears to differ from that on the Norwich Priory estates. The steward of Benet's Abbey insisted that the traditional manorial services and obligations were strictly enforced, and that built up resentment against the Abbey. The management of the Priory manors seems to have been more flexible, or perhaps lax, in the late 1380s. The Martham accounts for 1377-8 and 1379-80 (the only ones available for 1370s and 80s) show very small sums of money going to the Priory (£3 6s. and £1). Arrears of tenants' rents and dues mounted to £42 in 1380, and no serious effort seems to have been made to collect them. Only a few of the Priory manors seemed to have attracted the attention of the rebels, and when Litster's men seized Norwich they made no attempt to attack the Priory. Perhaps the strong Priory walls deterred them, or perhaps they had no serious quarrel with the monks. Yet it was the Prior, not the Abbot, who seems to have learnt the lessons of 1381, for in 1386 he made a new composition with his tenants at Martham. The old rents and services described in Chapter 7 were abandoned, and a much simpler pattern imposed. Rent was fixed at 12d. an acre with one harvest duty for every eight acres held. The new rent of 12d. an acre was a high price for the tenants to pay and brought the Monastery £47 10s. a year.

Peasants illustrated in stained glass in Ely Cathedral

A reminder that peasants were not all poor and starving. The officials of the Manor Court would not have worn rags to attend court.

13: The Fifteenth Century: Three Flegg Manors

In many ways the fifteenth century was a period of economic and social depression. The population of England, which had fallen by a least a third after the Black Death, did not begin to recover until near the end of the century. Spasmodic attacks of the plague and other diseases, some of them very localised, kept the population stagnant. These later outbreaks of plague did not spare Flegg. In 1471 Margaret Paston wrote that there was great mortality from the plague in Filby, Ormesby and Scratby, but that thankfully it had not reached Caister and Mautby. At the time people noticed that the fifteenth century outbreaks caused high mortality among children and young adults, the very group that would normally have become the parents of the next generation. The age of marriage appears to have risen in the fifteenth century also contributing to a lowered birth rate.

Foreign wars meant increased taxation, and localised disturbances associated with the Wars of the Roses brought temporary insecurity to many areas, including Norfolk. Despite a flourishing cloth industry, East Anglia suffered from the gradual shift of industry and commerce to the West Country. Yarmouth, which, according to taxation records, had been the fourth wealthiest town in the kingdom in the early fourteenth century, fell to the twentieth position in the fifteenth.[137]

Flegg continued to be a major corn producing country. In 1400 corn prices were at the pre-plague level of about 6s. per quarter for wheat, 3s. for barley and 4s. for malt, but they fell steadily during the fifteenth century. In 1461 John Paston reported that the price of barley was 1s. 4d. a quarter and malt 1s. 6d. or 1s. 8d. In July of that year he still had 160 quarters of old malt and 400 quarters of new malt unsold. He wondered whether to send the corn to London where the price was higher, but the cost of carriage would be 6d. a quarter. Gloomily he noted that the fields of barley looked good, which meant that the price would fall again after harvest.

137. For general background see Maurice Keen 1990. Information about the decline of Yarmouth from Paul Rutledge in a talk, 'Yarmouth in the 15th century' given to Yarmouth Archaeological Society, 1994.

Fifteen years later, in 1475, prices had not risen very much for Margaret Paston reported to her son Sir John Paston, that wheat was 4s. 8d. a quarter and malt only 1s. 8d. A military expedition to France was under consideration, and the letter finishes with a nagging worry that any mother will understand; 'For God's love, if your brothers go over seas, advise them as best you can for their safe keeping. For some of them are but young soldiers, and know full little what it means to be a soldier, and to endure as a soldier should do.' [138]

Yet all was not doom and gloom. The fall in grain prices and the rise in wages meant that much of the population could afford a higher standard of living. Consumption of meat increased and enterprising farmers turned to livestock farming. With vacant holdings on most manors, land was available for peasant farmers to enlarge their farms and make them more productive. After the Peasants' Revolt manorial obligations and restrictions were relaxed. It is against this picture of the fifteenth century that we must look at life in Flegg.

The Priory Manor at Martham

At the beginning of the fifteenth century the Priory manor at Martham gave every appearance of a prosperous estate. In 1380 the Priory had acquired the Cobham manor. (See page 126) The 'Composition' of 1386 meant that bond tenants now held their land by a fixed rent and a reduced number of harvest services. (See page 159) The new arrangements must have been easier for both the bailiff and the tenants, although 12d. an acre was a high rent for a peasant farmer to pay. The new rental produced £42 a year for the Priory, compared with £9 16s. 7½d under the old arrangements.[139]

The bailiff continued to run the estate as he and his predecessors had always done. Prices were fairly steady at the beginning of the century, and corn sales brought in about £20 each year. The manor reduced the number of livestock, perhaps

138. Ed Roger Virgoe, *Illustrated Letters of the Paston Family* Guild Publishing, 1989, page 240.

139. Martham Account Rolls for 15th century, NRO. 1400-1429, NRS/ 20 D2/ 5904-D/3/5920.

because of the cost of labour. The number of plough horses and the dairy herd were maintained, but the numbers of pigs, geese and swans declined, and the money from the sale of livestock decreased. However income from the marsh grazing improved in the early years of the century when the fishery at Cobham's Weir came to the manor with the Cobham lands, and was let for £5 6s. each year.

Yet the bailiff had his problems. All labour was expensive and wages continued to rise. A farm labourer in regular employment on the manor earned 11s. 7d. a year in 1400, by 1424 he was paid about £1. The harvest wage increased from 7s. in 1400 to 10s. or 12s by 1423. Casual labourers were paid 2½d. a day for breaking up the clods in the fields and 3d. a day for ditching. In the fourteenth century they would have earned 1d or a 1½d. for such tasks. The manor economised by reducing the number of regular farm workers from six to four and employed less casual labour. The productivity of the manor suffered.[140]

The cost of labour was not the bailiff's only problem. It was not always easy to find tenants for the land in the lord's hand. Bad weather and rising water levels meant that some pastures were flooded and could not be let, or only at a reduced rent. The rent for the fishery at Cobham's Weir, which in 1400 was £5 6s. per annum, fell to £4 13s. 4d. by 1418, and £3 6s. 8d. by 1436. It was often difficult to collect the rents and the fines imposed by the manor court. The fifteenth century accounts end with a catalogue of money which the bailiff and his predecessors owed to the lord, mounting to £100. Some of these debts were six or more years overdue, and were never likely to be collected.

In 1425 the Priory followed the example of many fifteenth century landlords and leased the demesne to a farmer. At Martham Thomas Drake, the bailiff, took a five year lease on 207 acres of demesne and another 154 acres of land in the lord's hand for an annual rent of 177 quarters of barley, that is approximately four bushels of barley per acre. (At 3s. a quarter for barley the Prior could expect to raise £26 6s. 6d. if he sold all the grain.) As lessee the farmer would have to foot the wages bill. He also rented the

140. Campbell. B.M.S (1983) 'Agricultural Progress in Medieval England' p.39 for the decrease in employment on the manor and subsequent fall in productivity.

fishery at Cobham's Weir and continued to act as bailiff, drawing his 26s. 8d annual salary. For its part the Priory received the tenants' rents, the fines from the manor court, and of course the barley that Thomas Drake and others paid for the land they rented.

For many years the Priory retained responsibility for certain aspects of manorial management; it provided the farmer with seven plough horses and twenty two cows, and was responsible for the up-keep of the manor house and farm buildings including the mill. In 1429 Thomas Drake's lease was renewed for another five years, with the Priory still responsible for the maintenance of the farm buildings. This could be quite a financial burden, for in 1429 the manor had to spend the large sum of £9 12s. 1½d. on re-building the mill. In giving short leases and remaining responsible for livestock and buildings, the Priory Steward must have hoped that a change in the economic climate would make it possible for the Priory to take the manor back in hand and run it profitably again. Had that occurred the Priory did not want to receive a dilapidated estate with derelict buildings and insufficient plough beasts. However the Priory never took back the management of the manor. Prices of agricultural produce remained low, wages still rose, and gradually the farmer became responsible for all aspects of the management of the estate, including the buildings and the livestock. He rented for cash the herbage and the pasture, the fishing and the mill, and received the fines paid by the tenants for harvest services which they no longer performed. The Priory's income from the manor consisted tenants' money rents for their bond and free land , the profits of the manor court and the barley and cash paid by the farmer for his lease. Fines from the manor court decreased and rents fell from £42 to £36 a year by 1471. The receipts from both these sources had fallen still further by the end of the century. The Prior, as lord of the manor, continued to control the manor court. In this way the Priory acted in many ways as a magistrate, controlling the social and economic activities of the community, as will be apparent in the next chapter.[141]

Readers may wonder how the farmer, Thomas Drake, could

141. Building the mill at Martham 1449 NRO Bailiff's Accounts NRS 20 D35920. This entry gives a good example of building methods and materials of the 15th century.

make a success of the demesne farm when the monastic landlord found it uneconomic. The Priory had a large establishment in Norwich to feed, extensive buildings to keep in repair, and a prestigious position in society to maintain. Thomas Drake, like the many other well-to-do tenants, would have a modest home, a family upon whom he could probably call for a contribution to the labour needed on the manor and a comparatively simple life style. Landlords seldom had difficulty getting farmers for their manors, although Margaret Paston found it impossible to let Mautby manor in 1460.

St Benet's Manor of Flegg in the 15th Century

The manor of Ashby and Thurne may never have fully recovered from the troubles of 1381. A new agreement was made between the tenants and the Abbot of St Benet's in 1402, but it did not make the clean break with the past that the 1386 'Composition' had done at Martham. (See page 159) No explicit record of the agreement appears in the court rolls or the accounts, but the rents must have been raised considerably because the income from that source increased from about £8 in the fourteenth century to £12 14s. 2½d. in the fifteenth. The number of manorial services were substantial reduced, but none were abolished. They still provided most of the labour on the manor.[142]

The manor did not prosper in the fifteenth century. The annual receipts from all sources of income fell from an average of £80 in the late fourteenth century to £50 in the fifteenth, and the main source of income, the sale of corn, fell by a half during this period. However expenses remained fairly constant at around £35 a year. The average sum of money sent each year to the Abbey fell from £25 to £8 2s.

Activities on the manor were reduced. Only two thirds of the demesne was cropped each year, leaving fifty acres uncultivated. The lord already had about the same amount of unclaimed bondland on his hands, and it was very difficult to find tenants for the surplus acres. Unlike Martham the cost of labour does not seem to have been a very serious problem at Ashby and Thurne.

142. Accounts for St Benet's manor of Ashby and Thurne NRO Diocesan EST 9/12 -21; Court Rolls NRO Diocesan EST 8/1424-1454.

The manor was remote from Yarmouth, and perhaps inflationary wage demands were not felt there. The bailiff continued to receive £2 14s. 10d. a year as wages throughout the first thirty years of the fifteenth century and the annual wages of the regular farm labourers remained at 10s. The harvest wage rose slightly from 6s. to 6s. 9d., occasionally to 8s. The manor still relied on the tenants' services for much of its labour. This proved unreliable in some years and the Abbey had to send its own workers to help with the harvest.

The manor turned to the landlord for financial help in other ways. The Abbey bore the cost of re-roofing the stable and the grange, and in some years paid the shepherd's wage of £1 a year, later to be reduced to 13s. 4d. Livestock numbers declined and sales were few. The marshes at Thurne suffered from severe flooding during the fifteenth century and in many years could not be let. It is not surprising that in 1429 the Abbey farmed out a 101 acres of demesne to John Edward for ten years for a rent of 63 quarters of barley a year (5 bushels an acre). Gradually more of the land and the livestock and services were farmed to local men.[143]

Only sheep farming seems to have prospered, but it was the Abbey, not its manors, which controlled the flocks of sheep. In 1385 the Thurne Court Rolls recorded that the Abbot had fold courses at Ashby, Thurne and Oby. A fold course in East Norfolk, unlike those in North Norfolk, only gave the landlord the right to pasture his flocks on the open fields of a village for a defined length of time after harvest, the time of 'shack' as it was called. In the fifteenth century the Abbey rented fifteen acres of the surplus demesne land at Ashby for the lambing season. The villagers were also turning to livestock farming. There are the usual complaints against men who overstocked the common with geese, pigs, cows and horses, and men from Repps frequently brought their animals to pasture on the Thurne commons. It seems that the small farmers of the locality were vying with each other for a share of the common grazing along the river Bure.

Yet the court rolls give the impression of a community in decline. After the Peasant's Revolt, 103 tenants came to claim their land. Fifty-eight years later, in 1439, only 49 tenants came to

143. Ashby and Thurne Accounts NRO Diocesan EST9/ In 1426 18 workers were sent from the Abbey to help with the harvest.

atourne, that is to pay homage to the lord of the manor. Even allowing for the inevitable absentees, it looks as though the number of tenants had declined substantially.

In the late fourteenth century only one or two bondmen are recorded as leaving the manor. By 1406 fourteen men had left and were liable to pay chevage. Their names are repeated year after year until they either died, or the authorities had lost track of them. Most had not moved far; Billockby, Upton, Rollesby, Martham, Yarmouth and Norwich were their destinations. No one appears to have left the county, but other tenants probably left the village leaving no record of their departure.

Other entries in the court records suggest that the community was declining. There are constant complaints about the non-payment of rent, of abandoned holdings, of buildings not maintained or even pulled down and thistles growing in the fields. In 1449 Ashby was the only place in Flegg that was given relief from taxation because of a decline in population. It seems that, as the peasant farmers left the village, yeomen and gentry farmers took over the vacant land and created larger farms of twenty, thirty or fifty acres. Thurne did not suffer in the same way. Fewer tenants left the village. Its position on the River Bure must have given easier contact with Yarmouth and Norwich, and the marshes provided the holders of small farms with grazing for livestock and a ready supply of other wetland products.[144]

A Lay Manor: Ormesby

The manorial pattern of Flegg was changing in the fifteenth century. The lordships of many of the lay manors and estates were coming, either by marriage, inheritance or purchase, into the hands of two gentry families, Paston and Clere. After the marriage of John Paston to Margaret de Mautby and the inheritance of the Fastolf lands, the Pastons held manors in Caister, Mautby, Filby, Winterton, Herringby and lands in Runham and Repps, as well as many other estates in Norfolk. The main branch of the Clere family lived at Ormesby (now Ormesby St Margaret), and held land in Ormesby, Burgh, Somerton and Winterton. Another other branch of the family, the Cleres of Stokesby, held the manors of

144. *Norfolk Archaeology XXXI part 1* Allison 'Lost Villages of Norfolk'.

Stokesby and Thrigby, and estates in Filby, Caister and Runham. I will not write at length about the Pastons because there are two books, *The Pastons and Their England,* by H.S.Bennet and *The Illustrated Letters of the Paston Family* by Roger Virgoe, which give a detailed picture of the family and the society in which they lived. The Clere family is less well known and it is their manor at Ormesby that I have taken as an example of a lay manor. [145]

The manor of Ormesby Kingshall, was one of the largest in Flegg. A good run of bailiff's accounts has survived from 1423 to 1458. In the 1420s and 30s the manor was in the hands of Lady Elizabeth Rothenhale, who lived at Caister, and who was always referred to as 'the Lady' in the accounts. Her first husband had been John Clere. Their son Robert Clere lived at Ormesby Hall with his family and inherited the Ormesby estate when his mother died in 1437. The manor house stood to the north of the village on the road to Hemsby. No traces of the buildings remain today, but the name survives in Clere House, an Old People's Home on the Rollesby Road.

The Ormesby accounts begin in the 1423, just two years before the Priory gave up the direct farming of the demesne at Martham and leased the land to Thomas Drake. Ormesby manor, with its resident landlord, appears to have been a much more successful enterprise than the Priory manor at Martham or St Benet's manor at Ashby and Thurne. About three hundred acres was cultivated by the manor each year. Not surprisingly the regular labour force was much larger than at Martham. It consisted of a bailiff, four ploughmen, four general labourers, a maltster, a shepherd and a laundress, a very necessary servant for a resident family. The usual crops, wheat, barley, peas and oats were grown, with barley predominating. After the household had been supplied, the surplus grain was sold and raised well over £50 in most years. Although income from corn sales fell on the monastic estates, at Ormesby the income remained remarkably constant even when corn prices fell after 1440.

More detail is given about the sales of corn at Ormesby than for any other manor I have come across. Local men, whose names and villages were always recorded, bought small quantities of wheat,

145. PRO Ormesby Account Rolls 1423-1458 PRO SC6/ 939/1 - 941/3.

barley or malt. The Prior of Yarmouth and the Abbot of Langley Abbey in South Norfolk also purchased their wheat and malt from Ormesby manor. There were large consignments of forty or fifty quarters of malt sold to merchants from Covehithe, Dunwich, Colchester, and from unspecified places in Essex. These men were often described as 'crayermen'; a crayer was a coastal trading vessel, working up and down the North Sea. The Account Rolls do not record where the transactions between the Ormesby bailiff and the crayermen took place, nor who paid for the carriage of the grain to the port. Discount was certainly given for bulk purchases. Corn prices remained stable with wheat at 6s. a quarter and malt at 4s. until the 1440s when wheat fell to 4s. a quarter and malt to 2s. and the crayermen ceased to figure so prominently among the purchasers. However the total amount of malt sold was not significantly reduced. There is apparently only one instance of corn being sold to a foreigner, when in 1437 a Dutchman bought malt from the manor.[146]

Ormesby is one of the few manors in Flegg where a flock of sheep is recorded. In 1423-4 the manor had a large flock of 776 sheep, which included 12 rams and 253 ewes. The household was supplied with mutton for the table and fleeces for spinning. In 1424 twenty four sheep were sold to Thomas Brimblekin, butcher of Great Yarmouth, and John Cross of Beccles bought wool and sheep skins. Sheep and wool sales brought in £10 2s. 6d. that year. However the next year the flock was struck by disease. One ram, ten sheep and twenty-nine ewes died. Sixty of the remaining ewes were sterile, fewer lambs were born and, of those, seventy-three died. The decision seems to have been taken to get rid of the flock. Fifty-three sheep were sold that year to Yarmouth butchers, and more mutton was eaten at Ormesby and Caister. Sixteen pounds of wool went to both manors for the ladies to spin, and wool and sheepskins worth £3 10s. were sold.

In future years the flocks from Ormesby and Caister were combined and 'the Lady' at Caister took responsibility for the whole flock. Although sheep were no longer recorded in the list of livestock at Ormesby, a shepherd was employed in the autumn, winter and early spring when a flock from Caister was folded on the Ormesby demesne to manure the soil. The shepherd's wage of 10d.

146. For Crayer, crayermen see Shorter Oxford Dictionary, 1936.

Caister Castle before recent reconstruction
Margaret de Mautby preferred living in the smaller Mautby Hall which was warmer

a week was more than doubled to 22d. in February and March during the lambing season. Ormesby manor retained an interest in sheep for in 1430-31 the bailiff of Ormesby sold eighty sheep from Caister to a Norwich man. The flock was replenished in 1442-3 when hundred and seven ewes were bought, eighty from Edmund Clere of Stokesby.

There is some evidence that in the late 1450s sheep had returned to Ormesby. In 1457 twenty eight sheep appeared on the list of livestock and the next year summer pasture in Fulholm marsh was rented for 230 sheep. Six men were employed to shear them and the fleeces were then sold in Yarmouth. Other sales of sheep that year brought in at least £3 13s. 6d. As the price of grain fell in the mid fifteenth century the decision may have been taken to invest in sheep farming.

I would have liked to study the Ormesby manorial records more fully, but they are in the PRO and my time in London was limited. Throughout the first half of the fifteenth century the Ormesby manor seems to have been profitable and well run. Someone, perhaps Robert Clere himself, had the initiative to establish regular sales of malt to the Essex crayermen. The presence of a resident lord must have encouraged the bailiff to attend to the details of management - note his careful record of the purchasers of Ormesby produce. The manor court met at least twelve times a year, compared with only four times at Martham. The frequency of the courts would have made it difficult for tenants to evade paying rents and fines. The impression gained from the bailiff's accounts is that Ormesby with its resident landlord was a better managed and more productive estate than either the Priory manor at Martham or St Benet's manor at Ashby and Thurne.

In 1437 Lady Elizabeth Rothenhale died and the Ormesby estate reverted to Robert Clere, her son by her first husband. He died ten years later, leaving the estate to his widow, Elizabeth. In 1458, the date at which the bailiff's accounts stop, she leased the manor farm at Ormesby to Walter Haigh of Filby for seven years. The estate consisted of 246 acres of arable, five enclosed fields, a pasture called Brakenham and a 'gret medew callyd Snekkes medew'. The land was clearly in good heart; sixteen acres had been dunged with farmyard manure, forty-seven acres folded with sheep and thirty-one acres of fallow had been ploughed seven times. Walter was to have the use of the farmyard with all the buildings

Photo: J.C.Barringer 2000

Ormesby Church

The Perpendicular tower was built in the fifteenth century. Elizabeth Clere left £10 to the 'Tower of Ormesby Church' in her will (1492). This legacy may have paid for the figures of the Four Fathers of the Church on the pinnacles of the tower, since the tower itself was probably already built by 1492.

and barns, but Elizabeth was to live in the manor house. He agreed to find her straw and whins for her brewing and baking as long as she lived at Ormesby, and to give her a fat boar each year for brawn at Christmas.[147]

Although Elizabeth leased the demesne to Walter Haigh in 1458, she was still actively engaged in the management of the estate. In 1466 she made an agreement with her tenants that in cases of dispute they should choose two or three of themselves 'to set them through the said trouble', or if they could not agree among themselves, 'to abide and fulfil the ordnance and rule of the said Elizabeth and her son', Robert. The tenants covenanted not to take their disputes to any court except Ormesby manor court, yet as tenants of the King's ancient demesne, they had in certain cases a right to use the King's courts. Over a hundred years later this agreement was cited when a group of Ormesby yeomen tried to get

147. Lease of Ormesby manor to Walter Haigh, See *Catalogue of Ancient Deeds* Vol. 5 No 12188.HMSO.

justice in the King's court against Sir Edward Clere who they claimed had taken away their rights of common.

Elizabeth was a very capable woman, and unusually for a young widow she never remarried, but lived for the next forty-five years at Ormesby, directing the family fortunes until her death in 1492. Thanks to her, the Clere family weathered the problems of the fifteenth century successfully. Elizabeth Clere, although a very rich heiress, seems to have husbanded her wealth. Being a widow she was not tempted to play any great part in local or national politics, although she was quite a forceful woman in many ways. She was a friend of Dr Caius, who called her 'the nurse and almost mother' of the college he founded at Cambridge. She paid for the building of one side of the college court, and gave a further legacy to the college in her will. She seems to have lived in a comfortable, but fairly modest style at Ormesby on the income from her many manors. In her will in 1492 she left £10, a large sum for those days, to the church tower at Ormesby St Margaret. In the sixteenth century the Clere family became more involved in Court life with all the expense that entailed and were constantly in debt.[148]

Ploughing

From the Gorleston Psalter

148. For the Clere Family see Yarmouth Archaeology 1982, Cornford. B. 'The Cleres of Ormesby'.

Chapter 14: Village Life In The Fifteenth Century

The Village Community

The peasant farmers of the sixteenth century, faced with landlords who arbitrarily raised their rents and enclosed the commons, always looked back to the fifteenth century as a golden age, when land was plentiful, rents were fixed, wages good and prices stable. One of the demands of the men who joined Kett's rebellion in 1549 was that the rents for copyhold land, meadow and marsh should return to the level of 1485. This chapter looks at the realities of peasant life in Flegg in this 'Golden Age'.

The community in Martham in the fifteenth century consisted of both bond and freemen. Bond status does not seem to have been a great disadvantage. Many of the services, charges and restrictions that had been the lot of bondmen had been abandoned, or were ignored or only irregularly imposed. However since most land on Martham manor was bond land, almost all tenants, whatever their status, held some land by bond tenure and were expected to be responsible for the services and charges attached to it. All transactions of bondland were recorded in the manor court and the tenant was said to hold his land by copy of court roll, hence the term, 'copy hold', given to this type of tenure. All copyhold tenants were expected to attend the manor court and to abide by its regulations.[149]

The high death rate in the Black Death period and the slow recovery of the population in the fifteenth century had a lasting impact on the land holding pattern of Martham manor. At the end of the thirteenth century 375 tenants had held 830 acres on the manor. The average size of a holding had been about three acres and more than half the tenants had held less than two. Many tenants redistributed their land among members of their families in order to spread their land as widely as possible among their relations. (See Chapter 7) A hundred years later surplus land could easily be rented or bought and livestock farming or a trade or craft might provide a better income than corn growing. A rental of the tenants of Martham manor, recorded at the end of the fifteenth

149. See Chapter 8. Copyhold tenure was only legally abolished in 1922.

century in 1497, can be compared with the 1292 survey. This rental names eighty-five tenants who hold 735 acres, and includes four parish gilds holding six acres between them. The size of holding ranges from two tenants with 20 perches each to four tenants with holdings of over thirty-five acres. Table 14.1 of the distribution of the size of holdings in Martham in 1497 is found below.

Table 14.1 Holdings in Martham 1497

Size of holdings	Number of tenants
Over 30 acres	4
20 - 29 acres	6
10 - 19 acres	15
5 - 9 acres	24
2 - 4 acres	15
1 - 2 acres	10
under 1 acre	8

In Martham many holdings were still small, but over half the tenants held more than five acres, and nearly a third held over ten. In fact the 1497 rental underestimates the actual size of many peasant farms in Martham for tenants could rent or buy land from the demesne. Campbell has shown that in the fifteenth century tenants tended to buy land rather than lease it, and so increase the size of their holdings permanently. It is clear from their wills that some tenants also held land in other villages.[150]

In Martham there was considerable migration both in and out of the village. The lists of bondmen owing chevage show that most emigrants went to Yarmouth or to local villages, but one or two went to Lynn and one man, Robert, son of Thomas Amound was living in London in 1385. The Herman family is interesting. In 1388 John, Robert and William Herman, bondmen, left the village, abandoning their eight acre holding, and went to Yarmouth. By 1399 they had all moved well away from Yarmouth and taken up different trades; William Herman was a tailor in Halesworth, Robert, a cordwainer in Ely and John, a barker (tanner) in Sybertoft in Northamptonshire. We do not know where they learnt their crafts, but they had the initiative to travel and settle in places

150. 1497 Rental, NRO, DCN 27655 (R32D).

outside Norfolk. Once they had established themselves away from the village, I think it unlikely that they ever came back or paid chevage to Martham.[151]

It is more difficult to find information about people who moved into the village, but sometimes the records of other manors are helpful. The first fifteenth century record of the Ashby manor court show that John Edward had already left that village by 1424 and had settled in Martham. As a bondman of blood he owed chevage each year to the Abbot of St Benet's, the lord of Ashby and Thurne. In 1423 a man called John Edward had married in Martham and the court rolls described him as 'free of blood' since he was not a bondman of the Prior. He may well have been the man who came from Ashby to Martham, but it is impossible to determine whether he was also the John Edward who rented a hundred and one acres of demesne at Ashby six years later in 1429. (See page 165) In most cases bondmen who migrated from their native manor must have been classed as freemen in their new homes. Another family, the Lounds, also settled in Martham. The Lound family left Forncett in 1401 and, after some time in Norwich, came to Martham. The Forncett court rolls show that they were liable for chevage at Forncett until 1555, but as far as I know, do not record any payment. Their descendants still live in Martham. Certainly there must have been considerable migration into Martham, for many unfamiliar surnames appear in the Court Rolls. On the whole the men who settled in the village after the Black Death, seem to have prospered and often held official positions, for example Thomas Drake, the bailiff and farmer of the manor.[152]

Peasant Agriculture in the Fifteenth Century

In the fifteenth century while the manor was reducing its agricultural operations, the tenants were expanding their activities especially into livestock farming and the exploitation of the

151. For details of the Herman brothers, see NRO. Martham Court Rolls, N.R.S. 20 D 3 5927, 5929.

152. For John Edward, who had left Ashby by 1424, see NRO. DN EST. 8 /16. It is possible, but unlikely, that he was the same man who leased the Ahsby demesne in 1429. NRO N.R.S. 20 D4 5937 for John Edward's marriage. For Thomas Lound, see Davenport, Frances 1906.

common. The court records show that pigs, geese, cows and horses all made themselves a nuisance in the fields and on the common. Sheep were kept in larger numbers, for their wool rather than their meat. Tenants were often accused in the manor court of overcharging the common with sheep. Flocks from neighbouring manors, 'foreign sheep' as they were called, were brought to feed on the extensive common at Martham. In 1398 the Rollesby shepherd had sixty sheep on Martham common where they had no right to be. In the 1420s the Martham manorial shepherd, Roger Clark, a relatively prosperous tenant who held at least fifteen acres of land, combined his manorial duties with keeping a flock of his own and other men's sheep. In 1423 he was presented for overcharging the common, and in 1425 for the same offence with forty 'foreign sheep'. I have found no record of his death, but he may have been a man of some wealth, for about 1449 a man of the same name ordered a window to be made in the newly-built church in Martham in honour of the Blessed Mary. Unfortunately the window has long since disappeared.[153]

The common and the marshes were intended only for the use of tenants and their families. In the fifteenth century a growing market for rushes, reeds and peat meant that tenants cut these marsh products for sale in the neighbouring villages and towns. For example, in 1442 John Pery cut reeds on Martham common and sold them in Yarmouth, for which offence he was fined 6d., a sum that must have been well covered by the money he received from the sale. From 1452 Fen Reeves were appointed each year to regulate the cutting and disposal of the marsh products and to control the fishing. Certain nets, such as steel nets, (nets held by stakes in permanent positions across dykes) and wayndraggs, (dragnets) were banned from use.[154]

153. Simon Cotton. 'Martham Church Redated' in *Narg News No 33* 1983.

154. John Pery fined for cutting reeds 1442, See Martham Court Rolls NRO N.R.S.20 D 4 5942. Fen Reeves appointed, see NRO N.R.S. 209 D 4 5947.

The Wealthier Tenants and the Manor Court

It is very clear from the Court rolls that the community contained a group of wealthy tenants.[155] These more prosperous farmers were usually freemen and often held the official positions in the manor court. As Capital Pledges they were responsible for the good behaviour of the community and would present tenants accused of breaking customs and regulations, which they frequently they ignored themselves. Thomas Drake, who was a Capital Pledge and bailiff of the manor in 1420, became the farmer of the demesne in 1425, and is typical of this group of wealthy tenants. He may have been a newcomer to the village because his surname does not appear in the court rolls before 1416, when he bought a cottage and nine acres of land for 50s. He must have amassed land in the next twenty years for he had a holding of 30 acres at his death in 1435. Like many other tenants he often broke the regulations of the court or ignored its orders. In 1416 he cut down two ash trees and a poplar worth 3s. 4d. and sold them outside the manor without permission. For this offence he was fined 3s.4d., the value of the timber. He delayed for at least two years before repairing his bakehouse that had been destroyed by fire. He did not make up the bank between his land and the common, nor maintain his gate on to the common. However these were relatively minor offences compared with those of John Maynard and John Richer.

The Maynard family had been in Martham since the Black Death and had frequently been in trouble in the manor court. In 1416 John Maynard and a man from Potter Heigham took a crop of hay from another man's meadow without permission and sold it outside the manor. He was fined 6s. 8d. He tried to enclose a piece of common and add it to his own land without permission. Despite his infringements of the rules of the manor he filled two official positions on the manor. He was a capital pledge at Martham and at Ormesby, where he also held land. He was also chosen as one of the Martham Fen Reeves in 1452. (See list of Manorial Officials on page 194)

A companion of John Maynard was John Richer who had friends and interests all over Flegg. He was the executor of the will

155. Mention of John Coping, 'yoman', July 1416. Ref. NRO N.R.S. 20 D4 5934 Court Monday prx ante St Marg.

of William Mundes of Mautby and part owner of a marsh and turbary in Ormesby. Like John Maynard he was a capital pledge in Ormesby as well as Martham. In 1423 he was accused of making an enclosure on the common at Damgate and adding it to his own land. The capital pledges were ordered by the court to set the boundaries between his land and the common, but were very reluctant to do so. He had also occupied a common fishery for his own use for several years and enclosed a pit for his eels. He had been fishing with an illegal wayndragge and had refused to surrender it to the bailiff, for which he was fined 40s. In the same year he assaulted the bailiff, Thomas Drake, in church calling him 'a false rustic', while his son attacked the chaplain and stuck a dagger into the bailiff. Father and son were fined 3s. 4d. for each assault. John Richer continued to flout manor regulations. He obstructed a path and allowed his sow to wander in 1435; two years later he destroyed and stole the growing crops of two tenants. In 1438 he was accused of claiming that his bondland was free land, stealing hay and selling it outside the manor and insulting and attacking another tenant by breaking two bows across his head. He died in 1452, leaving his son, another John, 1½ roods of land. The rest of the son's inheritance may have been free land and so was not recorded in the court rolls. The records of the manor court reveal that many prosperous and influential men thought nothing of flouting the regulations of the court in their endeavours to further their own fortunes.

Martham Church and Martham Heretics.[156]

In the fifteenth century a new church was built in Martham in the Perpendicular style on the site of the old round-towered church. (See page 79) It is only from the late fifteenth century that the word 'church' appears in place names, as 'Church Gate' on Heygate in 1497, and 'Church Field' and 'Church Hill' to the west of the Church on the old Fendrove Hill.

The new church is a light and lofty building. It has a seven sacraments font and some fine stained-glass windows. Three centuries of neglect and abuse had taken their toll of the glass by

156. For the early church at Martham see pp. 122-3.

1856 when the chancel was rebuilt and the church refurbished. Most of the remaining stained glass was collected and reinstated in the east windows of the aisles, not always correctly. There you can see St Michael with his scales and a delightful Eve spinning in a flowery meadow. However the window of Adam was taken by the curate to Mulbarton when he moved to that church in the mid nineteenth century.[157]

The inhabitants of Martham must have been proud of their new church, and showed their devotion to it in ways that were customary at the time. Many wills give legacies to the church or to the four guilds, of which the most popular was the guild of St Blide. She was reputedly the mother of the eleventh century St Walstan of Bawburgh and is said to have been buried in Martham. Her feast day was on the first of August when a fair was held in the village.

Devotion to the saints was clearly not to the taste of all the inhabitants of Martham. A group of men and women rejected the teaching and ritual of the Catholic Church when they came under the influence of the Kentish religious leader, William White, whose beliefs were more extreme than those of the fourteenth century Lollard, Wycliffe. Fearing prosecution under the harsh heresy laws of 1414, William White left Kent and travelled through Essex and Suffolk to the Waveney valley where he and his companions established heretical congregations in a number of villages by 1428.

There was a group in Loddon that met in the house of Thomas and Hawisa Moon. The Moons had contact with William Baxter of Martham, described as a wright, a craftsman in wood or iron. A meeting was arranged between Baxter and White, the Kentish heretic, at the house of the vicar of Halvergate. Following this meeting, the house of William Baxter and his wife Margery became the centre of religious discussion and teaching in Martham. William White stayed for five days in hiding in the Baxter household and Margery was greatly influenced by him and his teaching. Information about the activities and beliefs of the Norfolk

157. Simon Cotton 'Martham Church Redated'. in Narg News 33. 1983. A Victorian curate took the stained glass window of Adam with him when he went to Mulbarton where it can be seen in the south aisle window.

Norfolk heretics is to be found in the record of their trials in the Ecclesiastical Court in Norwich from 1428 to 1430.[158]

William White condemned almost every aspect of contemporary religious orthodoxy. He rejected the sacraments and the veneration of the saints. Crucifixes and images of saints encouraged idolatry. Pilgrimages were ineffective. There should be no swearing or taking of oaths. Killing, including capital punish-ment and fighting for king or country, was forbidden. Tithes should not be taken or given. Instead the poor should be relieved. Fasting was unnecessary on Fridays, in Lent or on Holy Days. Confession to a priest was pointless; confession should be made directly to God. There was no need of any intermediary between men or women and their God. All good men were priests, and only priests could enter heaven. His theology discarded all the visual, oral, personal and spiritual support that the contemporary church gave to the human soul. There were no ceremonies of baptism, marriage or membership for his followers. Unlike the fourteenth century Cathars in South Western France, there were no special rites for the dying. White's beliefs were very similar to those of the Adepts of the Free Spirit, who were active in North Germany and Bohemia in the fourteenth century. [159]

This robust religion seems to have made an appeal to the artisans in the villages of South and East Norfolk. Shoemakers, glovers and other craftsmen were among its adherents, men who had skills, a moderate income and some status in the community. The gentry were not touched, although one or two priests, such as the vicar of Halvergate, appear to have been sympathetic. There is no evidence that the poor were attracted to heretical theology. White's teaching appealed to the same section of society as those who joined the Peasants' Revolt, craftsmen like William Baxter and men, such as John Pery, who had held official positions in the Manor court. (See page 182) A local group usually met in the home of its most active member, and the entire household, including servants and apprentices attended. At these meetings White's beliefs were expounded and readings from religious works were given in English, especially from the New Testament. A meal,

158. Tanner.N.P. *Heresy Trials in the Diocese of Norwich, 1423-31*, Camden Society Fourth Series 20 1977.

159. Cohn, N. The Pursuit of the Millennium, Paladin Press 1970, p.248.

which always contained meat, was eaten, often on a day officially appointed for fasting, as if to emphasise the rejection of the ordinances of the Church.

In 1428 White was arrested, found guilty of heresy and burnt. Many of his followers, including Margery Baxter, were also arrested. She confessed that she knew him and that he had stayed in her house. She accepted his teaching, that only those who follow the precepts of God are true Christians. She condemned pilgrimages and the worship of images which, in her words, was 'the adoration of stokkes and stones and ded men's bones'. Joanna, wife of William Clifland, of Norwich, brought further evidence against her. Margery Baxter, described as 'lately living in Martham', appears to have moved to Norwich in 1429, and was living near her accuser. Joanna gives a vivid account of Margery's attempts to convert her and her two young servant maids. Condemning the worship of saints, Margery is reported as saying that 'lewed wrightes of stokkes (that is carpenters) hew and fourme such crosses and ymages, and after that lewed peyntors glory thaym with colours'. (Perhaps she was thinking of the newly built church at Martham). She continued 'if you would see the true cross I will demonstrate it to you in your own home'. Then Margery extended her arms in length and said, 'See this is the true cross of Christ and this cross you can see and adore every day in your own house. You labour in vain when you go into churches to adore or pray to any images or crosses'. Joanna's account gives a taste of the determination and passion with which Margery tried to convert her neighbour.

However Joanna decided to investigate Margery further. She sent her maidservant, Agnes, to Margery's house. Now let the deposition of fourteen year old Agnes Bethon tell the story: 'This witness said that on Saturday after Ash Wednesday when she was sent to the house of the said Margery by her mistress to fetch an onion, she saw a copper pot standing on the fire, covered and boiling. The said Margery not being at home, this witness uncovered the pot and saw in it a piece of bakon boiling in water with oatmeal'. The Saturday after Ash Wednesday was, of course, in Lent when meat should not have been eaten. This was added proof that Margery and her household had rejected the ordinances of the Church.

Margery, like other heretics examined by the Ecclesiastical Court, pleaded guilty, recanted and purged herself. Her punish-ment was to be whipped in solemn procession round Martham church on four successive Sundays. She had to walk barefoot and clad in white with uncovered head and shoulders, carrying a candle weighing a pound. She was also to be whipped twice round Acle market. Similar punishments were given to the other convicted heretics. Margery's husband, William Baxter, seems to have escaped arrest, for there is no record of his interrogation or trial. Three other inhabitants of Martham, John Pyrye, Robert Gryggys and Isabella Chapleyn were accused, found guilty and recanted. They were sentenced to punishments rather similar to Margery's.

I could find very little about the Martham heretics in the Court and Account Rolls of the early fifteenth century. There was a family of Baxters in Martham, but the only William Baxter I can find seems to have come from Bastwick or Repps. He and his brother, Robert, inherited five acres in Martham on the death of their father, John Baxter of Bastwick, in 1427. Probably the same William Baxter, described as 'of Repps', died in 1449, leaving 10 acres. His wife at the time of his death was Katrina; she may have been his second wife, but there is no suggestion that he was a craftsman or that he had held heretical beliefs.

Two other Martham men were named as heretics in the Ecclesiastical Court of 1428-9, Robert Griggys and John Pery. Gryggys appears in the court rolls twice for minor offences. John Pery, or Pyry, was a capital pledge and a juror in 1435. At his trial for heresy he was accused of eating meat with Margery Baxter on Fridays, sometimes at her house and sometimes at his. On one occasion they dined on roast goose which he had caught on the marsh. I think he may have been the same John Pery who was fined 6d. in 1442 for selling reed in Yarmouth. (For information about John Pery, see page 176).

The heresy trials throw light on various aspects of fifteenth century society. John Pery's activities reveal how the marshes could contribute to the income and wellbeing of members of the rural community. The heretics, who regularly dined off roast goose and boiled bacon, provide an example of the improvement of nutrition in the fifteenth century. Some of the heretics had a degree of literacy and read from religious texts in English at their meetings, which were followed by exposition and general dis-cussion. One imagines that the heretics moved easily about east Norfolk. Isabella Chapleyn had connections with both Martham and Loddon. Margery Baxter speaks as though she knew Hawisa Moon of

Loddon personally. William Baxter was acquainted with the vicar of Halvergate, about fifteen miles distant from Martham, and it is known that Thomas Moon of Loddon travelled widely in this part of Norfolk. Women took played an important part in heretical circles. Margery Baxter, Hawisa Moon and Isabella Chapleyn were all articulate women who took an active role in the group's activities. Even if, according to Joanna Clifland's testimony, Margery's efforts to convert her became frantic and hysterical, there is no doubt of Margery's energy and deter-mination. She should join the growing company of assertive women of the fifteenth century along with those very different Flegg ladies, Elizabeth Clere and Margaret de Mautby. (See page172)

There is a stark contrast between the colour and theatre of Catholic worship in Martham church and William Baxter's kitchen where a small group gathered to hear William White's exposition of the relationship between man and God. He must have been a man of considerable charisma. His teachings have more in common with the Ranters of the seventeenth than the fifteenth century, but after his death and the conviction of heresy against many of his followers, no continuing legacy of dissent appears to have survived in East Norfolk. No connection has been found between William White's group and the Protestant martyrs who were burnt in Norwich in the early sixteenth century.

Fifteenth Century Wills 1424 - 1505[160]

In the fifteenth century it became the usual for the well-to-do tenants to register their wills in the Church Courts. The early fifteenth century wills do not usually deal with land, but with personal gifts of clothing and small sums of money. A typical will is that of Margaret Maynard, who died in 1424 and may have been the mother, or possibly the wife, of John Maynard, the Fen Reeve of Martham. Her first legacies were to the parish church. She left 3s.4d. to the altar, 6s. for the upkeep of the church, 2s. to the light

160. Wills mentioned in the text, 1424, *Margaret Maynard.* 1467, *William Spencer,* Stokesby, Cons. Jekkys 95; 1465 *Thomas Fuller* , Stokesby, Cons. Cobold; 1464 *Walter Shipdam* Filby Cons Jekkys; 1473 *Christina Love* Martham. Cons. Paynot; 1475 *John Salmon* Caister. Cons. Gelour 1445-6; 1429 *Robert Draycot* Stokesby Cons. Surflete 126; 1442 *Robert Drye* Filby. Cons. Wylby 110; 1498 *Godfrey Candeler* Martham. Cons. Moulton 103; 1505 *Dionisie Candeler* DCN wills. 1501.

of St Mary, 2 lbs of wax to burn before the image of St Blide, 6d. to the clerk and 3d. to the sexton. Then came legacies for the welfare of the community, 13s.4d. to the poor, 'where most need is', and 8s. to the repair of Wey Bridge causeway, that is the road to Acle bridge. Her personal gifts were a gown with a hood to John Faukener of Hemsby and gowns and kirtles to three women. She left small legacies to the churches of Tunstall and Cantley with which she must have had some connection. The residue of her goods she left to her executors to sell and use the money for the health of her soul, in other words for prayers for her passage through purgatory. She seems to have ben a wealthy woman by fifteenth century standards.

Like Margaret Maynard, almost every testator left some money to the parish church, to the parish guilds, or candles for the lights of saints. A man with a personal interest in the image of St Mary at Stokesby was William Spencer who, in 1467, left 4 lbs of wax to the light of our lady 'which I did make'. Had he perhaps painted her image or made some part of her 'light'? Legacies to the poor were not so common, except among the gentry and the clergy, who usually left a few shillings to the poor of their parishes. In 1465 Thomas Fuller of Stokesby, like Margaret Maynard, left gifts of his clothes. His best cloak and boots went to his son, his other cloak to a friend and the rest of his clothes to the poor. Legacies to roads and bridges are fairly common, with Wey Bridge and its causeway on the road to Norwich attracting more gifts than any other highway.

The Acle Causeway, towards Acle Bridge

Some wills throw light on the homes of the testators. The most common domestic utensils left in wills were brass pots used for cooking. Brass pots could be bought in Martham Fair, for in 1480 Robert Ansell was accused of forestalling brass bowls at the feast of St Blide. He had bought up the bowls before they came to market with the suspected intention of raising the price later in the day. As the century progressed, feather beds, blankets and coverlets were frequently given as legacies.

Walter Shipdham's will, dated 1464, is one of the very few which give information about his home. He was a wealthy man who, with John Richer of Martham, had held 'the waters, turbaries, reed grounds, and fisheries in Ormesby'. Although he was buried in Filby church, his main house was in Ormesby, which he left to his son, John, while providing his wife with one of his other properties for life. His home included a hall, a chamber, store room, kitchen and bakehouse. He left his wife and daughter six silver spoons each, but all the rest of his silver, including 'a flatpiece with a cover', was to be sold. Eleven acres of his Ormesby land was to be sold to pay for his son, Thomas, to finish his apprenticeship as a raffman. (See page 97) Walter had a '*domus*' in Yarmouth, probably a shed or small building, perhaps on the quay or near the market. His property in Yarmouth and his remaining land was to be sold to pay his debts and to provide money for legacies to various churches and to the Houses of Friars in Yarmouth. The residue was to be distributed to the poor.[161]

Another Will, that of Christina Love of Martham, dated 1473, gives a good list of domestic utensils including a silver mazer (bowl), candlesticks, salt cellar and spoons, all of silver, a pewter vessel, three kettles (large saucepans) and necklaces of jet and coral. It is unlikely that many inhabitants of Flegg had so large an establishment as Walter Shipdham, or so much silver and household equipment as Christina Love, but probably these were the standards to which an increasing number of well-to-do farmers aspired.[162]

Wills do not give much information about the size or location of the testator's property. The death of a person holding bondland

161. Reference to Wills: NRO Cons = Consistory Wills. D&C = Dean and Chapter Wills. 1424 *Margaret Maynard*, Martham, Cons. Hyrning 134.

162. Alms given at Ormesby in 15th cent. Margaret Paston's concern for her tenants. *Paston Letters* Gardiner 4 vols.

and the inheritance of his or her heir would be registered in the manor court and would not necessarily be repeated in the will, unless the testator had property in more than one village. Like Walter Shipdham, four other testators had 'buildings' in Yarmouth, which in every case, were to be sold. Small personal gifts of grain, usually malt, were given to the parish guilds or to relatives. A prosperous farmer sometimes bequeathed larger quantities of corn along with horses, carts and ploughs to the son who had inherited the farm. Cows and sheep in small numbers were left as personal gifts particularly to daughters. Money does not feature in wills as often as livestock and household goods, although daughters were often provided with 40s. on marriage, and younger sons sometimes received a gift in cash.

Perhaps the will of John Salmon of Caister who died in 1475 gives some idea of equipment and livestock to be found on a typical mixed farm. His oldest son, Robert, was to have twenty acres of land, two quarters of wheat and fourteen of barley, a plough, a cart and four horses. He was left thirty ewes, two cows, two heifers and a sow with two piglets. He also had a brass pot, pewter dishes, two candlesticks, two tables and some bedding. His kitchen equipment included two ale stands, three tubs and a flesh trough (for salting meat). He was to have 20s. upon marriage. John Salmon's wife inherited his messuage with livestock and equip-ment very similar to Robert's, and all the family linen, wool and household utensils. She was apparently expected to run the farm and to look after his other two sons and three daughters. The children, two of whom were under sixteen, were each left a cow or a heifer, and, as so often, sheep: thirty for the oldest daughter and ten or fifteen for the others. They were all given some bedding and 20s. upon marriage. John Salmon was a very substantial farmer indeed.

Like John Salmon most testators tried to make some provision for each son and daughter. Sheep feature more than any other livestock in the wills of both prosperous and not so prosperous men. Typical of the latter was Robert Daycot, whose legacies in 1429 consisted of 6s. 8d. to his parish church, two sheep to his son Richard, and all his domestic utensils to his wife Custance. William Drye of Filby, who died in 1442, was a much wealthier man. He divided his estate between his wife and his four sons. Margaret, his wife, was to have his 'headplace' in Filby for her life, and he left land to three of his sons. To the fourth son, John, he left a flock of 120 sheep on condition he resigned all claim to the rest of the estate. What family history lies behind this bequest? Possibly, like Roger Clark, the Martham shepherd of the 1420s, John was already a professional shepherd, making his living through the sale of wool and sheep skins.

Some families specialised in a trade or craft. Godfrey Candeler of Martham, who died in 1497, held fifteen acres in Martham according to the 1497 rental, but his will shows that he also held land in Rollesby, Horsey, East and West Somerton and, further a-field, in Aldeby. The will of his wife (1505) indicates that the family were chandlers or raffmen, for her son, Sebastian, inherited all stuff belonging to a 'Chamder's or Rafman's trade' which seems to have been a lucrative occupation from the thirteenth century onwards, for in 1299 Adam Raffman of Martham was able to buy his freedom from the Prior for £2 (See page 97). In 1464 Walter Shipdham, a wealthy man from Ormesby, paid for his son to finish his apprenticeship as a raffman. Raffmen appear to have dealt in timber, tallow and probably candles as the surname 'Candeler' suggests; they might be described as chandlers or general merchants.

Winterton offered the opportunity for other specialised trades.The old village, which lies between the church and the sea is a huddle of narrow lanes and little cottages, reminiscent of the fishing villages of north east England and unlike the pattern of tofts and messuages in other Flegg villages. By the fourteenth century fishing from Winterton was important enough for the Crown to have established a toll on boats. In 1334-5 the Hemsby Manorial Accounts record the receipt of 5s. 6d. from the tolls of eleven boats at Winterton, and later in the fourteenth century Dionysia Clere of Ormesby claimed 'Havencourtes', which is described as a Botetoll in Winterton. The fishing and the coastal trade must have stimulated the market at Winterton. It attracted trade from surrounding villages. Clement Paston went to Winterton from Paston to sell his grain and to meet his bride, the daughter of Geoffrey of Somerton. In the early fifteenth century John Locke, a Winterton crayerman, was buying malt from Ormesby manor, for export or the coastal trade.

Some local farmers combined farming with fishing. Richard Parker of East Somerton who had three farms and a flock of a hundred sheep, left a boat called 'le Trinyte' to his wife, and a boat called 'le Kasche' and his share in three small fishing boats called 'cokkys' to his son. Less wealthy men gave fishing nets or their share in the profits of a boat to their wives or to the local guilds.

Yet there were many who had very small holdings. Not everyone was able to get his foot on the ladder of prosperity. Disease, poor harvests and plain ill luck still dogged the small farmer. The 1497 Rental shows that most tenants at Martham held under ten acres. Occasionally manorial records provide evidence of hardship. In 1430-31 at Ormesby three barrels of herrings were bought and distributed to the poor at the manor gates and seven years later faggots were bought for alms. In 1465 Margaret Paston commented on the poverty of their tenants, and hoped her husband would not let a certain marsh that year 'so that the tenants might have rushes to repair their houses and windfall wood, that is not of great value'. Many testators were aware of the poverty of their neighbours and some gave legacies of clothes or money, 'where most need is'. The grinding poverty of the early fourteenth century seems to have been a thing of the past. No longer are the comments 'cannot be levied' and '*pauper*' written beside the fines in the manor court records at Martham.

Nutrition and living conditions were improving. Houses were more solidly constructed and household goods, such as brass cooking pots, blankets, coverlets and feather beds, more numerous. The ubiquitous cottage pig provided meat and the rivers and marshes, fish and game. The increase in the con-sumption of meat and the drinking of ale provided calories, protein and fat, all lacking in the medieval peasant's diet.[163]

The conditions of the fifteenth century, particularly the availability of land and the loosening of the ties of serfdom, enabled many tenants to increase the size of their farms and to diversify into livestock. We would call such men 'yeomen', although the term does not seem to be in very general use in the fifteenth century. I have only found two mentions of yeomen in the Flegg. Thomas Coping 'yoman' of Winterton was accused of taking two hares in the Lord's warren at Martham in 1416. A mid-fifteenth century Schedule of the Clere lands in Winterton and Somerton shows that members of the Coping family rented land on the Clere Estate in Winterton. They seem to have been a fairly well-to-do family. The

163. Christopher Dyer, *Standards of Living in the later Middle Ages*. O.U.P. 1989.

The other mention of a yeoman is John Lubbock, who in his will is described as 'yeoman of Runham'. In his will of 1470 he left his son 3 acres of arable land, and brass dishes to his other two children. He does not appear to have been a very wealthy man, beside such men as Walter Shipdham of Filby, or John Salmon of Caister, but he may well have held more land than the few acres he bequeathed to his son. Campbell discusses the economic and agricultural circumstances leading to the emergence of this yeomen class at the end of the fifteenth century. The yeomen, secure in their copyhold tenure and with mixed agriculture on their farms, were to dominate rural society in Flegg for the next two centuries.[164]

Lovers meeting

From the Gorleston Psalter

164. B.M.S.Campbell 1983 Economic Historical Review 2nd Series 1983. 'Agricultural Progress in Medieval England' p44.

15: Four Centuries of Flegg History

There appear to be many similarities between the eleventh century Domesday freeman who had his own meadow, his oxen and his saltpan, and the fifteenth century peasant farmer with a mixed farm, a diversity of economic options and considerable freedom from servile obligations. Yet the world of the of the eleventh and twelfth century freemen and sokemen was very different from that of countrymen four centuries later. During the twelfth and thirteenth centuries many of the Domesday free tenants became absorbed in the manorial system and bound by the terms of their tenancy to do manorial duties. A very productive system of intensive farming was practised on the manorial demesnes, dependent on cheap labour, which was supplied by a substantial growth in population. By the thirteenth century all the suitable waste had been brought into cultivation to provide additional holdings. At Martham, and on other manors in eastern Norfolk, the existing tenant holdings were divided by partible inheritance and, with the help of an active land market, provided holdings for the growing population. Most communities in eastern Norfolk seem to have maintained a degree of stability during the thirteenth century.

A series of bad harvests and high prices at the end of the century made it very difficult for many tenants to provide their families with even a minimum standard of living. The Black Death of 1349 had a profound effect on this impoverished population. Most communities in Flegg probably lost up to half their population, but only Ashby seemed to have been in danger of becoming a deserted village. The Black Death affected landlords as well tenants. The manorial lord, whether lay or ecclesiastical, could no longer rely on a supply of cheap labour which had made the intensive cultivation of the demesne so successful. However once the immediate impact of the disease had abated the tenant had many advantages. He could easily acquire land which the manorial lords were willing to sell or farm out, and craftsmen could demand higher wages. The nutrition and living conditions of countrymen were improving. Travel was easier and the population was becoming more mobile. The Herman brothers of Martham may have been exceptional (see page 174), but many tenants left the villages to make a new life in new surroundings.

Improvements in communications led to the spread of news and ideas. The speed with which information about the Peasant's Revolt reached Thetford (barely two days after the men from Kent and Essex reached London) shows how quickly news could spread especially when it concerned the interests of rural communities. The enthusiastic acceptance of William White's heretical ideas by small groups in Loddon and Martham shows a willingness to receive new intellectual ideas, which may at first have seemed disturbing.

By the end of the fifteenth century Bartholomew Diaz had rounded the Cape of Good Hope and Vasco de Gama had sailed to the coast of India. Five years before the Martham Rental was written in 1497, Columbus had discovered the West Indies. The pattern of English trade begin to shift westwards from the North Sea port of Yarmouth to Bristol and Plymouth. Knowledge of the new discoveries and their effect on trade and commerce must slowly have penetrated to Norfolk. Flegg, like the rest of Norfolk, remained relatively prosperous. Arable farming flourished, providing barley for both the home and overseas markets. Although there is no evidence of much weaving in Flegg, many farmers kept sheep mainly for wool for which there was a ready demand. perhaps from weavers in Aylsham and North Walsham. Increasingly Flegg yeomen were fattening beef on the marshes for sale further afield.

The geography, economy and landscape of the area had changed significantly over the centuries. Whatever direction the Thurne and the Bure had taken in the earlier centuries, by the fifteenth they flowed in the course familiar to us. The Thurne flowed from the marshes between Winterton and Horsey and went westwards and then southwards to join the Bure at Thurne Mouth. Grubbs Haven, the earlier mouth of the Bure, on the coast between Caister and Yarmouth, had silted up about two centuries earlier, and the Bure followed its present course to enter the eastern end of Breydon Water, giving a through waterway between the Flegg villages and Yarmouth.

The climatic changes at the end of the thirteenth century had caused a rise in water levels and flooded the peat diggings in the Muck Fleet valley, in fact forming broads, although that term was

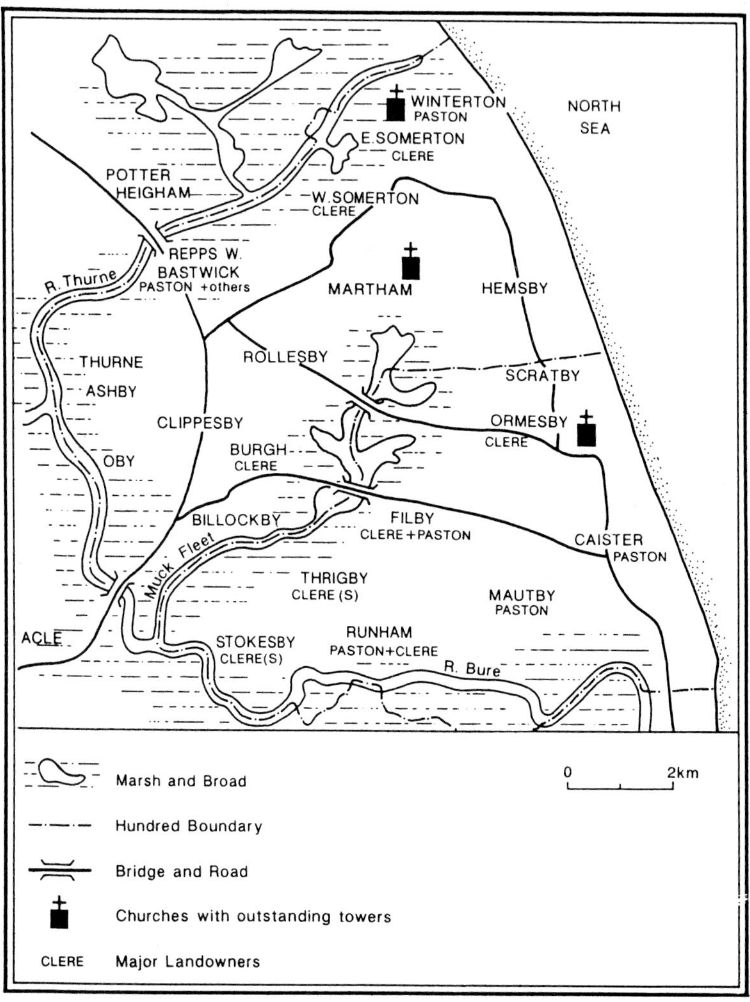

Map 15.1. Flegg at the end of the Fifteenth Century
'Clere S' indicates the Cleres of Stokesby

not used until the next century. The best peat from the deep Flegg turbaries had to be dredged up from the flooded turbaries, ferried to the dryer land and there formed into the turves or blocks of peat. Increased labour costs meant that large scale production of peat decreased. By about 1380 the Cathedral Priory turned from peat to wood as a source of fuel for its kitchens. However peat was still dug from the shallower turbaries and turf pits for everyday use in Flegg villages for another three centuries. The manors with marsh pastures, such as Martham and Thurne suffered from frequent flooding. At Martham considerable sums were spent on clearing the ditches and raising the banks round individual pastures, but the raising of the river banks along the Bure and the Thurne was never undertaken until the seventeenth century.

Salt production from the saltpans of the Bure estuary, so valuable in the earlier centuries, does not seem to have survived the period of the Black Death, though some salt-making may have continued on a small scale in the coastal villages. Sheep, another economic asset in Flegg for the wealthier Flegg manors at the time of Domesday, were still present four centuries later. Norwich Priory had a flock based at Fulholm pasture near Yarmouth and a very small flock at Hemsby. The Abbot of St Benet's had fold-courses in Oby and Ashby, where the sheep spent the lambing season on the vacant demesne lands. The Clere estates at Ormesby and Caister were increasing their flocks in the mid-fifteenth century. Tenant farmers of the later fifteenth century also kept sheep, usually in fairly small numbers. However, sheep farming was never as important as it was in North Norfolk, and a textile industry never developed in Flegg.

Two innovations in farming had taken place in the twelfth and thirteenth centuries, windpower for milling and horses for ploughing. By the fifteenth century windmills were universal for milling grain. Horses probably replaced bullocks more gradually, but by the fifteenth century they pulled the ploughs on both the manorial demesnes and tenant farms, and increasingly in the next century young bullocks were fattened for beef on the marshes. Road transport had certainly improved by the fifteenth century. Substantial stone bridges at Acle and Bastwick were built in the fourteenth century, structures that survived into the twentieth century.

The pattern of land-ownership had changed. In 1086 ten major landowners held the Flegg manors, including the King as part of his royal demesne, the Bishop and the Abbot. In 1500 the Abbot and the Bishop still held their estates, but two families, the Pastons and the Cleres dominated Flegg as is shown in map 15.1 (page 192). Other manors were in the hands local landowners. Billockby, for example, was held by de Martham, a descendent of the Gunton family. Both the Cleres and the Pastons left Flegg early in the next

Potter Heigham Bridge
Photo: Eastern Counties Newspapers

Photo: J.C.Barringer

West Somerton Church
The tower is twelfth century with a fifteenth century hexagonal addition. Nave and chancel are thirteenth century.

century and moved to North Norfolk where both families developed great houses with extensive grounds, the Cleres briefly at Blickling, and the Pastons more permanently at Oxnead. After the move, both families tended to ignore their Flegg possessions. Perhaps arable fields in Flegg pressed too close to the manor house to allow a great mansion and its estate to be created there.

The number of churches built or renovated in the Perpendicular style testifies to the wealth of the larger communities in Flegg in the fifteenth century. The fine tall tower of Winterton church from which a beacon shone out to ships at sea is an example of this new wealth and confidence. Martham church was was completely rebuilt in the new style. A new tower was built at Ormesby, while less wealthy communities like Mautby (see page 46), Rollesby and West Somerton, built new square towers, upon their existing round ones (see page 194). These fifteenth century towers still dominate the landscape of Flegg, along with the wind turbines of the late twentieth century.

Winterton Church and the Wind Farm

The fifteenth century tower carried a beacon for the guidance of boats at sea.

Glossary

1. Manorial Officers.

Officers appointed by the lord of the manor.

The bailiff was responsible for the over-all management of the estate, and lived in the manor house. He either presented the annual accounts or testified to their accuracy. At Martham and Hemsby the bailiff was usually called 'Serviens' (usually translated as sergeant in Account Rolls) although he occasionally appears as 'Baillivus'. Adam de Bawdswell was Bailiff of both manors from about 1287 to 1312-13. He was paid 6d. a week at Martham and occasionally was given a gown and a pair of shoes. At the larger manor of Hemsby, he was paid 12d. a week.
The keeper of the grange is found at Martham and Hemsby. He was responsible for receiving the corn at harvest time, seeing to its safe storage and disposing of it during the year, and for keeping a detailed record for all these duties for the Annual Accounts. He was paid 10½d. a week at Martham in the thirteenth century. There is no record of this officer after the Black Death at Martham and the post seems to have died out. In Adam de Bawdeswell's time the keeper of the grange and the beadle presented the annual accounts and the bailiff testified to them. At Martham the keeper of the grange was not a local man.

Officers chosen from the tenants

The beadle was primarily an officer of the Manor Court who delivered summonses to court and collected the fines. In Martham he is often called the 'collector'. (In Hemsby these seem to have been two separate officials) It is not clear whether he was appointed by the lord or chosen by the tenants. He did not receive any pay, but may have been excused his manorial services for the year he was in office.
The reeve was responsible for the work in the fields and in particular for organising the manorial services of the tenants, and seeing that they performed their duties.

The hayward or messor was responsible for keeping the hedges in good repair and looking after the meadows and pastures. It was he who impounded straying cattle. In Martham the reeve was chosen each year from among the tenants of one of the ten-acre tenements and the messor from the tenants of a twelve-acre tenement. In this way the existence of the old twelfth century tenements survived into the fifteenth century. Usually it seems that the man with the largest acreage of land in the tenement was expected to take on the duty. The reeve's job was very unpopular and he usually paid to be excused his duties. For example in 1289 William Herbert paid 8s. and in 1290 Robert le Webster paid 13s. 4d. to be relieved of their duties. The messor appears to have performed his duties regularly. In the late fourteenth century the messor replaced the reeve as the chief village official, and was chosen by the manor court. At that time he is associated with the bailiff in presenting the annual accounts.

Tithing and tithing men. Social control was exercised through the tithing. At the age of fourteen all male tenants were placed in a group called a 'tithing'. The tithing was jointly responsible for the good behaviour of the group. One of the members of the group would be chosen as tithing man. He would present to the manor court any member who broke any regulations or who acted anti-socially.

2. Weights and Measures

Measures of Corn

Thrashed corn and peas were measured by volume in bushels and quarters. Eight bushels made a quarter. The grain was usually stored in large comb sacks holding four bushels. A peck, sometimes found in medieval accounts, was a smaller measure used in the household, two gallons made one peck, and four pecks one bushel.

2 gallons = 1 peck
4 pecks = 1 bushel
4 bushels in a comb sack
8 bushels or 2 combs = 1 quarter

Pounds and stones were used for weighing cheese and other foodstuffs.

14 lbs. = 1 stone

In the nineteenth century some farming manuals converted the old measures into weights. It was accepted that a comb of wheat weighed about 18 stone, a comb of barley about 16 stone, a comb of peas or beans about 22 stone, a comb of oats about 12 stone. If a comb sack of medieval barley weighed the same as a nineteenth century comb, a bushel of barley weighed 4 stone or 56 lbs., a comb of barley 16 stone or 224 lbs., a quarter barley 32 stone or 448 lbs. (about a fifth of a ton). Medieval grain may not have been so well thrashed and winnowed as grain in the nineteenth century. Therefore the comb sack of barley would have contained more straw and chaff, and may have weighed less than 16 stone, perhaps a sixth or even an eighth of a ton would be nearer the mark.

Linear Measure

Land was measured by the rod. A standard rod was 5½ yards or 16 ½ feet in length. An acre was notionally four rods wide by 10 in length, in other words 22 yards by 220.The acre was divided into four roods; each rood was a strip measuring 1 rod by ten rods, with an area of a quarter of an acre. The perch, which was a fortieth of a rood, measured smaller areas of land. The smallest plots were measured by feet. Surprisingly the yard was never used.

40 perches = 1 rood
4 roods = 1 acre

The rood, a square measure is often confused with the rod, a linear measure, and acreages are given in acres, rods and perches.
The rod was also used to measure buildings. Many medieval houses are one rod in width and two or three in length.

Local Measures

Some communities did not use the standard rod of 16½ feet. On the Priory estate in Martham the rod was 18½ feet long. The rod of 18½ feet also measured the land belonging to the Clere family in Burgh, Somerton and Winterton. (In South Norfolk where the width of old houses is often about15 feet, the traditional rod may have been that length) I do not know when the rod of 16½ feet became accepted in Flegg. The Hemsby Field Book (1422) states that land is measured by the standard rod of 16½ ft; I do not know whether the long rod was ever used at Hemsby.

Bibliography

Standard Works

Allison, K.J. (1957) 'The Lost Villages of Norfolk', *Norfolk Archaeology xxxi* pp116-62

Blomefield, F. (1711) *Essay towards a Topographical History of Norfolk* Vol xi Hundreds of East and West Flegg

Browne, Philippa ed. (1984) *Domesday Book, Norfolk* in *History from the Sources,* ed. J.Morris, Phillimore, Chichester.

Campbell, B.M.S. (1980) 'Population Change and the Genesis of Common Fields on a Norfolk Manor' in *Economic History Review, 2nd series.*

(1983a) 'Agicultural Progress in Medieval England: Some Evidence from Norfolk' in. *Economic History Review 2nd series.*

(1983b) 'Regional Uniqueness of English Field Systems: Some Evidence from Norfolk'. in *Agricultural History Review*

(1984) 'Population Pressure, Inheritance and the Land Market' in (ed.) R.M.Smith. *Land, Kinship and Life Cycle .* Cambridge

Clarke, R.Rainbird. (1960) *East Anglia* S.R.Publishers Ltd.

Coles Bryan P.L. & Funnell Brian M. (1981) 'Holocene Palaeoenvironments of Broadland, England.' in *Specs. Publs. int Ass. Sediment.*

Cornford B. (1984) 'Hemsby in the later Middle Ages' in *Norfolk Research Committee Bulletin 2nd Series No 32.*

Darby H.C. (1971) *A Domesday Geography of Eastern England* Cambridge.

(1977) *Domesday England.* Cambridge.

Davies R.H. (1954) 'East Anglia and the Danelaw' in *Trans.Royal Historical Association Series 5* pages 23-29 .

Davenport, F. (1906) *Economic Development of a Norfolk Manor 1086-1565* Cambridge.

Dawson, P. (1980) 'A Hill in Broadland' in *Narg News.* no 22, (Sept.1980).

Dodwell, Barbara. (1941) 'The Free Peasant in East Anglia' in *Norfolk Archaeology* No. 27.

(1952) *Feet of Fines, Norfolk. 1198-1202.* Pipe Roll Society 27

(1958) *Feet of Fines Norfolk. 1201-1214.* Pipe Roll Society 32

(1965 'The Honour of the Bishop of Thetford/Norwich in the late 11th and early 12th century' in *Norfolk Archaeology* No.33.
(April 1967) 'Holdings and Inheritance in Medieval East Anglia', in *Economic Historical Review*.
(1984) *Charters of Norwich Cathedral Priory* Pipe Roll Society 40.
(1985) *Charters of Norwich Cathedral Priory* Pipe Roll Society 46.
Douglas, D.C. (1927) *Social Structure of East Anglia.* Oxford
Funnell, B.M. (1979) 'History and Prognosis of Subsidence and Sea-Level Change in the Lower Yare Valley, Norfolk' in *Bulletin of the Geological Society of Norfolk* 19.
Gairdiner, James ed. (1910) *The Paston Letters* 4 vols.
George, Martin. (1992) *The Land Use, Ecology and Conservation of Broadland* Packard.
Glasscock, R.E. (1963) 'Distribution of Wealth in East Anglia in the early Fourteenth Century' in *Trans. and Papers of the Institute of British Geographers* 1963.
Gurney, David. (1990) 'Caister-on-Sea' in *Narg News* 59.
(1996) 'The Saxon Shore in Norfolk' in *A Festival Norfolk Archaeology,* pub. Norfolk and Norwich Archaeologoical Society and authors.
Hanawalt, Barbara. *Crime in East Anglia 1307-1316 Norfolk Record Society* .vol xliv.
Harvey, P.D.A. (1951) 'English Inflation of 1180-1220' in *Peasants, Knights and Heretics,* ed. R.Hilton.
Hood, C.M. ed.*The Chorography of Norfolk. An historicall and chorographicall description of Norfolk.* Norwich (1938). Written c.1600. Attributed to John Norden.
Kealey, Edward.J. (1987), *Harvesting the Wind.* University of California.
Keen, Maurice (1990) *English Society in the Later Middle Ages.* Penguin.
Lambert J.M. et al. (1960) *The Making of the Broads,* R.G.S. Research Series No3.
Lawson, A. (1981) 'The barrows of East Anglia' in *East Anglian Archaeology No 12.*
Macdonald, J and Snooks, G. (1986) *Domesday Economy.* Oxford.
MacKinley, R. (1975) *Norfolk and Suffolk Surnames in the Middle Ages.* Phillmore.

Margeson, S. (1996) 'Viking Settlement in Norfolk' in *Festival of Norfolk Archaeology* pub. by Norfolk and Norwich Archaeological Society and authors.

Mortimer Richard. (1980) 'The Prior of Butley and the Lepers of West Somerton' in *The Bulletin of the Institute of Historical Research vol.liii No127,* (May 1980).

Sandred, K.I. (1987) 'Some Reflexes on Old Anglian and Viking Settlement in Norfolk Place Names' in *Norfolk Research Committee Bulletin 2nd Series No 38.*

(1996), *Norfolk, Place-Names of East and West Flegg, Happing and Tunstead Hundreds.* English Place Name Society.

Saunders. (1930) *Introduction to the Obedientiary and manor rolls of Norwich Cathedral Priory.* Norwich.

(1939) 'First Register of Norwich Cathedral Priory' *Norfolk Record Society vol xi.*

Smith, A.H. (1956) *English Place-Name Elements,* English Place Name Society. Cambridge University Press.

Stenton F.M (1922) 'St Benet's at Holm and the Norman Conquest' in *The English Historical Review Vol 37.*

Tanner, N.P. (1977) *Heresy Trials in the Diocese of Norwich 14232-31,* Camden Society, 4th Series 26.

Virgoe, Roger (1991) 'The Will of Hugh Atte Fenne 1476' in *Norfolk Record Society* vol lvi

West R.G (1932) *Register of the Abbey of St Benet at Holm.* Norfolk Record Society Vols 2 & 3.

Williamson, Tom (1993) *The Origins of Norfolk.* Manchester University Press.

Yaxley, David (1988) *The Prior's Manor-houses.* The Larks Press.

Original Documents

The British Library

Survey of manors belonging to the Norwich Cathedral Priory 1292. Stowe 936 Microfilm copy in the Norwich Record Office MF 514

Public Record Office

Calendars of Inquisitions Post Mortem, published by the Public Record Office, give a summary of each Inquisition

Inquisitions Post Mortem for Runham. in PRO
1272, C133/3/12, Calendared vol 2
1300 C133/122/7 Calendared vol 4
1307 C/133/123 Calendared vol 4
1316 C/ 134/48 Calendared vol 5
1327 C 135/13/14 Calendared vol 5
1340 C135/58/17 Calendared vol 8
1351 C 135/100/12 Calendared vol 8

Norfolk Record Office. (NRO)
Cathedral Priory Documents Reference DCN (Dean and Chapter).

Hemsby manor
Bailiff's Accounts 1265 - 1335. DCN 60/15/1-16.
Priory Inventory of Manor House 1351 DCN.
Hemsby Field Book 1422 Middleton Killin & Bruce, 19/11/68.

Martham
Martham Court Rolls and Bailiff's Accounts are in two different Archives, Dean and Chapter of Norwich DCN and Norfolk Record Society, NRS. It is quite difficult to follow the references.
Court Rolls 1288/9-1420-21, DCN 60/22/ 1-33.
Court Rolls 1350-1480 NRS 11312 20 B3 onwards.
Account Rolls 1261/2-1349/50 and some later D.C.N 60/23/25.
Account Rolls 1323/4, and 1355-1441/2 N.R.S. 5889 onwards.
Rental of Martham 1497 DCN 2765 (R 232 D).

Ormesby Account Rolls DCN 61/39 for 1296; 61/40 for 1305; 61/41 for 1339

Scratby Account Rolls DCN 60/ 31/ onwards.
Proficuum Maneriorum (The Prior's own Account Roll of Priory estates). DCN 40/13 onwards.

Magister Camera Rolls (The Rolls of the Master of the Cellar) 1265 D.C.N.1/1/ onwards

Somerton

Lease for 7 years from William Boleu, Prior of Butley Abbey, to Edmund Palmere of Wytton next Broomholm of the Manor of West Somerton NRO 16214 32 B2.

St Benet's Abbey

Manorial Accounts

Ashby, Oby, Thurne Accounts 1245, Diocesan EST/1.

Flegg Manor, that is Ashby and Thurne, Accounts 1341-1422 EST/9.

Court Rolls 1381-1457 Diocesan EST/8.

Mautby Bailiffs Accounts. Mich 1335-15 Jan 1336 Phi. 489 578 x 1;1336/7 1337/8 Phi 490 578 x 1.

Repps with Bastwick Field Book 1466/7 EVL584 463 x 6.

Field Book 1572 EVL 585 463 x 6.

Index

Alan, Count, 38, 41, 43, 48, 53
alms, 120, 121, 123, 138, 151, 185 188
anlipemen, 149
Ashby, 16, 19, 35, 41, 47, 53, 59, 60, 61, 121, 128, 130, 139, 145, 152, 153, 155, 157, 158, 164, 165, 166, 167, 170, 175, 190, 193
Bacon family, 153, 154
Bailiff's Accounts, 54, 57, 58, 59, 60, 61, 67, 69, 70, 73, 91, 94, 101, 103, 104, 107, 108, 109, 120, 121,136, 137, 140, 142, 143, 144, 148, 152, 158, 159, 162, 164, 167, 170
Bastwick, 21, 25, 48, 51, 59, 129, 149, 182, 193
Baxter, Margery and William, 179, 180, 181, 182, 183
Black Death, 12, 51, 57, 66, 68, 73, 88, 105, 107, 110, 121, 136, 138-41, 144, 145-6, 147, 148, 149, 160, 173, 175, 177, 190, 193, 196
Bigot, Roger, 44, 47, 48, 49, 67
Boyes Manor, Rollesby, 119, 139-40
Boys, John, 155, 156, 157, 158
bridges, 14, 16, 36, 53, 66, 184, 195
Bure, River, 14, 16, 18, 22, 36, 39, 43, 47, 49, 50, 59, 61, 66, 70, 105, 138, 152, 165, 166, 191, 193
Burgh, 21, 32, 36, 53, 59, 60, 61, 65, 127, 128, 129, 130, 131, 132, 139, 166
Butley Abbey, 72, 74
Candeler, Godfrey, 187
Cess (Ses), 25, 77, 78, 79, 81, 82, 85, 117, 125, 151
chaplains, 113, 125
churches, 18, 25, 39, 45, 46, 58, 59, 64, 69, 72, 74, 77, 79, 124, 125, 126, 127, 172, 176, 178, 179, 180, 181, 182, 183, 184, 185, 186, 187, 195
Clere family, 124, 127, 128, 129, 131, 132, 154, 166, 167, 170, 171, 172, 183, 187, 188, 192, 193
Clippesby,28, 32, 41, 47, 48, 49, 59, 61, 128, 129
Cobham manor, 126, 127, 161, 162, 163 See also Moregrove
Cope, John, 98, 112
craftsmen, 97, 98, 99, 147, 174, 180, 190
crayermen, 168, 170
Damgate (Damiottofts, 24, 77, 82, 178
Danes, Danish, 14, 16, 21, 22, 23, 24, 25, 29, 31, 53, 77
Daycot, Robert, 186
de Evermure family, 64, 65, 66
de Gunton family, 89, 124, 125
de Hil family, 87, 88, 110
de Martham family, 124, 126
de Mautby family, 55, 67, 70
de Ness family, 49
diet, 19, 51, 56, 57, 60, 68, 69, 72, 73, 87, 88, 93, 97, 101, 103, 104, 106, 107, 109,116, 117, 119, 121, 128, 136, 137, 138, 141, 142, 144, 150, 151
Drake, Thomas, 162, 163, 164, 167, 175, 177, 178
Drye, Robert, 183, 186
Eccles, 94, 155

Edward III, 70
Erl family, 114, 119, 147, 149, 150, 151
faldage, 104, 150
famuli, 106
Fastolf family, 70, 74, 129, 155, 166
fen reeves, 176, 177
ferries, 16, 23, 77
fines, 65, 93, 94, 111, 112, 113, 118, 119, 120, 123, 139, 141, 143, 144, 147, 148, 150, 151, 152, 156, 162, 163, 170, 178, 188, 195: chevage, 94, 140, 143, 149, 166, 175, 176: heriot, 118, 142: merchet, 118, 148
fisheries, fishermen, fishing, 22, 29, 30, 36, 39, 51, 53, 56, 79, 94, 97, 105, 119, 128, 134, 150, 151, 152, 158, 163, 167, 185, 187, 188
Fleggburgh, 11, 28, 129
Flemings, 140, 144, 145
fold-courses, 193
Forncett, 94, 175
Fulholm, 105, 129, 170, 193
Great Famine, 121, 123, 136, 137, 138
Gunton manor, 78, 96, 125
Gyrth, 26, 27
harvest, 66, 88, 93, 94, 97, 99, 103, 105, 115, 117, 120, 121, 136, 137, 140, 141, 142, 144, 145, 147, 150, 162, 165,188, 190; harvest meal, 60, 87, 104, 107: harvest services, 44, 87, 90, 106, 119, 125, 131, 143, 148, 149, 152, 157, 159, 161, 163
Hemsby, 14, 18, 19, 21, 27, 41, 43, 44, 45, 47, 52, 55, 56, 57, 58, 61, 67, 78, 85, 89, 94, 97, 99, 101, 106, 109, 115, 123, 128, 129, 133, 136, 137, 138, 149, 151, 167, 184, 187, 193
Herman family, 174, 175, 190
Herringby, 19, 28, 32, 36, 38, 41, 43, 53, 74, 133, 139, 166
Hickling, 11, 35, 38, 81, 127, 158
Hil, see de Hil family,
Horn family, 114, 147
Horsey, 11, 14, 124, 126, 127, 187, 191
Hundreds, 16, 19, 24, 30, 31, 33: courts, 24, 29, 31
Ingham, 35
inheritance, 24, 63, 67, 71, 93, 94, 96, 99, 110, 112, 118, 124, 128, 142, 149, 151, 166, 178, 186, 190
Inquisitions Post Mortem, 63, 65 70, 133, 134, 139
Knight family, 88, 92, 112-13, 114-116, 118, 119, 120, 147
Knightlys manor, 127
Langley Abbey, 168
leases, 62, 96, 124, 126, 149, 163
Litster, John, 153, 154, 158, 159

livestock, 13, 20, 38, 50, 51, 52, 56 60, 66, 68, 69 ,77, 79, 89, 106, 115, 117, 118, 144, 147, 149, 161-62, 165, 166, 173, 175, 186: cattle, 16, 22, 30, 33, 35, 38, 39, 43, 49, 51, 52, 57, 60, 69, 97, 104, 116, 117, 129, 136, 137, 142, 143, 144, 163, 165, 176, 186, 190,: horses 38, 39, 43, 53, 57, 60, 68, 70, 73, 103, 104, 129, 142, 144, 162, 163, 165, 176, 186, 193: peacocks, 56, 60-61, 105: pigs, 16, 35, 38, 39, 43, 45, 51, 57, 60, 69, 104, 105, 116, 142, 150, 162, 165,

171, 176, 188: poultry, 56, 57, 60, 61, 69, 78, 104, 105, 107, 150, 162, 165, 176: sheep, 36, 38-9, 44, 45, 46, 47, 51, 63, 104-5, 116, 117, 141, 143, 150, 165, 168, 170, 176, 186, 187, 188, 191, 193: swans, 56, 69, 73, 105, 106, 162
London, 11, 64, 74, 153, 160, 170, 174, 191
Long family, 92, 97, 105, 106, 113, 119, 120, 147
Lound family, 175
Love, Christina, 183, 185
manor courts, 12, 57, 65, 66, 76, 93, 94, 100, 101, 110, 111, 113, 114, 116-18, 120, 123, 129, 134, 141, 142, 143, 144, 145, 148, 150, 151, 156, 157, 158, 159, 162, 163, 170, 171, 173, 175, 176, 177, 178, 186, 188, see also fines, services
markets, 20, 54, 56, 64, 65, 66, 70, 93, 94, 99, 104, 137, 150, 176, 182, 185, 187, 190
Martham, 11, 12, 16, 18, 19, 21, 22, 24, 25, 27, 32, 33, 35, 45, 48, 49, 55, 56, 58, 61, 63, 67, 68, 69, 75-100, 101, 102, 103, 104, 105, 106, 110-27, 128, 129, 130, 131, 132, 133, 136, 137, 139, 140-44, 145, 146, 147-51, 152, 153, 155, 158, 159, 161-64, 166, 167, 170, 173-75, 176, 177, 178, 179, 181, 182, 183, 185, 187, 188, 190, 191, 193, 195: Survey of, 16, 19, 66, 76, 77, 84, 85, 87, 90, 92, 94, 96, 97, 98, 101, 104, 110, 113, 114, 124, 125, 127, 143
Mautby, 21, 23, 27, 32, 35, 36, 41, 46, 47, 49, 50, 55, 61, 63, 65-9, 70, 71, 101, 104, 129, 133, 139, 154, 160, 164, 166, 169, 178, 183, 195
Maynard family, 177, 178, 183, 184, 185
mills, 29, 30, 35, 36, 46, 53, 66, 101, 106, 119, 163
Moon, Hawisa and Thomas, 179, 182, 183
Moregrove, manor of, 63, 78, 81, 89, 115, 124, 125, 126, 127, 129
Muck Fleet, 19, 22, 26, 36, 39, 53, 105
murrain, 137
Ness, 28, 32, 49, 50, 51
Norwich, 14, 16, 19, 24, 36, 38, 41, 54, 55, 58, 59, 61, 66, 67, 72, 87, 88, 90, 91, 92, 96, 104, 105, 143, 147, 153, 155, 159, 164, 166, 170, 175, 180, 181, 183, 184
Norwich, Bishops of, 44, 54, 73, 89, 124, 125, 153-4, 155
Norwich Cathedral Priory, 54, 55, 56, 57, 58, 59, 67, 73, 76, 78, 88, 89, 90, 92, 96, 98, 101, 103, 104, 105, 109, 114, 118, 123, 124, 125, 127, 128, 129, 133, 134, 135, 136, 140, 141, 143, 144, 147, 149, 159, 161, 162-3, 168, 171, 192, 193
Oby,28, 32, 38, 41, 47, 48, 59, 60, 61, 156, 165, 193
Paston family, 70, 74, 160, 161, 164, 166, 167, 185, 187, 188
Peasants' Revolt, 19, 62, 63, 93, 116, 133, 147, 153-9, 161, 162, 180

peat, 14, 18, 19, 39, 58, 59, 69, 78, 79, 97, 106, 141, 176, 191, 192
Pecke family, 92
Pery ,John, 176, 180, 182
Pickerell Holme, 35, 36
population, 19, 30, 44, 54, 55, 82, 90, 91, 92, 93, 94, 98, 101, 110, 116, 121, 132, 139, 143, 146, 160, 161, 166, 173, 190
prices, 54, 55, 56, 65, 87, 88, 91, 93, 99, 101, 103, 109, 120, 121, 123, 131, 136, 137, 138, 147, 148, 150, 152, 160, 161, 167, 168, 170, 173, 185, 190
Ralph, Earl, 35, 42, 45, 46, 47, 52, 65, 89
Ralph the Staller, 27
rathmen (raffmen), 97, 187
Rede family, 92, 111, 112
rents, 30, 43, 44, 49, 53, 55, 61, 62, 64, 65, 66, 67, 69, 74, 76, 78, 79, 82, 87, 88, 90, 92, 93, 94, 96, 98, 100, 105, 110, 116, 118, 127, 129, 130, 131, 136, 137, 141, 148, 149, 159, 161, 162, 163, 164, 165, 166, 170, 173, 174
Repps, 18, 21, 32, 41, 47, 48, 59, 61, 72, 77, 78, 111, 128, 129, 165, 166, 182
Richer, John, 114, 177, 178, 185
Runham, 16, 18, 22, 27, 41, 46, 47, 63, 64, 65, 66, 68, 70, 71, 117, 133, 134, 139, 166, 167, 189
Salmon, John, 183, 186, 189
saltpans, 30, 36, 51, 63, 193
Sco, 25, 32, 45, 78, 82, 111, 112
Scratby, 27, 28, 32, 58, 94, 121, 122, 123, 129, 136, 137, 139, 160
serfs, 29, 30, 33, 44, 47, 153, 156
services, 31, 44, 52, 62, 65, 69, 76, 87, 88, 89, 90, 91, 92, 94, 96, 100, 104, 110, 114, 118, 119, 125, 128, 129, 130, 131, 132, 134, 135, 140, 141, 142, 143, 144, 147, 149, 152, 159, 161, 163, 164, 165, 173, see also harvest.
Ses, see Cess
Shipdham, Walter, 185, 186, 187, 189
slaves, see serfs
St Benet's at Holm, Abey, 26, 27, 31, 39, 43, 44, 45, 47, 48, 49, 52, 53, 59, 60, 61, 62, 82, 121, 128, 130, 133, 134, 145, 152, 153, 155, 156, 157, 159, 164, 165, 168, 170, 175, 193
Stanard family, 83, 112
Stefne,, 16, 59
Stigand, Archbishop, 26, 27, 42
Stokesby, 16, 22, 23, 26, 27,28, 32, 38, 41, 42, 47, 53, 133, 166, 167, 170, 183, 184, 192
surnames, 67, 92, 124, 157, 177, 187
Sutton, 35
Taillour, Thomas, 97, 147, 157, 158
tenants, 24, 29, 30, 31, 32, 33, 42-3, 45, 47, 48-9, 51, 52, 53, 59, 60, 61, 62, 63, 64, 65, 66, 69, 71, 76, 78, 79, 85, 87-98, 100, 101, 104, 106, 107, 110- 120, 123, 125, 127, 128, 129- 132, 133, 134-35, 137-38, 139- 40, 141, 142-43, 145, 147, 148-53, 154, 155,

156, 157, 158, 159..161, 162, 163, 164, 165-66, 170, 171, 173, 174-5, 176-9, 184-90, 191, 193: bordars, 30, 32, 33, 43, 44, 45, 49, 52: copyhold, 173: freemen, 26-7, 29, 30, 31, 32, 35, 45, 46, 47, 48, 49, 51, 52, 53, 59, 64, 65, 89, 110, 114, 129, 134-5, 173, 190:sokemen, 29, 30, 31, 32, 43, 44, 45, 47, 48, 49, 51, 52, 53, 59, 89, 90, 130, 190: villeins, 29, 30, 31, 32, 33, 44, 45, 49, 51, 52, 88, 89, 94, 96, 104, 110, 114, 115, 125, 132 134-5, 147

tenements, 30, 32, 33, 44, 48, 49, 51, 59, 67, 82, 85, 87, 88, 89, 90, 91, 92, 93, 94, 96, 97, 98, 99, 110, 111, 112, 113, 114, 116, 118, 120, 125, 128, 129, 130, 131, 132 134, 137, 145, 149, 156, 157, 158, 173, 174, 177, 185

Thetford, 24, 27, 44, 153, 191

Thurne, River, 14, 17, 18, 19, 35, 36, 43, 44, 45, 47, 59, 60, 61, 77, 79, 85, 105, 126, 127, 128, 130, 145, 152, 153, 155, 156, 157, 158, 164, 165, 166, 167, 170, 175, 191, 193

turbaries, 39, 53, 58, 78, 80, 185, 192

wages ,55, 69, 70, 104, 105, 107, 142, 144, 145, 148, 149, 161, 162, 163, 165, 168, 173, 190

Waryn family, 157, 158

White, William, 69, 70, 179-81, 183, 191

Winterton, 11, 16, 19, 20, 21, 22, 24, 45, 49, 62, 63, 65, 77, 99, 104, 128, 129, 138, 150, 154, 166, 187, 188, 191, 195, 198

women, 31, 48, 51, 62, 69, 73, 98, 111, 116, 119, 143, 168, 179, 180, 183, 184

Yare, River, 19, 129, 138

yeomen, 166, 171, 188, 189, 191